REVELATION

REVELATION
The Human Drama

Stan A. Lindsay

Lehigh
University
Press

Bethlehem: Lehigh University Press
London: Associated University Presses

Associated University Presses
440 Forsgate Drive
Cranbury, NJ 08512

Associated University Presses
16 Barter Street
London WC1A 2AH, England

Associated University Presses
P.O. Box 338, Port Credit
Mississauga, Ontario
Canada L5G 4L8

The paper used in this publication meets the requirements of the American National Standard for Permanence of Paper for Printed Library Materials Z39.48-1984.

Library of Congress Cataloging-in-Publication Data

Lindsay, Stan A., 1949-
    Revelation : the human drama / Stan A. Lindsay.
      p. cm.
    Includes bibliographical references and index.
    ISBN 0-934223-71-8 (alk. paper)
    1. Bible. N.T. Revelation—Criticism, interpretation, etc. I. Title

    BS2825.52.L56 2001
    228'.066—dc21   2001023430

Adam had Eve.
God had Israel (and the first Jerusalem).
Jesus has the church (the 144,000, the New Jerusalem).
I have Linda.

This is dedicated to my bride.

Contents

Preface

DUE TO THE NUMEROUS CITATIONS HEREIN FROM THE MAJOR WORKS of Kenneth Burke, I utilize a parenthical reference system for quotations from Burke's books of criticism and his novel. The abbreviations that I employ for Burke's books in the parenthetical references are to be found on the first pages of the bibliography. The abbreviations used are in bold letters and in parentheses following the corresponding full bibliographic entries. References to biblical texts and to classical texts are also listed parenthetically. All other quotations, including those from Burke's essays and articles, are referenced by endnotes. Biblical citations are generally from the New International Version. Comments are based on the Greek and Hebrew texts of the New and Old Testaments respectively. The texts of the original languages are cited in transliteration and translated when necessary to present observations that may be missed otherwise in the English translation. Occasionally, the Greek text of the Septuagint (hereafter LXX) is cited. The Septuagint is a Greek translation of the Hebrew Old Testament, produced two or three centuries before John wrote Revelation. Although John writes in Greek, he may be thinking in Hebrew. Therefore, correspondence between Greek and Hebrew terms often points to important issues.

Acknowledgments

No one was more keenly aware of the debts each human owes to other humans than was Kenneth Burke. Each of us is deeply indebted not only to our contemporaries but also to those "symbol-users" who lived before our time and left behind so vast a store of thought and information. Among those who lived before my time, I owe thanks to a man known only by the name of John who left behind one of the richest and most fascinating Symbols in all of history, the Book of Revelation. Among those who did not live quite long enough for me to meet them personally, I feel deeply grateful to Kenneth Burke, whose "animality" ceased shortly after I began my Ph.D. studies at Purdue University. How empty my pre-Burkean understanding of Symbols and symbol-users seems in retrospect!

While I regret not having the opportunity to meet Kenneth Burke personally, I am extremely gratified to have studied under Professor Don Burks, who was a close personal associate of Kenneth Burke. I thank Professor Henry Fischel of Indiana University who introduced me to biblical scholarship. I thank Professor John Patton (now of Tulane University) who, as my advisor at the University of Illinois, introduced me to the works of Kenneth Burke.

Of course, I thank Jesus of Nazareth, to whom the Gospel of John refers as Logos (John 1:1), an extremely important passage for understanding Burke's "logology," whose symbol-use of nearly 2000 years ago prompted his followers to write the New Testament. The study of the symbol-use of the New Testament continues to occupy some of the best minds in academia. I consider it a supreme honor to be a student of Jesus.

The Regents of the University of California own the copyright and have given permission to use approximately 1700 words of text from *Philosophy of Literary Form: Studies in Symbolic Action. 3rd edition, revised* (1973) and approximately 700 words of text from *Language as Symbolic Action: Essays on Life Literature, and Method* (1966). Ken-

11

neth Burke authored both books. The University of California Press publishes both books. Doubleday and Company owns the copyright and has given permission to use approximately 600 words of text from *Revelation* (1975), authored by J. Massyngberde Ford.

REVELATION

1

Introduction

THIS BOOK IS AN ATTEMPT TO PROVIDE A FRESH FRAMEWORK FOR interpreting the Revelation to John. Revelation was written in the last half of the first century A.D. The author, a Jewish Christian prophet known only by the name John, was adept at the use of figurative language. This use of figurative language has allowed many far-ranging interpretations of Revelation to be produced. Some believe the book incorrectly predicts the Roman Empire will fall in A.D. 100. Some believe the book predicts the return of Christ in the twenty-first century A.D. Some believe the book is an allegorical account of God's battle with Satan.

Using Burkean methodology to understand various levels of symbolic meaning, this study shows that John creates a form of transcendence for early believers. This extends into a pattern of continuity that other approaches to Revelation do not offer. The notion of drama is central to all of this. Kenneth Burke views language as a form of dramatic action and by taking us into the biblical text through that particular window readers are better able to understand how the language of Revelation works inside the text. Readers can understand how the notion of drama gives readers an extrahistorical, transcendent framework for being in the world.

Revelation is John's version of the human drama. He views that drama as having a beginning, a middle, and an end. He views the beginning (in act 1) as the Genesis account of the creation of heavens and earth. He looks forward to act 3—the reign of Christ and his followers on the earth. He foretells the end of the drama (in the epilogue): the destruction of heavens and earth and the creation of a new heavens and new earth inhabited by a new Jerusalem. John spends most of his time, however, detailing the events at the end of act 2 of the human drama—the transition from the suffering of old Jerusalem/Israel to the triumph of New Jerusalem/the Church.

The events of the drama that John supplies may be set forth

briefly. The structure of Revelation is based primarily on groups of
seven (an important number symbolizing completion/perfection—
based upon the seven days of creation in Genesis). The first group
of seven in chapters 2 and 3 sets forth letters to seven churches in
Asia Minor. Most of the churches have good and bad traits. The
churches are encouraged to repent from their bad traits so they
will be prepared for the coming "end" of act 2. Chapters 4 and 5
describe an important shift in the heavenly economy. In chapter 4
God alone is worthy of worship in heaven. In chapter 5, the Lamb
who was slain (a very important character in the drama) also becomes worthy of worship. This Lamb's accomplishments have allowed him to open a scroll that begins to unfold the drama to John
and his audience. Chapters 6 through 11 describe the second group
of seven, the opening of the seven seals of that scroll. The prelude
to opening the seventh seal is comprised of a third group of seven,
the seven last trumpets. When the seventh trumpet sounds and the
seventh seal is opened, the "end" (of act 2) will arrive. Chapters 12
through 14 introduce (and reintroduce) most of the major dramatis personae of John's drama—woman, dragon, beast from the
sea, beast from the land (the false prophet), the Lamb (who was
initially introduced in chapter 5), and the 144,000 virgins (who
were initially introduced in chapter 7). The harlot Babylon is introduced more fully in chapter 17. These dramatis personae are involved in the drama presented largely in the second half of Revelation. The fourth and final group of seven, the seven last plagues,
are presented in chapters 15 through 18. This is the end of act 2.

Act 3: having destroyed the harlot Babylon in the battle of Ar-
mageddon, the Lamb and his bride celebrate and rule the earth in
19:1–20.6. The beast and the false prophet are cast into the lake of
fire. The dragon is confined for a thousand years to the abyss. The
Christian martyrs are resurrected and reign for one thousand years
with Christ. Revelation 20:7–15 describes the final events of humanity's earthly existence. After the thousand years, Satan is released to raise one final army to fight against the camp of God's
people, the city he loves. Satan's final world powers, Gog and Magog, are destroyed by fire. Satan and all whose names are not found
in the book of life are thrown into the lake of fire. Death itself is
thrown into the lake of fire. The epilogue, chapters 21 and 22,
describe the new heavens and new earth in which the Lamb and
his bride will spend eternity.

Revelation is the most difficult book in the entire Bible. The most
significant Revelation scholar of the twentieth century observes that

this conclusion is universal from the earliest ages of the Church: "School after school has essayed its interpretation, and school after school has in turn retired in failure from the task."[1] While that observation makes the task attempted here daunting it also makes it challenging.

I have personally experienced frustrations associated with reading the book from the persectives of Contemporary-Historical critics, allegorical interpreters, source-theorists, sectarian advocates, premillennialists, postmillennialists, and amillennialists. The commonly accepted date for the writing of Revelation is A.D. 96. The frustrations associated with reading Contemporary-Historical critics (those who apply the symbolism to historical events at the time the book was written) relate to the great difficulty with finding historical referents to the symbols in the last decade of the first century. The frustration associated with reading source-theorists (those who believe the book is compiled by various authors using various sources at various times) is the scholarly consensus that Revelation's unique grammar argues convincingly that it was written by a single author at a particular time. The frustration associated with reading allegorical interpreters, sectarian advocates, and premillennialists is that they are uncritical; they use no scientific method. They are free to attach almost any meaning to any symbol. The frustration with reading postmillennialists (those who regard the thousand years mentioned in Revelation 20 as figurative, referring to the long time that precedes the coming reign of Christ) is that Revelation clearly states that Christ will reign for a thousand years. The frustration with reading amillennialists (those who hold that the thousand year period is completely figurative) is that there is definite evidence of Jewish teachings in the first century that predicted a literal thousand or two thousand year reign of the Messiah. My research for the past thirty years has been from a less frustrating perspective. I have found that perspective in the methodology of the prominent literary and rhetorical critic, Kenneth Burke, quite arguably the most significant rhetorical critic/dramatist of the twentieth century. Using insights from Kenneth Burke, this book analyzes Revelation from four perspectives—poetic, psychological, sociopolitical, and rhetorical.

Revelation: The Human Drama is a scholarly study of the book of Revelation utilizing Burkean entelechial criticism, a critical method that is rather new to biblical studies. Burkean criticism provides insights into Revelation that have not been uncovered by other critical methods. Furthermore, many of the insights provided support a conservative, evangelical reading of the book. Burkean criticism helps tie up many loose ends while remaining faithful to established critical scholarship. In fact, Burkean criticism may provide a way of transcending the division currently existing between evangelical scholars and critical scholars on the interpretation of this difficult book. The book makes contributions to those in biblical, rhetorical, and literary-critical disciplines.

The term "drama" in the subtitle has threefold significance. First, Revelation contains many parallels to Greek drama. Second, Kenneth Burke's system of analysis is named "dramatism" based upon his dictum, "Things move, People act." Since Revelation is the "act" of a single human, Burkean "dramatistic" analysis is a particularly useful analytical and critical method to apply to Revelation. Third, as opposed to Greek dramas dealing with limited events in human history, Revelation appears to be implicitly summing up the entirety of human history. Revelation is not concerned with a short segment of human history (as is the *Oresteia*, for example). Revelation is concerned with the human drama.

Rhetorical criticism is now well-established in biblical studies and (since he is the most dominant rhetorical theorist of the twentieth century) Kenneth Burke's methods are somewhat known to biblical scholars. Yet, Burkean rhetorical criticism differs from (the currently emphasized) classical rhetorical criticism in its emphasis on the implicit. When Burke's grandson, Harry Chapin, penned the lyrics to the song "Cat's in the Cradle," he was using (and exemplifying) rhetoric. Here was powerful persuasion at work. But the persuasion was not explicit, it was implicit. According to Burke, Aristotle's rhetoric is explicit: "Here's what to say if you want to smear a man . . . to build him up . . . and so on." Burke, on the other hand, borrows the term "entelechy," which Aristotle uses to describe the implicit, predictable motions and changes of "nature," and better uses it to describe how humans persuade themselves and each other implicitly.

CHAPTER SUMMARIES

Revelation is analyzed here from four perspectives—poetic, psychological, socio-political, and rhetorical. The poetic analysis may be accomplished virtually without respect to the historical circumstances in which Revelation was composed. The text alone is necessary. Burke suggests that the psychological and sociopolitical perspectives require going beyond the text. The psychological perspective requires examining the context of the primary audience to determine what expectations might be aroused by the use of specific forms. The sociopolitical perspective requires examining the social order in which the work was produced to determine what reinforcements and/or changes of the status quo the author might be recommending. Hence, Burke recommends beginning with the poetics perspective, by ascertaining what is internal—that which exists if the work exists.

Before presenting these four perspectives on Revelation, three preliminary steps are taken. Since the audience for this book is comprised of both biblical scholars and rhetorical scholars, chapters are provided that introduce rhetorical scholars to Revelation scholarship and biblical scholars to Burkean methodology. Then the trope synecdoche (primarily, the sense in which the part represents the whole, and *vice versa*) is explained in accordance with Burkean use. This trope is of great significance in interpreting Revelation.

Chapter 2 presents the two fundamental premises of the reading supplied here. Premise one: John wrote the Book of Revelation in or around A.D. 69. John was anticipating the impending destruction of Jerusalem and was intent upon incorporating this most significant chapter of Jewish history into his view of the human drama. The premise that Revelation was written in A.D. 69 is not established as fact. At this stage of scholarship, it is the minority view among Revelation scholars. The majority view would place the writing of Revelation near the end of the first century. Yet, the majority view is frustrating. It is very difficult to make historical sense of the symbols of Revelation if one assumes with the majority it is written in A.D. 96. Chapter 2 does not attempt to resolve the difficult historical issues associated with determining the date of the writing of Revelation. However, the basic arguments favoring an early date and those favoring a late date are briefly explained in the chapter.

Premise two: the writing of Revelation is the act of a single author. This premise has achieved much wider acceptance among Revelation scholars of the last one hundred years than has the first premise. While earlier fragmentation-based theories of authorship have survived, the majority view now holds that the work is a unity by one author. In this regard, the nature of Revelation as an act of a single author is emphasized. As an "act," the work is open to what Kenneth Burke calls "dramatistic" analysis. For Burke, dramatistic analysis of human symbolic action suggests a cycle of at least five terms (pentad) implicit in an act—scene, act, agent, agency, and purpose. Burke borrows these terms from drama, which he, at first, holds to be a metaphor for human "action." Later, Burke modifies his dramatistic perspective to claim that "dramatism" is not a metaphor; that people do literally "act" (*Dramatism and Development,* hereafter DD, 12).

Chapter 3 is an attempt to provide a concise overview of Burkean entelechial theory and methodology. This is probably too ambitious a task for one chapter, so if the reader requires more background on Burke, s/he is referred to *Implicit Rhetoric: Kenneth Burke's Extension of Aristotle's Concept of Entelechy.*[2] Burke borrows the terminology of entelechy from Aristotle. Burke understands Aristotle's entelechy to involve the process of *kinêsis,* which implies for Aristotle both action and motion (but with the emphasis on biological motion). By contrast, Burke's entelechy emphasizes action almost exclusively.[3] Action requires freewill on the part of the agent; motion (biological) is deterministic. Form, for Burke, becomes not the future shape of a mature plant, but the "chronology" of a drama. Form becomes "the arousing and fulfilling of expectation" drawn out into an "arpeggio." Likewise, "material [*hulê*]" in drama is not the fixed material of a biological organism. "Material" in drama is composed of words, symbols developed not unilaterally or automatically, but cooperatively. The audience participates in the production of the words, tropes, grammar—the *hulê* from which the drama is constructed. Chapter 3, therefore, provides Burke's methodology for analyzing this linguistic *hulê.*

In Chapter 4, Burke's view of the trope synecdoche is applied to Revelation. George Kennedy credits Stoic grammatical studies for producing "the theory of tropes, which is first expressly mentioned in a rhetorical treatise by Cicero (*Brutus* 69)."[4] Burke, in his theorizing, narrows the list of tropes from the eight of the "grammatical treatises" to four master tropes—metaphor, metonymy, synecdoche, and irony (GM 503). Of these four, Burke shows a marked preference for synecdoche. Burke claims that synecdoche is the key trope for handling matters of representation.

Two levels in which John employs synecdoche in the imagery of Revelation are presented. John's first-level use of synecdoche is to be found in his choice of a primary representative anecdote, the Eve versus serpent anecdote of Genesis. This anecdote, with the help of a plot twist from John, provides the story John dramatizes. John's second-level use of synecdoche is evident in the synecdochic fashion in which his specific heroes and villains are brought forth from the magma of his two major streams, only to melt back into the magma and reemerge later as different entities, which hold synecdochic relationships with the earlier entities. This second-level employment of synecdoche requires a more extensive explanation. The former level is set forth rather succinctly.

The *Poetics* perspective is the perspective of John, the author of Revelation. Chapter 5 presents a twofold poetics argument: (1) that John employs mirror-image symmetry to perfect a plot for his human drama, and (2) that he tracks down the implications of his two primary characters (woman and serpent) to perfect the dramatis personae of his human drama. This chapter seeks to answer the question, What does John do for John?

Chapter 6 takes the psychological perspective. The chapter turns from a consideration of the perspective of the author of Revelation to a consideration of the perspective of the readers comprising the primary audience of Revelation. It seeks to answer the question, what does John do for his audience? Such a move necessitates going beyond the text to find other historical materials. Materials exist that make such a move possible. Judeo-Christian scriptures, which were formative for John's primary audience, emphasize the expectations implicit in the "seven" structure, the creation week archetype. Hence, chapter 6 considers the seven structure (or, more specifically, the number six) as an example of entelechial criticism from a psychological perspective. Following Burke's definition of form/psychology, the chapter considers what expectations are aroused and fulfilled in Revelation.

Criticism from a sociopolitical perspective in chapter 7 requires significantly greater access to extratextual material. Furthermore, sociopolitical criticism requires a precise assessment of the sociopolitical context in which the literary work is produced. At this point the perspective presented here begins to take a route substantially different from the route taken by the majority of Revelation scholars. Chapter 7 posits that Revelation was written in an intra-Jewish sociopolitical context prior to the fall of Jerusalem in A.D. 70. Following Leland Griffin's adaptation of Burkean theory into a social movements model, first-century Christianity is presented as a social movement within Judaism. Revelation is then placed within this intra-Jewish sociopolitical context and an entelechial critique from a sociopolitical perspective is provided.

Chapter 8 supplies a rhetorical perspective on Revelation. Since the time of Aristotle, the rhetorical perspective has been characterized by the term "persuasion." Aristotle defines rhetoric as "the faculty of discovering, in any given case, the available means of persuasion" (*Rhetoric* I:2:1). Aristotle's definition of rhetoric conceives of persuasion as the *telos*, the goal for which the available means of achievement is to be found. Burke extends Aristotle's concept of rhetoric, recommending the addition of the strategies of identification and transcendence. John uses strategies similar to Burkean identification and transcendence as the means of persuading his audience to take the ultimate action, death as a martyr.

OTHER DRAMATISTIC APPROACHES TO REVELATION

Biblical scholars have seen that John writes a drama. Revelation scholar and former president of the Society of Biblical Literature, Elisabeth Schüssler Fiorenza, states that Revelation interpreters have claimed that Revelation is strongly patterned after the Greek drama.[5] Yet, the vast majority of Revelation interpreters are content to consider the book in the time-honored fashion—writing commentaries. Little elaborate dramatic critique of Revelation has been presented. Fiorenza's own book does not present an elaborate dramatic critique. *The Book of Revelation: Justice and Judgment* indicates that Fiorenza is interested in the methodological, historical-theological, and literary problems of Revelation.[6] Her book is a collection of scholarly essays she published over a period of twenty years on such issues. She sees them functioning as a preliminary introduction to her commentary on Revelation.[7]

Revelation scholar Adela Yarbro Collins sounds Burkean when she claims, "The Revelation to John makes use of holy war traditions to *interpret the situation* of its first readers [emphasis mine]."[8] In 1931, Kenneth Burke states in *Counter-Statement* (hereafter CS) that a Symbol (such as a drama) "appeals: *As the interpretation of a situation* [emphasis Burke's]" (CS 154). Burke's elaboration of the way in which a Symbol appeals as the interpretation of a situation is enlightening. Burke points out that a Symbol "presenting in a . . . consistent manner some situation" helps "give simplicity and order to an otherwise unclarified complexity." Surely, the original audience of Revelation (as well as audiences in subsequent generations) found itself in a situation with some unclarified complexity. To this complex situation Revelation gave simplicity and order. Part of the complexity encountered by the audience was due to the "irrelevancies" in its situation. With the "elimination of irrelevancies" the audience is enabled to interpret its situation in a consistent and idealized Symbol/drama. Burke's term "consistent" is of overwhelming importance in understanding Revelation. Whereas the various commentaries demonstrate the *diversity* of opinions regarding the many aspects of the book, a dramatistic analysis would look for the *consistency* in the book. Yarbro Collins's approach to Revelation suffers because she finds too much *inconsistency* in the book.

Yarbro Collins claims biblical critics have learned a great deal from literary critics, philosophers, and others. Her problem is that some people are apt to say Revelation is "only a symbol," and therefore it is not to be as highly regarded as inspired scripture or empirical proof. For true believers what Yarbro Collins wants to do with Revelation is unacceptable because believers do not want to found their lives "on something less than absolute bedrock."[9] One flaw in Yarbro Collins's handling of Revelation is that she herself views Revelation historically as "something less than absolute bedrock." After granting some validity to the classic historical-critical approach,[10] she retreats to a "perceived crisis" discussion.[11] Her perception of Revelation appears to be rather along the lines of her lay critics' comments—that it is "only a symbol." She writes: "It is not because I believe that the author of Revelation was intentionally deceptive or that he was a psychopathic personality. It is rather because he was a human like the rest of us." Her historical quest leads her to a quite difficult position—an inconsistency. On the one hand, she cites external evidence for "a date [of writing] of about 95 or 96"[12] under the reign of Domitian. On the other hand, she knows that "[t]here is insufficient evidence to warrant the conclusion that Domitian persecuted Christians as Christians."[13] She points out that many interpreters see Revelation as a response to this situation: Domitian was persecuting Christians, even forcing them to worship the emperor. She says this entire scenario is false.[14] Yarbro Collins claims the crisis addressed in Revelation is more perceived than real. This is frustrating. A more elaborate dramatistic analysis is possible if scholars revisit the dating of Revelation. More historical consistency may be found by dating the writing in A.D. 69. A more consistent and elaborate dramatistic analysis of Revelation is what this book attempts to accomplish.

2

Revelation Background

AT ABOUT THE TIME JOHN WROTE THE BOOK OF REVELATION, A RE-
spected school of rabbinic (jewish) thought, the school of Elias,
was teaching a peculiar interpretation of history that attempted to
sum up all of human history—past, present, and future. In some
respects, this interpretation of history resembles Greek drama. The
German scholar Paul Billerbeck observes that, according to the
school of Elias, humankind would exist on earth for a total of six
thousand years. Two thousand years would be spent without the
Law; two thousand years with the Law; and two thousand years
would be spent under the rule of the Messiah.

The school based its interpretation of history partly upon the
Biblical formula found in Psalm 90:4 that "a thousand years in
[God's] sight are like a day that has just gone by." According to
the various calculations of the school, the Jewish people had been
punished by God (i.e., had been under the domination of foreign
powers) for a total of one thousand years, beginning with the four
hundred years spent in Egypt from the time of Joseph to the time
of Moses. Because Israel had been punished for one thousand
years, Rabbi Yehoschua, from the late first century A.D., reasons that
the messianic period (the earthly reign of the Christ) should last
for two thousand years. Along with other rabbis, he observes that
Psalm 90:15 petitions God: "Make us glad for as many days as you
have afflicted us, for as many years as we have seen trouble." Yehoschua finds it striking that, according to his calculations, the Jewish people had been "afflicted" or had "seen trouble" for one thousand years—the formulaic "day" of the Lord from the earlier
passage in the same Psalm. Hence, he anticipates at least a "thousand years" of messianic reign. However, Yehoschua also observes
that the word "day" in 90:15 is plural, whereas in 90:4 it is singular.
Therefore, Yehoschua opines that there should be "two" days of
messianic reign, rather than just one. Thus, the reign of the Christ,
he thought, should last for two thousand years.[1]

Since one "day" equals "one thousand years" in this system, the "seven" pattern of the Sabbath "week" is next called into play. According to some calculations of biblical history, there were approximately two thousand years from Adam to the beginning of the Covenant (the time of Abraham). These years would amount to the "two days without the Law." Furthermore, approximately two thousand years had passed from the time of Abraham to the first century A.D., when this school and its view flourished. These years would be the "two days with the Law." If the messiah comes soon, they speculate, the final two thousand years of history will be spent in the reign of the messiah (or Christ). These six thousand years equal six days, according to the Psalm 90 formula. And, six days was the amount of time that God took to create the world. On the seventh day (Sabbath), God rested. The school of Elias thus anticipated, according to Billerbeck, a *weltensabbat* (a cosmic Sabbath) when all humanity would "rest" from labor—beginning at the end of the six thousand years.

At least two New Testament writers (John and the author of 2 Peter) connect a "thousand year" formula to speculation concerning future divine activity. Second Peter warns, "But do not forget this one thing, dear friends: with the Lord a day is like a thousand years, and a thousand years are like a day.... But the day of the Lord will come like a thief. The heavens will disappear with a roar; the elements will be destroyed by fire" (2 Peter 3:8 and 10).

Billerbeck acknowledges that John may be aware of Yehoschua's interpretation of history. Yet, John does not explicitly paint himself into a corner regarding time frames, as do Yehoschua and the school of Elias. John does indicate that there would be at least one "thousand years" period. During these thousand years, "the dragon, that ancient serpent, who is the devil, or Satan," would be "bound" and thrown "into the Abyss . . . to keep him from deceiving the nations anymore until the thousand years were ended" (Revelation 20:2–3). Following these "thousand years," however, John does not appear to promise an immediate end to human history. Instead, "After that, [the dragon] must be set free for a short time" (Revelation 20:3). John predicts: "When the thousand years are over, Satan will be released from his prison and will go out to deceive the nations in the four corners of the earth [or 'land']" (Revelation 20:7–8). An indeterminate amount of time follows the "thousand years" of the Book of Revelation. John's Revelation does not preclude the claim of Yehoschua and it is at least possible that John's vision partially corroborates the view of Yehoschua and/or the school of Elias.

My major professor in Hebrew at Indiana University, Henry A. Fischel, frequently asserts that New Testament writers knew rabbinic teachings, rabbinic writers knew Christian teachings, and they all knew Greek teachings. Fischel states:

> It is fortunate that at this stage of scholarship no further defense has to be made for the assumption that Greco-Roman situations were well-known to the creators of the Midrash, i.e., the literature that modifies the word and world of Scripture by interpretation, explicitly or implicitly. Rather the problem is how far this knowledge went, how much of Greco-Roman academic procedure and philosophical quest was used in that on-going process, in which the culmination of the tannaitic culture, c. 200 A.D. (the codification of the Mishnah) and that of the Palestinian amoraic culture, c. 400 (Jerusalem Talmud) were important stages.[2]

Among those "Greco-Roman situations [that] were well-known" to John and, I think, also to the school of Elias, are Greek dramas. As stated earlier, Elisabeth Schüssler Fiorenza claims, regarding Revelation: "Interpreters have not merely acknowledged the dramatic character of the book but have maintained that Rev[elation] is patterned after the Greek drama, since it has *dramatis personae*, stage props, chorus, a plot, and a tragic-comic ending."[3]

Both Greek drama and the *weltwochenschema* (cosmic week cosmology) of the school of Elias were possibly well-known to John. There are indications that John is writing some important episodes of the "human drama" based upon an implicit dramatic pattern quite similar to the pattern taught by the school of Elias. Essentially, the pattern of human history used in the Elias schema is tripartite followed by a fourth part that consists of undefined celebration and rest. Compare this schema to the Greek trilogy-turned-tetralogy. There also is a tripartite schema followed by a fourth part (a Satyr play), which is a(n admittedly obscene) celebration.

John is plausibly presenting his futuristic episodes as somewhat mirror-imaged (chiastic) developments of past history. Perhaps the frequent references to "the Alpha and the Omega, the First and the Last, the Beginning and the End" (Revelation 22:13, et al.) are allusions to the chiastic organization of John's implicit drama. The biggest hint that John provides of his mirror-imaged (chiastic) schema is that he concludes with a new creation. Revelation chapters 21 and 22 are, thus, mirror images of Genesis chapters 1 and 2.

Revelation begins with epistles (Revelation chapters 1–3), possibly indicating that what is closest to the mirror (chronologically, for John) is the diaspora age of the church (the church scattered across the Roman Empire) represented by the epistles. Next, John moves to a further history of the Lamb's exaltation in Heaven (Revelation chapters 4–5)—a mirror image of the oral narratives later written down in the gospel and Acts accounts of Jesus' earthly life and ascension. John then considers the Old Testament prophets and their prediction of the divorce of Israel, God's bride (Revelation chapters 6–11). This mirrors the books of prophecy in the Old Testament. And, before John concludes with the new creation, he tells of the last plagues (Revelation chapters 12–19), a clear mirror image of the Exodus. But John's view of the human drama remains more implicit than explicit. He does not begin his account of the human drama at Genesis. That much of the story has already been told. John picks up the human drama at the point at which he is writing. The Old Testament and the other books of the New Testament have brought the readers to John's point in history. So, what is John's current vantage point for relating new episodes in the great human drama?

The Scene

The year was A.D. 69. Fewer than forty years earlier, Jesus of Nazareth had been crucified. His followers were convinced that he had also been resurrected from the dead. The execution of Jesus had been accomplished by means of an alliance between the Jewish high priestly party and the local representatives of the Roman Empire— Herod Antipas and Pontius Pilate. It was common knowledge among Jewish leaders that the high priestly family was indebted to Herod's family for its prestige and power. Antipas' father, Herod the Great, had deposed the then-current (Hasmonean) high priestly family in the years preceding Jesus' birth. In its place Herod (the Great) had installed a high priest from among the Jews of the Babylonian diaspora (those Jews who had been "carried away" into Babylon in the sixth century B.C. and who had not yet returned to Palestine). It is possible that the term "Babylon" in Revelation and 1 Peter is a code word for this high priestly family and/or Jerusalem, the city controlled by the (Babylonian?) high priestly family.

According to Gospel accounts, prior to his death, Jesus had predicted that within a generation the walls of the Temple in Jerusalem would be brought down. Jesus is quoted as alluding to a prophecy of Daniel concerning an "abomination of desolation" that would be in control of the Temple in Jerusalem. The Gospel of Luke interprets the prophecy as a promise that armies would surround Jerusalem before the (then present) generation passed away. And in A.D. 69, there the armies were! Jerusalem was a city under siege! War with the Roman Empire had begun three years earlier, in A.D. 66, when the Jewish nation declared its independence from Rome. Within one year from 69, Jerusalem would, in fact, fall to the Romans. The Temple would, in fact, be torn down, as Jesus of the Gospels had prophesied. By A.D. 73, the Jewish-Roman War would be completed as Rome seized Masada, the final Jewish stronghold.

What was the significance of the war that was in progress in A.D. 69? Perhaps to the Roman armies, the significance was comparable to swatting a small but bothersome mosquito; to Judaism the significance was immense. The destruction of Jerusalem and the Temple spelled an end to all sacrificial worship. Never again in history would Judaism practice animal sacrifice. The war thus effectively ended the Jewish priesthood. The war very nearly ended Judaism altogether. From the ashes of Temple worship, two forms of Judaism would arise. Rabbinic Judaism would shed virtually all influence from the high priestly party. This form of Judaism—what some have called "normative" Judaism—would arise as primarily a product of the pharisaic party. The Sadducean party (so prominent in the New Testament writings and even in the Jewish government during the war) would virtually disappear. The Essene party (from which John the Baptist may have come) would scarcely be mentioned again, until the discovery of the Dead Sea Scrolls. The Zealot party (from which came one of Jesus' disciples, Simon the Zealot) would disappear along with a subgroup, the Sicarii (from which Judas came?). Rabbinic Judaism after the destruction of Jerusalem would be vastly different from what had preceded. The second form of Judaism that would arise was a Judaism that held appeal also for Gentiles: Christianity.

That John wrote the Book of Revelation in or around A.D. 69 is a major premise of my reading of Revelation. John was anticipating the impending destruction of Jerusalem and was intent upon incorporating this most significant chapter of Jewish history into his view of the human drama. Many of the conclusions drawn in this analysis of Revelation are based upon the acceptance of this premise. Nevertheless, I dutifully acknowledge that this premise is by no means established as fact. At this stage of scholarship, it is not even the majority view among Revelation scholars. The majority view would place the writing of Revelation near the end of the first century. In this study I do not attempt to resolve the difficult historical issues associated with determining the date of the writing of Revelation. I note, however, that historical scholars such as Robert M. Grant would admit the A.D. 69 premise as a possibility. A brief sketch of some issues pertaining to the date of writing is in order.

Although Adela Yarbro Collins concludes that Revelation was written around A.D. 96, she presents a balanced discussion of the external evidence in dating the book. Yarbro Collins writes:

> The earliest witness is Irenaeus, who says that the Apocalypse was seen at the end of the reign of Domitian. Since Domitian ruled from 81 to 96, Irenaeus' comment refers to 95 or 96. . . . [Yet,] Irenaeus is not reliable on figures of the first century. . . .
>
> Victorinus, who . . . died in 303 . . . and Eusebius say that Revelation was written during the reign of Domitian. They add that John was banished to Patmos by Domitian. . . . [Yet,] [c]ommentators have disagreed about whether this tradition of John's banishment is reliable historical information or a legendary motif inspired by Rev. 1:9. . . .
>
> A few late sources date Revelation to the time of Claudius, Nero, or Trajan. These texts show that there were traditions about the date that were apparently independent of Irenaeus. . . .
>
> Irenaeus' testimony has been questioned recently on the grounds that he believed both Revelation and the Fourth Gospel to have been written by the apostle John. If Irenaeus was wrong about authorship, so the argument goes, he may have been wrong about the date too. . . .
>
> Another objection to Irenaeus' dating could be raised on the basis of Domitian's portrayal as the second persecutor, a new Nero. . . . There is extremely little evidence that this tradition was accurate.[4]

In fairness, despite some difficulties, the external evidence favors a date of A.D. 96.

The internal evidence gives another story. Yarbro Collins argues that John's use of the term Babylon provides evidence for a later date. Unfortunately, her reasoning is somewhat circular. She points out, "Most commentators agree that 'Babylon' . . . is a symbolic name for Rome."[5] This is circular reasoning since most commentators also place the date of writing at A.D. 96. To her credit, Yarbro Collins observes:

> Most of the occurrences of Babylon as a symbolic name for Rome in
> Jewish literature are in the Apocalypse of Ezra . . . , the Syriac Apoc-
> alypse of Baruch . . . , and the fifth book of the *Sibylline Oracles.* . . .
> [T]he context makes it abundantly clear . . . Rome is called Babylon
> because her forces, like those of Babylon at an earlier time, destroyed
> the temple and Jerusalem.[6]

This is an interesting and valuable observation which pertains to
the interpretation of the term Babylon. But, in her greatest use of
circular reasoning, Yarbro Collins concludes, "It is highly unlikely
that the name would have been used before the destruction of the
temple by Titus. This internal evidence thus points decisively to a
date after 70 C.E."[7] Has Yarbro Collins completely missed the point
(she personally implied) that since Babylon is never associated in
Revelation with "destroy[ing] the temple and Jerusalem," Babylon
in Revelation is not Rome?

Babylon in Revelation is called a harlot. J. Massyngberde Ford
points out, "The harlot . . . is also a Jewish OT theme depicting Jerusalem . . . and there is no clear indication that Babylon is Rome
as in the Christian Sibyllines."[8] Ford further states regarding the
harlot epithet, "[A]ll idolatry was considered as adultery or fornication. . . . [T]he faithful community is the spouse of the Lamb . . . ;
Babylon is its antithesis and is presented as a prostitute . . . , as is
the faithless Jerusalem."[9] Reflecting on the teachings of Qumran,
Ford concludes, "These texts together with the OT ones indicate
that the harlot in Rev 17 is Jerusalem, not Rome. . . . [T]he harlot
depicts particularly the condition of the high priesthood."[10] Yarbro
Collins's observations, which link the late meaning of Babylon with
Rome just as easily (or perhaps more easily), lead to a dating of
Revelation prior to the fall of Jerusalem in A.D. 70.

Virtually every Revelation scholar weighs in on the claim that the
seven- or eight-headed beast of Revelation is Rome. The heads are
kings. Five have fallen. In terms of dating the book, the book claims
to be written during the reign of the sixth head. Hence, calculations
ensue to determine the date of the book. It is difficult to see how
the head count could begin before Julius Caesar. If Julius were head
one, head six would be Nero who died in A.D. 68. Since Julius was
never officially an emperor, it seems more likely that Augustus is
head one, and that Galba who reigned only in A.D. 69 is head six.
Since Tiberius was the first emperor following Jesus' birth, he might
be head one, in which case Otho who reigned only in A.D. 69 is
head six. Skip Tiberius as head one and you have Vitellius, who

reigned only in A.D. 69 as head six. How many heads may be skipped before this clue of John's becomes meaningless? It appears that John is claiming that the book is being written around A.D. 69. There certainly are elaborate ways of making Domitian equal head six, but it seems much easier to conclude that A.D. 69 is the date John claimed to write.

Revelation 11 discusses the measurement of the temple. Is it possible to speak of measuring the temple after A.D. 70, the year it was destroyed? Yarbro Collins states that "before 1882, this passage was used to date the book as a whole before 70 C.E."[11] She points out, "Recently, J. A. T. Robinson has revived the argument that Revelation as a whole was written before 70"[12] based somewhat upon chapter 11. It takes something of a compilation theory for commentators (including Yarbro Collins) to get around the clear suggestion of an early date in this instance. Yarbro Collins hedges here somewhat on her assertion, "I express my conviction that the book was given something very close to its present form by a single author at a particular time,"[13] in so doing. Yarbro Collins sees that (at least part of) chapter 11 refers to Jerusalem: "The earthly Jerusalem is referred to later in ch[apter] 11 as Sodom and Egypt, the place where the lord was crucified (v[erse] 8)."[14]

Beyond her quite significant dismissal of a historical persecution of Christians under Domitian, Yarbro Collins offers one more ambivalent piece of evidence: "Laodicea suffered a serious earthquake in 60/61 C.E. Nevertheless, it is addressed in Revelation as an affluent church. The earthquake is not mentioned or alluded to in Revelation. . . . [Yet, t]he fact that the citizens did not need imperial help to rebuild is an indication that a date in the late 60's is not impossible."[15]

This brief sketch is offered so that the reader might understand the complexity of issues involved in determining the correct date for the writing of Revelation. Although various commentators have taken positions on the dating issue, no knockout blows have been delivered to proponents of either the A.D. 69 or the A.D. 96 dates. Either date is still possible. One might even view the dating problem as being at an impasse, but this problem does not stop a Burkean. Of course, it is necessary to provide a specific historical context in order to perform socio-political or rhetorical critique, but Burkean method supplies the next step.

As Kenneth Burke says, "A way of seeing is also a way of not seeing—a focus upon object A involves a neglect of object B" (*Permanence and Change, An Anatomy of Purpose*, hereafter PC, 49). I confess to neglecting object B (the circumstances surrounding the later date) in my focusing on object A (the circumstances surrounding the earlier date). I may do this as a Burkean because I understand that all seeing is partial, perspectival. If I look at a soda can from only the side perspective, I see only a rectangle. If I look at it only from a top or bottom perspective, I see only a circle. If I look at it from an exterior perspective, I may believe it is solid. If I look at it from an internal perspective, I see that it is hollow or filled with liquid. No single perspective provides the full picture, that it is a hollow or liquid-filled cylinder. Every perspective is important. This study provides a reading of Revelation from the perspective that it may have been written in A.D. 69. Other perspectives are certainly welcome to Burkeans.

Furthermore, the arguments that I advance in my study are based more upon a "rhetorical" model of argumentation than upon a "philosophical" model (as Aristotle makes the distinction). Philosophy claims the ability to ascertain absolute truth. Rhetoric claims only the ability to ascertain probability. I am not hopeful that scholarship will soon achieve certainty regarding the dating of Revelation; hence, I am content to advance arguments based upon possibilities and probabilities. I fully recognize the fact that some scholars are heavily invested in a later date for Revelation. Those scholars who deem this premise impossible will find much of my analysis personally frustrating—perhaps even as frustrating as I find the analysis of those whose premise is that the book was written near the end of the century. Those who are at least open to the possibility of an early date may consider my arguments as contingencies. Those who are convinced that there is no possibility of an early date for Revelation will surely find ways of not seeing. But, lest later-date advocates find themselves inclined to totally dismiss my reading, I would propose that they view my reading from this perspective: if my early dating is wrong, John may have been a late-first-century apologist who was attempting to make sense of the events surrounding the fall of Jerusalem that happened a quarter of a century earlier. Yarbro Collins admits:

> such antedating is a common device in apocalyptic literature. Many Jewish apocalypses are indeed antedated. But usually the entire work is clearly set in an earlier time and the seer is a venerable figure of the distant past. Revelation does not have these characteristics.[16]

It is my position that Revelation was written in or around A.D. 69.

DRAMATISM

The second premise upon which my reading of Revelation is based is that the writing of Revelation is the act of a single author. This premise has achieved much wider acceptance among scholars of the last one hundred years than has my first premise. While earlier fragmentation-based theories of authorship have survived, the majority view now holds that the work is a unity by one author. In this regard, I particularly emphasize the nature of Revelation as an act of a single author.

As an "act," the work is open to what Kenneth Burke calls "dramatistic" analysis. Since Fiorenza has pointed out that interpreters have maintained that Revelation is "patterned after the Greek drama," Burkean dramatistic analysis is further justified. For Burke, dramatistic analysis of human symbolic action suggests a cycle of at least five terms (pentad) implicit in an act—scene, act, agent, agency, and purpose. Burke borrows these terms from drama, which he, at first, holds to be a metaphor for human "action." Later, Burke modifies his dramatistic perspective to claim that "dramatism" is not a metaphor; that people do literally "act" (DD 12).

Late in Burke's career, he begins to emphasize the relationship between his dramatistic perspective and Aristotle's theory of entelechy. Burke's entelechial theory differs from Aristotle's entelechial theory primarily in this respect: Aristotle's theory emphasizes the purely physical aspects of entelechy—what Burke calls the realm of "motion"; whereas Burke's theory emphasizes human "action" as being entelechial. Burkean entelechial criticism is a valid and useful method for shedding light on the Book of Revelation. Furthermore, Revelation is an excellent paradigm of entelechial motivation. The specific methods by which dramatistic and entelechial analysis is performed will be explained in chapter 3.

The Book of Revelation is unlike any other book in the New Testament. The first four New Testament books are placed together as Gospels. They provide accounts of Jesus' mortal life. The Book of Acts, while it appears to stand alone, is actually the second volume of the Gospel of Luke, and reports a continuing history of Jesus' work through his apostles. Hence, it follows the Gospels. The remaining books of the New Testament—with the exception of Revelation—are epistles. But what is Revelation?

Clearly, Revelation has elements that are common to epistles. Revelation seems to have a standard greeting very similar to that which Paul uses in his Epistles: "Grace and peace to you." Furthermore, John addresses the book to the "seven churches in the province of Asia" (Revelation 1:4). The book also contains seven letters to the "angels" of these seven churches (chapters 2–3) but the letters do not purport to be from John. They purport to be from someone "like a son of man" (Revelation 1:13). John presents himself as one who takes dictation for these letters.

It could also be argued that Revelation has elements that are common to the Gospels. Chapters 4 and 5 seem to contain a report on a further history of Jesus as he assumes a position in Heaven. He becomes "[w]orthy . . . to receive power and wealth and wisdom and strength and honor and glory and praise" (Revelation 5:12). Since God is the only other individual so "worthy," there are significant Christological implications here. However, these chapters seem to represent (for John) historical development rather than predictive prophecy.

Revelation certainly has elements that are prophetic in the tradition of the Old Testament prophets. Jonah and Haggai may be the only Old Testament prophetic books not cited or alluded to in Revelation. John refers most frequently to the books of Daniel and Ezekiel, followed closely by Psalms, Isaiah, and Jeremiah.

John makes a few historical allusions to events reported in Joshua, Judges, 1 and 2 Samuel, and 1 and 2 Kings, but he seems to be particularly interested in the Pentateuch, drawing especially from Genesis and Exodus. Elements of the Exodus (most notably, the plagues) are significant in Revelation. Clearly, creation becomes the dominant theme in the final two chapters, as John sees a "new heaven and a new earth, for the first heaven and the first earth had passed away" (Revelation 21:1).

Thus, Revelation has elements of creation story, exodus, prophecy, gospel, and epistle. Yet, it is difficult to make the case that Revelation is any single one of these types of literature. The literary genre in which Revelation is placed most frequently is the literary genre "apocalyptic." Even this placement, however, is somewhat tautological. The genre is named for the Book of Revelation. The Greek word for revelation is *apokalupsis.* Thus, the Book of Revelation became the paradigm for the genre classification "apocalyptic." There are, nonetheless, both Jewish and Christian "apocalypses" that parallel many of the features of Revelation and at least some of these apocalypses borrowed much of their form from Revelation.

What does it mean to identify a certain work as being of any given genre? For Burke, genre classifications would receive consideration in a discussion of "form"—specifically, "conventional form" (CS 126ff.). In chapter 6, some major "formal" (a term which Burke equates with "psychological") aspects of Revelation are considered. In the balance of the present chapter, the Burkean criticism of Revelation offered here is placed within the context of extant biblical scholarship and history. A brief overview of biblical scholarship on Revelation is provided before the presentation of my own views pertaining to Revelation.

BURKE'S METHOD IN THE CONTEXT OF REVELATION SCHOLARSHIP

Regarding his analytical method, Burke states:

I do not contend that the mode of analysis here proposed is automatically free of subjective interpretations. I do contend that an indiscussible dictionary is avoided. . . . To know what "shoe, or house, or bridge" means, you don't begin with a "symbolist dictionary" already written in advance. You must, by inductive inspection of a given work, discover the particular contexts in which the shoe, house, or bridge occurs. You cannot, in advance, know in what equational structure it will have membership. By inspection of the work, you propose your description of this equational structure. Your propositions are open to discussion, as you offer your evidence for them and show how much of the plot's development your description would account for. "Closer approximations" are possible, accounting for more. The method, in brief, can be built upon. (*Philosophy of Literary Form*, hereafter PLF, 89)

The Book of Revelation is indeed a most difficult book to interpret. Dr. R. H. Charles began his Lectures on the Apocalypse for the British Academy in 1919 with the words: "From the earliest ages of the Church, it has been universally admitted that the Apocalypse is the most difficult book of the entire Bible. School after school has essayed its interpretation, and school after school has in turn retired in failure from the task."[17]

Date of the Book

Is, then, scholarly consensus possible? There are, of course, those who would argue that the "essential" nature, date, and objectives of the Book of Revelation have been established. Elisabeth Schüssler Fiorenza claims that "New Testament scholars generally agree that the author of Revelation [was writing] . . . at the end of the first century."[18] If this general consensus view were correct, presumably the intended audience would be primarily gentile in makeup.

R. H. Charles, on the other hand, contends that the author of Revelation is Jewish[19] and J. Massyngberde Ford questions whether or not the work is Christian at all, or a *thoroughly* Jewish book.[20] If any portion of Ford's argument is accepted, what Fiorenza claims to be the consensus view regarding the date, and hence the intended audience of Revelation, needs to change. The Church at the end of the first century appears to be quite gentile in makeup. In this regard, S. G. F. Brandon notes:

> The author of the Acts in his presentation of the tradition of Christian Origins never gives any indication that the numbers of the Gentile converts were large, while he makes several statements about the considerable numerical strength of the Jewish Christians in Palestine, which . . . must be fairly interpreted as genuine indications of the comparative situation.[21]

Yet, Justin Martyr, writing in the second century at approximately A.D. 135,[22] can have a debate with Trypho, the Jew, in a context that seems to clearly indicate the almost total absence of Jews in the Church![23]

There have been two key issues in Revelation scholarship upon which virtually all other issues depend. The first issue, as previously noted, regards the date of the book's composition. The second regards the interpretive method. Of these two issues, the one regarding date has proved to be the more difficult to resolve. Determining the date of Revelation is very important for conducting any sociopolitical or rhetorical criticism of the book. Indeed, the date of the work, if understood to be different from Fiorenza's first generalized assessment, could dramatically alter not only perception of the conventional form, but also understanding of the psychology of the audience, the sociopolitical situation, and the rhetorical context. However, determining the date is less important for criticism from a poetics or psychological perspective.

Two major proposed dates for the writing of Revelation vie for scholarly acceptance. F. F. Bruce allows for the possibility that the book may have been written as early as A.D. 69 and as late as A.D. 96.[24] He also observes: "Hugo Grotius (1583–1645) . . . was the first

Reformed exegete to give up the identification of the Papacy with the Antichrist and he held that some of the visions of Rev[elation] reflect the period before, and others the period after, the fall of Jerusalem in A.D. 70."[25] Bruce continues, "[Grotius] may thus be regarded as the pioneer of the literary-critical approach to the book."[26] According to (an apparently private conversation with) John A. T. Robinson, Bruce "now inclines" in the direction of the earlier date.[27]

Robinson's own thesis is that Revelation (and all other New Testament books) should be redated prior to A.D. 70. Robert M. Grant severely criticizes Robinson's work, stating, "The case for placing all the NT books before 70 cannot be made by the methods employed here [in Robinson's book], and it has not been made."[28] Yet, Grant is only critiquing Robinson's book—he is not disavowing the possibility that the date of Revelation was prior to 70. Robinson even cites Grant as allowing for the possibility of an early date for Revelation: "Grant, INT, 237, is prepared to say 'a situation between 68 and 70 is not excluded.' "[29] While the reading presented here assumes an early date—a historical context in which the sociopolitical struggle is between the Christian Jews and the priestly party—there is no claim for the absence of subjectivity. As Burke advises, "By inspection of the work, you propose your description of this equational structure. Your propositions are open to discussion, as you offer your evidence for them and show how much of the plot's development your description would account for" (PLF 89).

It seems clear that any reading of Revelation must choose between the two proposed dates. There was tremendous sociopolitical change for Jewish audiences in the quarter of a century between the two dating alternatives. To posit an extreme dating divergence of 50 to 70 years prior to the A.D. 96 date (as does J. M. Ford for one major portion of the book) is not necessary for Revelation students to establish a dramatically different context from that of the A.D. 96 date.[30] Although only a quarter century separates the two dating extremes allowed by Bruce, the intervention of the fall of Jerusalem drastically changed the social, political, religious, and ecclesiastical landscape between Bruce's two dating extremes. Thus, the entire scholarly "consensus" regarding not only the date but also the genre and purpose (which Fiorenza claims) is on shaky ground if the earlier of Bruce's dates rather than the latter is correct.

As Charles asserts, the close affinity of Revelation to Jewish apocalypses indicates that (like Jewish apocalypses) Revelation should "be taken as referring first and chiefly to the times in which it was originally written."[31] This assertion by Charles summarizes the position of the Contemporary-Historical methodology of interpreting Revelation. Along with the scholarly consensus, the Contemporary-Historical methodology is followed here. Therefore, it is important to decide which of the two dating extremes is more acceptable.

In accepting the Contemporary-Historical methodology, the view that Revelation is "mere allegory or symbolical representation of the conflict of right and wrong"[32] is dismissed. Adherents to this "allegorical" view include Tyconius, St. Augustine, and the Roman Church until the 20th century. Likewise rejected is the attempt, begun in the Middle Ages, to apply the book to church history. This attempt, begun by Joachim of Floris and developed by his followers, the Franciscans, culminated in Peter John Olivi's identification of the papacy as the Antichrist.[33] These early attempts were like so many current uncritical and sectarian approaches to Revelation: "[They] had no scientific method to guide them—and were thus at liberty to attach almost any meaning to any symbol and to explain away any statement that conflicted with their theories."[34]

R. H. Charles excuses Revelation interpreters such as "Justin Martyr, Irenaeus, and Hippolytus" for producing unacceptable readings, stating that "a valid interpretation was wholly beyond their reach." With them he places 99 percent of all previous Revelation expositors. "They were without the necessary equipment," he states. The first piece of equipment Charles deems "necessary" is "a knowledge of Jewish Apocalyptic." Secondly, the Revelation expositors must possess a "knowledge of the unique grammar and style of their author," if they are to be considered qualified, according to Dr. Charles.[35]

Upon addressing these first two equipmental criteria, Charles instructs interpreters to adopt the Contemporary-Historical methodology, which he claims has "rightly achieved a permanent place in all scientific interpretation of the Apocalypse."[36] His two original equipmental criteria would be pressed into service in a "philological methodology" corrected from the failed philological methodology of the sixteenth-century reformers.[37] Using such a philological methodology, Charles (perhaps the most qualified practitioner, in light of his own criteria) proceeds to critique the next methodological development, the literary-critical methodology. A scholarly disagreement regarding the date of the Apocalypse continues to exist. Literary-critical methodology is one attempt to solve the problem.

According to Charles, the "three developments of this method that appealed to the suffrages of the learned world . . . were the Redactional-Hypothesis, the Sources-Hypothesis, [and] the Fragmentary-Hypothesis."[38] The redactional-hypothesis (which posits a plurality of editors) and the sources-hypothesis (which posits a plurality of independent sources) would solve the problem of the dating discrepancy by suggesting that different elements of the Apocalypse might have different authors/editors, dates, and contexts. However, Charles wholly rejects both methods on the grounds of linguistic unity, i.e., "the vocabulary, grammar, and style of the Apocalypse are unique over against all other Greek literature."[39] He recommends "in some form" the third hypothesis, which "maintains the relative unity of the book but assumes that its author made use of other materials." Yet, Charles accepts this hypothesis only as a "general explanation of the facts."[40]

Fiorenza's critique of J. M. Ford's commentary reasserts the linguistic unity argument, mentioned above. She rejects Ford's "peculiar form of the compilation theory": "It neglects the considerable linguistic evidence which compelled older commentators and most recent investigators of the language of Revelation to discard the source-theories and to maintain the compositional unity of Revelation. The unitary character of Revelation's language and symbol system argues against such an arbitrary dissection of the text."[41] Throughout her chapter, "The Composition and Structure of Revelation," Fiorenza champions the unity of Revelation from composition-critical and structuralist methodological standpoints: "The unitary composition of Rev[elation] does not result from a final redactor's arbitrary compilation but from the author's theological conception and literary composition."[42]

Burkeans try to "join in" the " 'unending conversation' that is going on at the point in history when we are born" (PLF 110). In a well-known passage, Burke explains:

> Imagine that you enter a parlor. You come late. When you arrive, others have long preceded you, and they are engaged in a heated discussion, a discussion too heated for them to pause and tell you exactly what it is about. In fact, the discussion had already begun long before any of them got there, so that no one present is qualified to retrace for you all the steps that had gone before. You listen for a while, until you decide that you have caught the tenor of the argu-

ment; then you put in your oar. Someone answers; you answer him;
another comes to your defense. . . . However, the discussion is inter-
minable. (PLF 110–11)

As in the "unending conversation" of which Burke speaks, credibility in Revelation scholarship demands that the difficult progress
that has been achieved be acknowledged and assimilated before
proceeding. Nevertheless, it seems equally important that Revelation research at least attempt to proceed beyond its present stage.
Concerning the scholarly "conversation" on Revelation, a fair
amount of inconclusiveness continues to cloud the fundamental
issues of Revelation studies. Scholars do not know conclusively the
date and, hence, cannot know conclusively the sociopolitical context of the work. The two dating extremes, while separated by only
one quarter century, would yield vastly divergent primary audiences
and issues.

The conversation is stymied. The methodologies utilized until
now have brought scholars to a very close (yet still unacceptably
imprecise) "knowledge" of this most difficult book. What is attempted here is a new methodological step. Using Burkean methodology,
no attempt is made to arbitrate between the alternative dates with
their respective audiences and contexts. Instead, one of the two
dates is chosen and what the message of Revelation would look like
if this date were correct is demonstrated.

Even if one does not strongly accept the premise that Revelation
was written in A.D. 69, it is worthwhile to see what the book would
look like *if* it were. Far more studies exist which attempt to demonstrate what Revelation would look like *if* it were written in A.D.
96. Therefore, on the grounds that the greater scholarly contribution would involve presenting a perspective that has been less analyzed, it seems useful to analyze the book using the A.D. 69 premise. If too many loose ends remain by the application of this
premise, scholars may use this work as an argument against the
early dating premise. If, on the other hand, the use of this premise
ties up a number of loose ends that exist in the application of the
A.D. 96 premise, scholars might reexamine the A.D. 96 premise and
perhaps even apply Burkean analysis to Revelation using the A.D.
96 premise to demonstrate what the book looks like with the later
date premise.

The Sociopolitical Scene in A.D. 69

The single most unanimous agreement of Revelation scholarship is that the beast is Rome. R. H. Charles surveys the theories of the scholars of his age. "Abbess and Spit," he says, see the context of the beast discussion in chapter 13 as "the reign of [the Roman emperor] Caligula, and reflecting the condition of Palestine in the years [A.D.] 39–41.... Caligula was ... the ... Beast."[43] Charles claims that Wellhausen sees a reference to "the destruction of Jerusalem in [A.D.] 70 in the 3½ years' war" according to which "the Beast is not Nero but the Roman Empire."[44] J. Weiss (along with many of his contemporary scholars) assumes a multisource origin for Revelation but concludes that "the final Apocalyptist made the entire chapter [13 of Revelation] refer to the Roman Empire."[45] In Charles's own view, "[t]he first Beast is the Roman Empire," which he equates with the fourth beast of Daniel.[46] He further finds in a survey of Jewish and Christian exegetes from the Hellenistic period that "from 30 A.D. onwards Jewish exegesis universally and Christian exegesis generally took the Roman Empire to be the fourth kingdom in Daniel."[47]

Caird comments: "Since the main trait of the monster's character is that it wages war on God's people, the emperor who best fits the specifications is Nero. His suicide in A.D. 68 could have been regarded as a deadly wound. ... Only with the accession of Vespasian did the monster come to life again."[48]

Ford seems to simply assume that the beast (from the sea) is one of the Roman emperors and proceeds to determine which one is intended.[49] Fiorenza, after surveying current scholarship, follows the same assumption, and observes that the problem is that "scholars ... do not agree whether or not to begin with Caesar, Augustus, Caligula, or Nero" in determining the date of the book by counting the heads of the beast.[50] The heads equal Roman emperors.

Whether the beast is a specific emperor or the empire itself, all are agreed that Rome is intended. The reading of Revelation developed here would certainly concur with this consensus. But, as Caird has seen, the clearest fit in terms of the monster's character would be Nero, the emperor who declared war on the Jews in A.D. 66. Vespasian was Nero's general whom Nero sent to besiege Jerusalem, and who in A.D. 69 became emperor after the Roman civil war that followed Nero's suicide (in A.D. 68). With Caird, I find Vespasian to be the best candidate for the head that "seemed to

have had a fatal wound, but the fatal wound had been healed"
(Revelation 13:3). No other candidate for emperor could more
clearly have represented Nero-returned-to-life to the Jews in A.D. 69
than did the general whom Nero sent to attack Jerusalem.

The beast/Rome was certainly a key problem for all Jews/Chris-
tians in the habitable world in A.D. 69. The question was, What can
be done about the beast? Jewish groups offered essentially three
different options: (1) we can beat them; (2) if you can't beat them,
join them; and (3) if you can't beat them, transcend them.

1. THE "WE CAN BEAT THEM" APPROACH

Some Jewish groups actually believed that they could defeat the
Roman Empire militarily. Louis Finkelstein summarizes some of the
events that led to the overtly rebellious activities of the Zealot party:

> After the death of Agrippa the country was once again reduced to
> the status of a province to be governed by procurators; for the next
> twenty-two years they did everything to make confusion worse con-
> founded. Fadus demanding that the High Priest's vestments be de-
> posited . . . with the Romans; Tiberius Alexander symbolizing apostasy
> triumphant; Cumanus . . . aggravating Samaritan-Jewish relations; Fe-
> lix outraging everyone and . . . ordering the imprisonment of excel-
> lent persons—these men destroyed every possibility for peace and
> established a precedent for pillage and anarchy.
>
> Such a state of affairs strengthened the Zealot group, and a number
> of extremists in their midst now abandoned restraint altogether. At
> every public gathering . . . these extremists created panic by stabbing
> their enemies with hidden daggers . . . Everyone trembled at the . . .
> Sicarii (. . . so called because of their murders with the sica, dagger),
> for their weapons were raised not only against Romans but against
> any Jews suspected of counseling "collaboration."[51]

It is probable that Jesus' disciple Judas, since he is surnamed
"Iscariot" (*iskariôtês*), was one of these "Sicarii." Another disciple,
Simon the Zealot (Luke 6:15, Acts 1:13), should be identified as a
member of the Zealot party.

2. THE "IF YOU CAN'T BEAT THEM JOIN THEM" APPROACH

A second group of Jews were convinced that there was no possibility of defeating the Roman Empire. Most notably, this group included the high priestly party. Rather than antagonize Rome, the high priestly party sought to ameliorate the tensions that existed between Jews and their Roman rulers. Evidence of their attitude is found in the Gospel of John:

> Then the chief priests and the Pharisees called a meeting of the San-hedrin. "What are we accomplishing?" they asked. "Here is a man performing many miraculous signs. If we let him go on like this, every-one will believe in him, and then the Romans will come and take away both our place and our nation."
>
> Then one of them, named Caiaphas, who was high priest that year, spoke up, "You know nothing at all! You do not realize that it is better for you that one man die for the people than that the whole nation perish." (John 11:47–50)

In another passage in John, Pontius Pilate has Jesus on trial. John claims that "Pilate tried to set Jesus free, but the Jews kept shouting, 'If you let this man go, you are no friend of Caesar. Anyone who claims to be a king opposes Caesar' " (John 19:12). Pilate responds to this premise with the assertion, " 'Here is your king. . . . Shall I crucify your king?' . . . 'We have no king but Caesar,' the chief priests answered" (John 19:14–15).

According to Louis Finkelstein, since the Seleucid-Ptolemaic pe-riod (third century B.C.):

> The intermediary between the royal government and the Jews was the High Priest, appointed by the king. Practically, the office was hereditary and was held for life. The high priests, responsible pri-marily for the tribute, also became accustomed under Egyptian [Ptol-emaic] domination to farm the other taxes. In this way, the High Priest became the political head of the nation as well.[52]

This political position is implicit in the mention of the "place" (in John 11:48, cited above), which it is feared the Romans would take away. The "place" is the Jerusalem Temple. Those who rule the Temple are the high priest and his family. It is understandable that those in positions of political strength under the Romans would be less inclined to wage war with Rome.

Even when the Judean state declared its independence from Rome in A.D. 66, the high priestly party was still covertly attempting to avoid war with Rome. Solomon Zeitlin states:

> On the 28th of Tebeth, the beginning of January 66, a great assembly was convened in the temple for the purpose of establishing a government to carry out the necessary preparations for the war. It chose as head of the government the High Priest Ananus, a Sadducee who inherently was for peace. . . . This government turned out tragically for the State of Judea. It played a double role. It thought it would achieve its goal by shrewdness. Speaking openly for war, inwardly it was for peace. It wanted to disarm the extremists so that it should have all power concentrated in its hands and thus be allowed to make peace with Rome. It failed utterly.[53]

3. THE "IF YOU CAN'T BEAT THEM TRANSCEND THEM" APPROACH

Finally, there is John's approach. While he is less opposed to the first approach than he is to the second, John considers a military victory over Rome to be impossible. His view of the inevitability of Rome's military triumph is indicated in Revelation 13:10: "If anyone is to go into captivity, into captivity he will go. If anyone is to be killed with the sword, with the sword he will be killed. This calls for patient endurance on the part of the saints."

John's true complaint is against the "if you can't beat them join them" approach. His favorite psalm is Psalm 2. According to Nestle and Aland, he cites this psalm eight times in the Book of Revelation.[54] For John, this psalm denounces an alliance between Jewish rulers and "the kings of the earth." As does the author of Acts, John considers this evil alliance to be the alliance between Roman "kings" such as "Herod and Pontius Pilate" (Acts 4:27) and "the rulers, elders and teachers of the law . . . Annas the high priest . . . and . . . Caiaphas, John, Alexander and the other men of the high priest's family" (Acts 4:5–6). The psalm ponders:

> Why do the nations conspire and the peoples plot in vain? The kings of the earth take their stand and the rulers gather together against the Lord and against his Anointed One.
>
> "Let us break their chains," they say, "and throw off their fetters."

The One enthroned in heaven laughs; the Lord scoffs at them.
Then he rebukes them in his anger and terrifies them in his wrath,
saying, "I have installed my King on Zion, my holy hill."
I will proclaim the decree of the Lord:
He said to me, "You are my Son; today I have become your Father.
Ask of me and I will make the nations your inheritance, the ends of
the earth your possession. You will rule them with an iron scepter.
(Psalm 2:1–9)

John defines worship of the beast/Rome as asking the questions:
"Who is like the Beast? Who can make war against him?" (Revelation 13:4). Hence, John is especially disgusted with "the great prostitute" with whom "the kings of the earth committed adultery"
(Revelation 17:1–2). This is sociopolitical commentary. John is identifying the dual enemy—Rome and the high priestly party, who
entered into an alliance with Rome at Jesus' crucifixion and who is
covertly seeking to enter into a new alliance with Rome in A.D. 69.

Rather than capitulate to Rome (as the high priestly party prefers
to do) or fight Rome militarily (as the Zealots prefer to do), John
is proposing a "transcendent" battle (in a Burkean sense). In chapter 8, John's strategy is explicated. For now, let it suffice to say that
John views the most significant battle not as physical warfare, but
as the battle of the human will. The true "conquerors" will "conquer" as Jesus did, by dying to their own will. They will be resurrected to reign with Christ.

JOHN'S VANTAGE POINT IN THE HUMAN DRAMA

If John is writing in A.D. 69 regarding the sociopolitical struggle
with Rome, how does John view his chronological position in the
great human drama? He is on the brink of the "end" (*telos*). In
chapter 6, John's use of the psychology of form to place his audience on the brink of the end is demonstrated. But *which* end? Many
Revelation interpreters have been confused by John's prediction of
a "time" that is "near" (Revelation 1:3, 22:10), of Jesus' "coming
soon" (Revelation 3:11, 22:20), of an earthbound dragon whose
"time is short" (Revelation 12:12), and of the "things that must soon
take place" (Revelation 22:6).

Just as there are multiple ends in Greek dramas, there are multiple ends in John's human drama. The Greek trilogy has three
ends, one for each of the three dramas that comprise the trilogy.

If John envisions a tripartite human drama, somewhat along the line of the tripartite *weltwochenschema* of the school of Elias, John would seemingly place himself at the end of part two. The period "with the Law" is drawing to a close. Temple worship will soon cease. The messianic reign upon the earth/land is beginning or has begun. John briefly outlines the messianic reign (Revelation 20: 1–9) and proceeds to briefly sketch the type of existence that will characterize the (Sabbath?) rest period, the new heaven and new earth (Revelation 20:10–22:5). But, for now, John's primary interest is in the *transitional period*, as the period with the law ends and the period with the Messiah/Christ begins. Revelation is primarily about the events surrounding the seven-year war from A.D. 66 to 73. He writes from the vantage point of A.D. 69, the year before Jerusalem fell and the Temple was destroyed.

Some Christians may be dismayed to see that premillennial, post-millennial, and amillennial approaches to Revelation are set aside in this approach. Unlike the famous Hal whose last name matches mine except for a spelling discrepancy, this Lindsay does not find it necessary to force upon the text twentieth- and twenty-first-century referents for John's symbols. Revelation's few references to "our" future are made more credible by correctly referencing the bulk of John's symbols historically. Virtually all of John's symbols from chapters 1 through 19 can be referenced within the context of the seven-year Jewish-Roman war and those events that preceded it.

Some Contemporary-Historical scholars may be confused to see that this reading does not share their pessimistic conclusion that John's predictions were erroneous. Martin Kiddle correctly observes that "it is needful to explain what [the New Testament writings] meant for the communities to which they were addressed in the first century."[55] Kiddle incorrectly suggests that "John was mistaken only in so far as he narrowed too closely the focus of his gaze into the future."[56] Indeed, Kiddle and others who place the date of Revelation in the last decade of the first century *do* find it difficult to locate fulfillments for John's prophecies in the events immediately following *their* proposed date for the book. They will find it much easier to locate historical referents in the seven-year Jewish-Roman war.

And, what about chapter 20? What about the thousand year imprisonment of the dragon? What about the release of Satan? What about Gog and Magog? What about the surrounding of the beloved city? Now, Hal Lindsey, you may try your hand. These were futuristic for John. The symbols used are much more ambiguous and, thus, open to speculation. Christians can surely supply interpretations that acknowledge the strength of the Contemporary-Historical method and yet preserve the expectant hope for the future triumphant return of Christ.

3

Burke's Statistical Method

BURKE NOTES IN THE FOREWORD TO PLF: "[T]HERE IS A TENDENCY for writers to feel that they have characterized a work intrinsically when they apply epithets of approval or disapproval to it (appreciation), or refer to it in tonalities meant to be in tune with the tonalities of the book itself (impressionism), or tell what it's about (reviewing), or classify it (bibliography)" (PLF xix). These methods are unsatisfactory, in Burke's view. In this chapter, Burke's approach to method is surveyed. Method is one of the nouns that Burke modifies with the adjective "entelechial." To place his statistical method in perspective, therefore, discussion of his method is prefaced with a definition of "entelechy/entelechial." Next, an overview of other terms that Burke modifies by the terms "entelechy" and "entelechial" is provided.

DEFINITION OF ENTELECHY/ENTELECHIAL

For a detailed explication of the meaning of the term "entelechy," the reader is referred to the book, *Implicit Rhetoric: Kenneth Burke's Extension of Aristotle's Concept of Entelechy.*[1] What is provided here is a brief overview:

> [T]he term entelechy may be defined as: *the process of changing from what something is into what something should become, which process is directed by an internal principle of change which allows the thing to possess internally the final form toward which the thing is changing....* Aristotle appears to have originally coined the term to explain the fact that a biological organism possesses within the very germ matter of the organism something like a blueprint—a fully determined plan regarding how that organism will develop....
> Aristotle thought of seeds, for example, as possessing within themselves the "final cause" or *telos*—the goal of what the mature plant

48

would be. He believed that there exists within a grain of wheat the formula that makes the seed first produce roots and a sprout, then grow a blade, which grows into a stalk, until finally an ear of new grain develops. The plan for the fully grown stalk with its ear of grain is implicit in the seed. To use a computer metaphor, the seed is "programmed" to produce a fully developed wheat plant. The *telos* (or goal) of the fully developed plant is held in the seed and in the plant throughout the growth process. Thus Aristotle called the process "entelechy." "En" means "within." "Tel" is short for *telos*, the goal. "Ech" means "to have." "Y" indicates "process." Thus, "En-tel-ech-y" means: the process of development (*cf. Attitudes toward History*, hereafter ATH, 107) while having one's *telos* within oneself.

We now know that there is, in fact, a code . . . that virtually directs the growth pattern and changes of all biological organisms. We call the code DNA.[2]

When Burke extends Aristotelian entelechy from the biological realm to the symbolic realm, he leaves intact most of Aristotle's definition:

Burke employs the term entelechy in his theorizing in 1945, where his comment on the matter is little more than a brief summary of Aristotle's use of the "concept of the 'entelechy,' which [Burke, then] might call the individual's potentialities for becoming a fully representative member of its class" ([*A Grammar of Motives*, hereafter] GM 27). Although Burke therein presents the notion that Aristotle's concept of entelechy was derived in a sense from a "Platonic theory of forms," he also distinguishes the "Aristotelian" view from that of the "realist" or the "nominalist." Later, in GM, Burke defines the Aristotelian entelechy as "the striving of each thing to be perfectly the kind of thing it was" (GM 249). This sometimes biological, sometimes physical, "striving" is, of course, a "temporizing of essence." Again, Burke distinguishes "Aristotle's more 'scientific' brand" from Platonism in that "the Aristotelian 'entelechy' resided in the things of sensory experience" as opposed to "the heavenly family identity" (GM 253). Still commenting on the Aristotelian entelechy, Burke offers one more definition of entelechy in GM: "having its end [or purpose] within itself" (GM 261).[3]

Burke finds it necessary, however, to replace the implicit determinism (such as that of a DNA code) with the implicit freedom of human action in his concept of entelechy:

Certainly, by 1961, Burke has put in place the logological framework
that will characterize the Burkean entelechy in its extension of the
Aristotelian entelechy. Burke here speaks of "terminologies that can
be developed in connection with the 'logic of perfection.' (A bright
Greek will treat it in terms of . . . the 'entelechy')" ([*Rhetoric of Religion*, hereafter] RR 300). And while Burke acknowledges that "[t]he
Aristotelian concept of the 'entelechy' is essentially a biological analogy," which locates the "entelechy . . . as residing not just in the . . .
seed, but in the . . . *process as a whole*" (RR 246–247), Burke is moving
to "extend" Aristotle's biologically-contextualized entelechy to his
own logologically-related entelechy. . . .

Burke later states: "By entelechy, I refer to such use of symbolic
resources that potentialities can be said to attain their perfect fulfillment" (DD 39). Since Burke's concept of entelechy is described in
the final clause in his definition of [hu]man—which definition, at its
outset, distinguishes between the human's biological nature (animality) and his/her logological nature (symbolicity)—Burke is concerned with tracking down the logic of perfection implicit in symbols,
terminologies, nomenclatures. This concern is Burkean, not Aristotelian.[4]

REVIEW OF ENTELECHIAL TERMS

Burke uses a variety of terms to characterize entelechy and entelechial:

Burke uses "entelechy" and "entelechial" to refer to a "term" (GM
261–262), a "concept" (GM 223, *Language as Symbolic Action*, hereafter
LSA, 69–70, 125), a "principle" (GM 249, LSA 19, 160–161), a "theory" (GM 261), a "pattern of thought" ([*A Rhetoric of Motives*,
hereafter] RM, 19), a "tendency" (RM 141, LSA 19), a "job" (LSA
17), a "motive" (LSA 69–70, 73–74), a "way of viewing" (LSA 380), a
"point of view" (LSA 390), and a "perspective" (LSA 390).[5]

Burke refers to entelechy as a theory in GM (261). The term
"theory" may be used to characterize Burkean entelechy as a whole.
The various other epithets that Burke applies to entelechy would
be synecdochic parts that represent this theoretical whole. Burke's
term "theory" is best defined with respect to its Greek origins. Theory is a noun of process that denotes a viewing or seeing. In the
sense in which Burke employs the phrase "entelechial theory" (or
"theory of entelechy"), he refers to the entire process of viewing

any given human action as a process that contains its *telos* within itself. When committing to this definition of entelechial theory, certain assumptions follow.

ASSUMPTIONS

It is assumed that an entelechial tendency (RM 141, LSA 19) does exist for human beings—that humans *tend* to act in accordance with a purpose (or *telos*), which exists within the mind of the specific human taking the action. This is true of the symbol-using animal and untrue of the non-symbol-using animals. It is assumed that there are points of view (LSA 390), standpoints (*The Complete White Oxen: Collected Short Fiction*, hereafter CWO, 272), or perspectives (LSA 390) from which this tendency may be observed. It is assumed that in order for an entelechial process to begin (i.e., for an action to commence), this tendency must somehow be activated. Something must start the action. This would be the Burkean equivalent of the Aristotelian *archê*, the principle or the primary or efficient cause.

The term "principle" is the key to unlocking what Burke means by the choice of *Grammar* as a title for his first volume in his proposed trilogy on motives. He contrasts the grammatical with the philosophical by contrasting principles with casuistries (GM xvi). *Webster's Seventh New Collegiate Dictionary* offers a negative connotation for "casuistry": "sophistical, equivocal, or specious reasoning." Burke would not be so negative. For him, philosophies are casuistries that "apply these principles [scene, act, agent, agency, purpose] to temporal situations" (GM xvi).

To illustrate the difference between principle and casuistry, Burke offers the term, "Scene . . . as a blanket term for . . . background or setting in general" (GM xvi). This term would be grammatical since the concept of scene is a general principle. Whereas, in "matters of 'philosophy' . . . one thinker uses 'God' . . . another uses 'nature,' a third uses 'environment,' or 'history,' or 'means of production,' etc." (GM xvii). Such specific scenic applications would be casuistic or philosophical.

Grammatical principles refer to those elements of motivation that can be detected in all discussions of motivation, not just in specific examples. Hence, Burke offers five terms that he calls "the generating principle" (GM xvi) of motivation. These five terms are interrelated. But all attributing of motives can be seen as generating from one or from a combination of them (with this qualification: Burke later "hexes" the pentad by adding attitude). Burke's "five terms would allow for ten" ratios: "(scene-act, scene-agent, scene-agency, scene-purpose, act-purpose, act-agent, act-agency, agent-purpose, agent-agency, and agency-purpose).

The ratios are principles of determination" (GM 15). One could say that each term in a ratio "determines" (GM 15) what the other term in the ratio will be like. Another way of putting this is to say that they are "principles of consistency" (GM 9) that bind each other together: "scene, act, and agent also lead to reverse applications. That is, the scene-act ratio either calls for acts in keeping with scenes or scenes in keeping with acts" (GM 9). Burke, in applying his representative anecdote—"drama" (GM 59–61)—to his analytical system, appropriates an important "principle of drama" to his method: "that the nature of acts and agents should be consistent with the nature of the scene" (GM 3). He calls this principle of drama a "principle of consistency" (GM 3, 7, 9, 77).

In this respect, the pentadic terms and their ratios could be said to have been generated from Burke's concept of form as "the arousing and fulfilling of expectations" (DD 16). Each term in a ratio arouses an expectation in the other term of the ratio. For example, not only does the "scene-act ratio" call "for acts in keeping with scenes," but also for "scenes in keeping with acts—and similarly with the scene-agent ratio" (GM 9). Burke also calls his pentadic ratios "principles of selectivity" (GM 18). In other words, various scenes/situations select ("call for") "cautious men . . . daring men . . . traditionalists . . . [or] innovators" as "the appropriate 'voice' " (GM 19) for that scene. To this extent the ratios select from the potentialities the appropriately consistent balance among its terms. Whether these ratios are called "principles" of "drama," of "selectivity," or of "determination," they remain "principles of consistency." Whenever the ratio relationships are observed in any pentadic set that results from action, the principle of drama, all of the interrelated pentadic terms will be expected to display consistency.

Since the "scene contains the act" (GM 3), discussions of the ratios lead to discussions of tropes. As Burke puts it, "the synecdochic relationship whereby a part can be taken as consistent with the whole" (GM 107) can surface in pentadic discussions. Normally such "synecdochic" relationships will bear out our expectations of consistency. However, Burke allows for "transformations" (GM 107) whereby this consistency principle can be severely tested. In some cases, it is possible that synecdochic relationships can become compensatory, rather than consistent. In GM (53–55), Burke discusses the transformation of his five key terms from principles of consistency into compensatory principles. This is possible due to the ambiguity of substance, as when nature is equated with God, as the scene of man's acts, then later God and nature are turned into agonistic terms. What had begun as a synecdochic relationship— the view that God created natural laws; hence nature could stand synecdochically for God—developed, due to the Occamite "principle" (GM 80–81), into the narrowing of a circumference of the scene to simply nature. The "natural" then became contrasted with a no-longer-necessary "supernatural" explanation. Thus two terms that had been consistent became compensatory. However, even compensatory terms may be seen as consistent. When Burke discusses the "political and economic agon," he understands such an agon to be "not simply ... differences, but ... antitheses" (GM 103). An antithesis shares a consistency with a thesis that a difference does not share.

Burke teaches: "The technical appeal of the symbol lies in the fact that it is a principle of logical guidance, and makes for the repetition of itself in changing details which preserve as a constant the original ratio" (CS 60). Burke sees the necessity of both "logical consistency" and "emotional consistency" within the symbol (CS 61). Burke calls this consistency demand a "generative principle" (CS 57), a "generative ratio" (CS 60), a " 'creative' or 'interpretive' principle" (CS 152), and a "generating principle which entails a selection" (CS 157).

Dramatic principles are also entelechial principles. Burke asserts: "A theoretically perfect Symbol would, in all its ramifications, reveal the underlying pattern of experience. . . . [A] wholly consistent . . . pattern is observable in such minute particles as the single word" (CS 158). What would be more entelechial in the Burkean sense than a "single word" that reveals "an underlying pattern of experience"? What would illustrate the entelechial process more than the producing of a "theoretically perfect Symbol" that would "in all its ramifications" adhere to an "underlying pattern"?

In Aristotle's realm of motion, the "generative feature" is termed by Burke the "principle of the entelechy, which represented the striving of each thing to be perfectly the kind of thing it was" (GM 249). In Burke's realm of action, the " 'entelechial' principle" corresponds with the " 'perfectionist' tendency for [humans] to attempt carrying out" the "various implications" that a "given terminology" "contains" (LSA 19). Apparently, for Burke, this " 'entelechial' principle" (LSA 161) exists when the latent entelechial tendency that lies otherwise dormant is given the specific *telos* toward which this tendency should act. Since this happens within the human mind, Burke characterizes this "moment" at which point in time the tendency is given a specific *telos* "the moment of the 'revelation'" (LSA 161). (Incidentally, this Burkean characterization may be in itself one of these types of revelations for those who would study Revelation.) The "moment of 'revelation'" is equated by Burke with the "Joycean use of 'epiphany,' the discovering or unveiling of a moment that stands for much more than its sheer materialism" (LSA 160).

However, the "'entelechial' principle" (LSA 161) in the Burkean system should not be reduced to the Aristotelian realm of motion. Burke writes: "The 'principle of perfection' could not be said to operate in any immediate purpose, as when a person reaches for something that he intends to eat" (LSA 160). I surmise that this application would be too close to human animality and Burke is interested only in human symbolicity. Yet, the eating example could be applied easily to Aristotle's concept of a primary cause, or *archê*. The hunger tendency, when combined with the sight of the food, could cause the beginning of the eating process. Certainly, animals other than humans participate in this process, based upon the same primary cause. In symbolic entelechy, terms generate consistent actions.

The term "cause," while it may fit the requirements of Aristotle's biological entelechy, is too simple a term for the complex motivational structure involved in human action. Burke suggests that the term "freedom" is an appropriate term to apply to human action since "no single terminology can be equal to the full complexity of human motives."[6] Human motivation, for example, cannot be reduced to the (biological) realm of stimulus-response, as in the eating example that Burke has offered.

In discussing the "entelechial motive," Burke complains that "Freud's overwhelming tendency to treat of motives in terms of the temporally prior ... might deflect our attention" (LSA 69). Burke's "'entelechy' ... [as] a species of Unconscious" would refer us to "'future possibilities' in a purely formal [= formal logic, here?] sense" (LSA 69). Burke offers Euclid's system as an illustration. Euclid's "propositions" were not temporally prior to "the definitions and axioms of his geometry." Rather, they were "deduced from" them (LSA 70). What was temporally later, however, is superior in the sense that it is a "'perfect' conclusion." This, Burke calls "the 'entelechial' motive, a motive intrinsic sheerly to symbol systems" (LSA 70). It is that "perfectionist" motive that causes writers of animal stories to develop an "entelechial dog" such as "Lassie" (LSA 74). It is the "motive" that seeks to develop any given terminology into its perfect expression.

As in the Euclid example, the entelechial motive may not at the time of the inception of action (the "epiphany" or "moment of revelation") contain within itself the exact form/*eidos* that the ultimate product of the action will have. This is due to the fact that, unlike the ideal forms of Plato, and the biological forms of Aristotle, the logological forms of Burke do not always have temporally prior existence. Aristotle's seed has its prior stalk, leaves, roots, etc. Plato's chair has its prior ideal chair in heaven. But, Euclid's geometry does not have its perfect conclusions/propositions prior to Euclid's development/deductions of them. What is implicit with Euclid's definitions and axioms is the "terminological" potential/ *dunamis*—the "future possibilities" (LSA 69)—for being developed into a "terminological" *telos*. And there is implicit in Euclid an "entelechial tendency" to develop his "terminological" potential into its "perfect" form (= *telos*). This is Euclid's "entelechial motive." The *telos* that exists in Euclid from the "moment of revelation" is not the "perfect" form that he developed. It is the notion of "perfection" itself that motivates humans to "attempt carrying out [the] implications" that a "given terminology contains" (LSA 19).

It is finally assumed, when speaking of an entelechial theory—a process of seeing human action—that there are more and less preferable ways of viewing the theoretical entelechial tendency. Method is therefore the subject of the present chapter.

ALTERNATIVE CRITICAL METHODS

As cited above, Burke comments:

> there is a tendency for writers to feel that they have characterized a work intrinsically when they apply epithets of approval or disapproval to it (appreciation), or refer to it in tonalities meant to be in tune with the tonalities of the book itself (impressionism), or tell what it's about (reviewing), or classify it (bibliography). (PLF xix)

The four current methods, Burke allows, "[a]ll . . . have value" (PLF xix). But Burke is critical of the way they have been practiced.

Burke calls his "article on Hitler's *Mein Kampf*... the most complete example" of his "theory of the criticism of books" in PLF (PLF
xviii). In that article, Burke characterizes those previous "reviewers"
who contented themselves "with the mere inflicting of a few symbolic wounds upon this book [*Mein Kampf*] and its author" as "van-
dalistic" (PLF 191). Yet, Burke's main criticism of this criticism
hinges on the word "hasty" and its synonyms. He refers to such
reviewers as "hasty." He refers to their "inattention." He alludes to
the limited "time at their [the reviewers'] disposal." The "appreciation" that these hasty reviewers have expressed, Burke calls "a few
adverse attitudinizings ... with a guaranty in advance that [their]
article[s] will have a favorable reception among the decent members of our population" (PLF 191).

THE BURKEAN METHOD

In PLF (191), Burke indicates what he considers to be the preferred objective of criticism—that is, "enlightenment." If theory denotes seeing, and perspective denotes that vantage point from
which seeing occurs, then method provides the light by which seeing occurs. Burkean method is not designed to gratify readers (to
reinforce attitudes readers already possess); it is designed to enlight-
en readers, to help them see things that they have not seen before.
Of course, some of the methods currently in use are capable of
providing "enlightenment." Reviewing or "telling what it's about"
certainly enlightens those who have not read a given book. A review
provided by a colleague provides one with a new perspective, and
is therefore enlightening. Yet, Burke seeks a method of enlightenment that will be able to go systematically deeper than the sheer
perspectives of various reviewers. "Classifying" comes closer to
Burke's goal of providing a method, but it may not, at times, provide as much enlightenment as "reviewing." Certainly, if a critic
classifies a given book as tragedy or comedy or satire, that critic is
contributing to the enlightenment of his readers, so long as the
readers are enlightened as to what expectations the various forms
arouse and fulfill. It accomplishes very little, for example, for a
critic to classify Revelation as either an apocalypse or a prophecy
or an epistle, unless that critic's readers share the meaning of the
implications of those conventional forms. Burkean method does, in
fact, classify. But it classifies with the objective of enlightenment
constantly in mind.

Burke is a "philosoph[er] of human relations" (LSA 54). He claims:

> Basically, the Dramatistic screen involves a methodic tracking down of the implications in the idea of symbolic action, and of [the hu]man as the kind of being that is particularly distinguished by an aptitude for such action. To quote from *Webster's Third New International Dictionary*, which has officially recognized "Dramatism" in my sense of the term, as treated schematically in my *Grammar of Motives*, it is "A technique of analysis of language and thought as basically modes of action rather than as means of conveying information." I would but note that such an "Ism" can also function as a philosophy of human relations. (LSA 54)

Burke's philosophy methodically "track[s] down . . . the implications" of two ideas—the "idea of symbolic action" and the idea of "[hu]man as . . . distinguished by an aptitude for such action." The bulk of this chapter is devoted to methods of "tracking down . . . the implications in the idea of symbolic action," but before moving to such methods, the idea of "[hu]man as symbol-user" is briefly outlined.

The Definition of Human

By 1935, Burke uses a "poetic or dramatic metaphor" to enlighten his readers concerning humans (PC 263). He explains that Unamuno lists several alternative metaphors for viewing humans:

> [T]he political being of Aristotle, Rousseau's signer of the social contract, the economic [hu]man of the Manchester school, the homo sapiens of Linnaeus, "or, if you like, the vertical mammal." He [Unamuno] votes for "the [hu]man of flesh and bone," as the romantic philosophers had stressed a concept of volitional [hu]man which reached its culmination in Nietzsche's metaphor, [hu]man as warrior. (PC 263–64)

To this list, Burke appends "[hu]man as mechanism," and then suggests "that the metaphor of the poetic or dramatic [hu]man can include them all and go beyond them all" (PC 264).

The adoption of such a metaphor, says Burke, means that we have "a vocabulary of motives already at hand" (PC 264). This vocabulary is the "whole vocabulary of tropes (as formulated by the

rhetoricians) to describe the specific patterns of human behavior"
(PC 264). Among these tropes, Burke manifests an interest both
early (PC 264) and late (GM 503ff.) in synecdoche, which is considered more fully in chapter 4 of this book.

By 1953, Burke argues that dramatism is not sheerly a "metaphor, but is strictly literal in reference" (CS 219). The human,
Burke continues, "is the specifically symbol-using animal, and a
'Dramatistic' theory of motives is systematically grounded in this
view of human essence" (CS 219). The sheer simplicity of Kenneth
Burke's definition of the human is at once obvious and yet deeply
fertile. In chapter 1 of LSA, Burke reiterates that "[The Hu]Man
is the symbol-using animal" (LSA 3). The present consideration
of the Apocalypse will illustrate this definition with thoroughness.
The Book of Revelation abounds in symbolic action. The very
thought of a lamb opening the seals of a scroll, of a seven-headed
dragon and multiheaded beasts, of heads that are kings one minute and mountains the next should indicate that John is a symbol-
user.

But Burke is not limiting symbolic action to the use of extrava-
gant metaphors and similes, which are common to the apocalyptic
genre. His book is called *Language—as Symbolic Action*. Burke is concerned with the "essential" nature of mankind (CS 219). He asserts
that "a definition of [hu]man is at least implicit in any writer's
comments on cultural matters" (LSA 2), and he thereupon serves
notice that he rejects the reductionism of the behaviorist view of
humankind (DD 11). It is human language that, for Burke, distinguishes humankind from all other animal life. Burke tells his audience at the Heinz Werner Lectures: "I had in mind the particular
aptitude that the human biologic organism has for the learning of
conventional symbol systems (such as tribal languages), our corresponding dependence upon this aptitude, and the important role
it plays in the shaping of our experience" (DD 15).

Implicit Rhetoric[7] considers the issue of determinism and freewill
in connection with Burke's preference for the term "motive" rather
than "cause" as an explanation of human action. In CS, Burke re-
frains from making a "plea for free will" (CS 81). He concedes, "It
may be true that, despite our 'illusion of liberty,' we are rigidly
determined in both our thoughts and our actions" (CS 81). Yet for
Burke, the key phrase in this sentence is "may be." Burke prefers
this "agnostic" stance (of the perhaps). However, he actually believes that human symbolicity implies free will. Otherwise, he would
not have taken "sides against behaviorist reductionism" (DD 11).

Yet, Burke accedes to biological determinism insofar as human animality is concerned. Burke locates the deterministic factor for humankind in the realm of human animality. He locates freewill in the realm of human symbolicity. Burke maintains:

> A Dramatistic terminology of motives, based on a generating distinction between action and motion, would not look for the ultimate roots of freedom in either physicist or biological notions of indeterminacy. As a matter of fact, along Spinozistic lines, Dramatism would feel safest if one could prove beyond all doubt (as one doubtless never will) that everything in the realms of physics and biology is inexorably determined. Insofar as a state of freedom is possible, Dramatism would seek it in the realm of symbolic action (the dimension that the determinist, Spinoza, called "adequate ideas"). (DD 30–31)

For example, a man may have a physical ailment that is determined through purely biological factors—he may have consumed a poison. But, the man overcomes this determinism through the development of an adequate idea. Some doctor or chemist may be able to discover what sort of poison is causing the problem. Once this discovery is communicated to the man (via language/symbols), the man is free to change his diet and thus overcome the deterministic circumstance.

It is not "signaling" (LSA 14) that differentiates humans from other animals; it is the human aptitude for using symbol systems. Dogs certainly bark, cats meow, birds chirp, and lions roar. But there is a fundamental difference between even "such complex sign systems as bees apparently have" and "what [Burke] mean[s] by the reflexive or second-level aspect of human symbolism" (LSA 14, cf. further the entire "Definition of [Hu]Man" essay). For all we know, the specific signals of animals are instinctive. A Japanese dog might well instinctively "know" the meaning of the bark or growl of a Brazilian dog. But humans must learn the often subtly variant implications of a particular word or idiom when used by humans of different nationalities, ethnic or religious backgrounds, cultures, and ultimately different individuals or the same individual speaking in different contexts. Words for humans do not carry immutable denotations in the same sense as a specific chirp of a mother bird attempting to lure the cat away from her young in the nest might.

Herein lies both the conquest and the quandary of humankind. Specifically, as regards the Book of Revelation, John is "free" to expound for his generation (and subsequent generations) those "adequate ideas" that he believes to have the capacity to release his auditors from their circumstances. Yet, these "adequate ideas" are relayed to his auditors in the form of language/words/symbols. John, no doubt, assumes that his primary audience shares fairly well and rather precisely the meanings of his words (the referents of his symbols). But to assume that there was perfect communication even with an audience of his own generation and culture (much less an audience separated by nearly two millennia) would be asking too much.

Humans, however, can function quite well by "approximation" in terms of communication (CS 79). And, as Burke has said, mankind has an aptitude for learning symbol systems. Any person's sense of reality is related proportionally to his/her successful development of this aptitude. Burke asks:

[C]an we bring ourselves to realize just . . . how overwhelmingly much of what we mean by "reality" has been built up for us through nothing but our symbol systems? Take away our books, and what little do we know about history, biography, even something so "down to earth" as the relative position of seas and continents? . . . [T]he whole over-all "picture" is but a construct of our symbol systems. (LSA 5)

To live as a human child is to gradually learn the symbol system of one's own tribe or country. To study a foreign language is to gradually learn that shared symbol system. And in the context of a study of Revelation, to study John's "unique grammar and style,"[8] as well as the apocalyptic, apocryphal, pseudepigraphal, rabbinic, Old and New Testamental, Near Eastern mythological, and sectarian literature with which John (and his audience) may have been familiar, is to gradually learn John's peculiar symbol system, and thus to share an ever-closer proximity in meaning with John.

This is the realistic goal of dramatistic analysis. The aim is not perfect communication but rather further enlightenment, closer proximity in terms of shared meaning. Burke provides enlightenment to the ways symbol systems work, by pointing out how they are constructed. Using Burke's statistical method, the terms of a given symbol system may be analyzed and the interrelations between those terms may be viewed.

Once Burke has identified the human as the symbol-using animal, he is free to move on to four additional clauses in his definition of the human. Burke's second clause, "Inventor of the negative" (LSA 9), is an adaptation of and accommodation to the chapter "The Idea of Nothing," from Bergson's work, *Creative Evolution.* Burke is struck by the notion "that there are no negatives in nature, where everything simply is what it is and as it is" (LSA 9). The "peculiarly human marvel, the negative," is demonstrated by Burke: "Look at any object, say, a table, and . . . remind yourself that, though it is exactly what it is, you could go on for the rest of your life saying all the things that it is not. 'It is not a book, it is not a house, it is not Times Square,' etc., etc." (LSA 9).

Burke proceeds to distinguish between the "hortatory negative, 'Thou shalt not,' " and what he suggests that Bergson stresses, "the propositional negative, 'It is not' " (LSA 10). The hortatory negative implies moral choice, which involves action. "Hence the obvious close connection between the ethical and negativity, as indicated in the Decalogue" (LSA 11). Finally, under this clause, Burke alerts his audience to the existence of "polar" terms such as "true-false, order-disorder, cosmos-chaos, success-failure, peace-war" (LSA 11), etc.

Earlier, the concept of the negative is developed by Burke—drawing on Nietzsche and Oswald Spengler—into a "perspective by incongruity," as he observes that certain clusters of terms automatically exclude certain other clusters of terms. Yet Spengler acquires a new perspective "by taking a word usually applied to one setting and transferring its use to another setting" (PC 89–90). This is identified as a " 'perspective by incongruity' since he established it by violating the properties of the word in its previous linkages" (PC 90). Burke notes that the "metaphor always has about it precisely this revealing of hitherto unsuspected connectives which we may note in the progressions of a dream" (PC 90). Burke's statistical method provides assistance in charting a "perspective by incongruity" in Revelation that is implicit when Caird in his commentary speaks of "the kaleidoscopic quality of dream imagery,"[9] which Caird sees in Revelation. Chapter 4 of this book deals further with Caird's "kaleidoscopic" model of Revelation imagery. There, I propose the replacement of Caird's model with a synecdochic model.

The third clause in Burke's definition of human "is designed to take care of those who would define [the hu]man as the 'tool-using animal' " (LSA 13). The clause reads: "Separated from his natural condition by instruments of his own making" (LSA 13). Burke argues that although "the human powers of symbolicity are interwoven with the capacity for making tools" (LSA 14), the symbolic nature of the very act of defining is prior to the instrumentality of tool-making.

In the fourth clause, "Goaded by the spirit of hierarchy," Burke handles the "incentives of organization and status" (LSA 15). He addresses the social hierarchy in RM and relates the concept to the heavenly economy in his RR. This concept proves helpful in considering the implications of the old and new orders that Revelation relates and develops.

The fifth clause is presented by Burke as a "final codicil [that] was still needed, thus making in all":

[The hu]Man is
the symbol-using . . . animal
inventor of the negative . . .
separated from his natural condition by instruments of his own making
goaded by the spirit of hierarchy . . .
and rotten with perfection. (LSA 16)

This final codicil is the point at which Burke indicates that he is attempting to adapt "the Aristotelian concept of the 'entelechy,' the notion that each being . . . is marked by a 'possession of telos within' " (LSA 17). Thus, Burke's definition of the human ends with the human's rotten penchant for chasing ends. Perhaps the irony of ending his definition with a clause indicating the rottenness of the human preoccupation with ends prompted Burke to call this a "wry codicil" (LSA 16). With the addition of this perfection codicil, Burke believes that he has perfected(?) a definition of mankind.

It may strike the reader as strange that Burke's "philosophy" has no need of a definitive position on human origins. Burke answers such a query:

Certain intradisciplinary decisions might be immaterial to a given philosophy. For instance, though specialists might quarrel as to just exactly where human culture began and exactly how it spread, many such decisions would be quite irrelevant to a philosophy of language which takes as its starting point a definition of [hu]man as [s/]he is, everywhere all over the world, regardless of how [s/]he came to be that way.[10]

As noted, Burke's philosophy methodically "track[s] down . . . the implications" of two ideas—the "idea of symbolic action" and the idea of "[hu]man as . . . distinguished by an aptitude for such action" (LSA 54). Now that the idea of "[hu]man as symbol-user" has been outlined, consideration will be given to the Burkean method(s) of "tracking down . . . the implications in the idea of symbolic action."

Analyzing Symbol Systems

Burke describes his method of criticism as follows:

> [T]he way primarily tried here . . . is this: To identify the substance of a particular literary act by a theory of literary action in general.
> The quickest way to sloganize this theory is to say that it is got by treating the terms "dramatic" and "dialectical" as synonymous. So it is, as you prefer, to be called either "dialectical criticism" or "dramatic criticism methodized" (i.e., a reasoned method for treating art as act). (PLF xix–xx)

Earlier discussion of clause two of Burke's definition of the human makes reference to the existence of "polar" terms such as "true-false, order-disorder, cosmos-chaos, success-failure, peace-war" (LSA 11), etc., wherein Burke observes that certain clusters of terms automatically exclude certain other clusters of terms. As mentioned there, these clusters of terms at times can be violated so as to produce a perspective by incongruity. But, usually, these clusters can be studied for the purpose of understanding the peculiar symbol system of a given author (or, more specifically, a given author within a given work) to find out which terms s/he automatically associates with which other terms. For Burke, "a book is a replica of the human mind" (DD 20). He would qualify the comparison by adding that "in a book," the "vast assortment of 'equations' " is "finished, whereas in life there is always the possibility of new situations which will to some degree modify such alignments" (DD 20). The mind is in a state of constant modification. Note, however, that for Burke, "Any work is a set of interrelated terms with corresponding 'equations,' sometimes explicit, but more often implicit" (DD 20). Such clusters of "implicit or explicit 'equations' " form a "structure of terms, or symbol-system" (PLF viii).

The associational nature of these equations, according to Burke, make them similar to what "contemporary social scientists call 'values' or what in Aristotle's Rhetoric are called 'topics' " (PLF ix). Otherwise put, the inductive procedure to which Burke adheres is capable of providing not only enlightenment regarding the specific text under consideration, but also of revealing a picture of the scenic background in which the literary act takes place (since Burke considers the scene to be the ideological background in which the act occurs, and values considerations are ideological). Ruth Anne Clarke and Jesse Delia comment: "Since the Classical period, rhetoricians have taught *topoi*, or commonplaces—general strategic approaches to be adapted to specific communicative needs."[11] The epideictic *topoi* of a given rhetorical handbook, for example, would provide a tool for an orator of the milieu in which the handbook is valid in order to persuade an audience from that milieu to either praise or blame the individual who was the subject of the epideictic speech. The *topoi* serve as indicators of the level of virtue of a person, according to the values which the audience accepts.

In the Hellenistic Greek milieu, with which (it might be argued) John was familiar, the *Rhetorica Ad Herennium* provides an interesting list of epideictic *topoi*. *Topoi* may vary greatly from age to age and from culture to culture, but the *Ad Herennium* epideictic *topoi* are at least indicative of what Burke means when he links topics/ *topoi* with values. The *Ad Herennium* divides the *topoi* of epideictic oratory into three categories: external circumstances, physical attributes, and qualities of character.[12] The *topoi* that the *Ad Herennium* lists under the heading of external circumstances are: (a) descent, (b) education, (c) wealth, (d) kinds of power, (e) titles to fame, (f) citizenship, (g) friendships (3:10). Further elaboration is probably unnecessary. In the list of *topoi* are revealed the sort of values that were held in esteem in this milieu.

These *topoi* work quite well when judging the virtues of Alexander the Great as presented by Plutarch. The values indicated in the *Ad Herennium* are reflected clearly in Plutarch. However, some important differences in values may be noted when attempting to utilize the Hellenistic *topoi* of the *Ad Herennium* to examine the virtues of Jesus of Nazareth in the gospel accounts. Although both works (Plutarch and the Gospels) are produced in roughly the same age, they differ in cultures. The Gospels provide virtually no physical attributes of Jesus whatsoever. There is no clue concerning his height, weight, relative handsomeness, color or length of hair, etc. Whatever exceptional physical feats he accomplishes (walking on water, healing, calming storms) are attributed in no way to his physical attributes. Hence, an entire major category of *topoi* is missing. Certainly, other *topoi* such as "wealth" and "citizenship," which were important for Plutarch's primary audience, are unimportant or even anathematized in the Gospels. Quite obviously, an alternative value system/symbol system/epideictic *topoi* system is at work in the

Gospels, despite the fact that the *Ad Herennium* is from roughly the same age as the New Testament. So, how is Burke's method to be used to become enlightened concerning the values and associations of New Testament authors?

In charting the specific symbol system of a given author, Burke's method requires "objective citation":

> Now, the work of every writer contains a set of implicit equations. [S/h]e uses "associational clusters." And you may, by examining his [/her] work, find "what goes with what" in these clusters—what kinds of acts and images and personalities and situations go with his[/her] notions of heroism, villainy, consolation, despair, etc. And though [s/]he be perfectly conscious of the act of writing, conscious of selecting a certain kind of imagery to reinforce a certain kind of mood, etc., [s/]he cannot possibly be conscious of the interrelationships among all these equations. Afterwards, by inspecting his[/her] work "statistically," we or [s/]he may disclose by objective citation the structure of motivation operating here. There is no need to "supply" motives. (PLF 20)

Burke includes the proviso, "by objective citation," and his elaboration, "There is no need to 'supply' motives," as an answer to and protection against his method being "characterized as 'intuitive' and 'idiosyncratic,' epithets that make [him] squirm" (PLF 68). Biblical interpreters, utilizing some other method(s), might do well to add the "objective citation" proviso to their method(s). At times, interpreters have found it convenient to posit motives that might explain the texts, and then to proceed to interpret the specific text in question, as well as other texts, on the assumption that their hypothesis has now become fact, by virtue of its pragmatic usefulness. To cite an extreme example of such methodical impropriety, one might quote R. H. Charles's criticism of so much of the Revelation scholarship that preceded him: "These early attempts had no scientific method to guide them—and were thus at liberty to attach almost any meaning to any symbol and to explain away any statement that conflicted with their theories."[13] Consequently, I not only adhere to Burke's "objective citation" proviso, I recommend that other interpreters hold to the same standard.

Burke would begin his search for "equational clusters" by watching "for the dramatic alignment. What is vs. what" (PLF 69). Another way of considering this first step is as a search for polarities. When Burke says that he might "sloganize [his] theory . . . by treat-

ing the terms 'dramatic' and 'dialectical' as synonymous" (PLF xx),
he implies that there are "two quite different but equally justifiable
positions . . . in [his] approach" (LSA 54):

> There is a gloomy route of this sort: If action is to be our key term,
> then drama; for drama is the culminative form of action (this is a
> variant of the "perfection" principle . . .). But if drama, then conflict.
> And if conflict, then victimage. Dramatism is always on the edge of
> this vexing problem, that comes to a culmination in tragedy, the song
> of the scapegoat.
>   There is also a happy route, along the lines of a Platonic dialectic. . . .
> [T]his happier route . . . states the problem in the accents of an ideal
> solution. (LSA 54–55)

Whether Burke's method is called dramatic or dialectical, the implicit antithetical nature of Burke's method may be noted. In drama, the antithetical hero and villain are present. Burke can speak
of "the 'villain' that makes the total drama go" (ATH 343). In Platonic dialectic, something similar to the "opposite banks of a
stream" is present. The antithetical nature of the "opposite banks"
may be transcended by the "reality" of the whole stream. It is not
necessary in dialectic to disprove one bank of the stream, in order
that the opposite bank may be true. Still, in both the "dramatic"
and the "dialectic" separate "bins" (ATH 135) are present. Polarities
are present. The question, "What is vs. what?" is present.

As a paradigm for utilizing Burkean analysis, Burke would himself
recommend his analysis of Hitler's *Mein Kampf.* Therein, Burke
seems to follow his own advice. He sees several polarities. There is
the polarity of the single mecca, Munich, as opposed to the discord
of the parliamentary wrangling of Vienna. There is the "dominating
male" (Hitler himself) who "woos" the feminine masses," as contrasted with "the rival male, the villainous Jew," who would "seduce"
them (PLF 191–95). There are the "many voices in dispersion,
placed in . . . opposition to the one voice of Hitler" (PLF 69).

Once Burke has located the polarities, he notes "the sets of 'equations' that reinforce each of the opposing principles" (PLF 69). By
way of illustration, with the "one voice of Hitler," he sees that:

> Hitler's inner voice, equals leader-people identification, equals unity,
> equals Reich, equals the mecca of Munich, equals plow, equals sword,
> equals work, equals war, equals army as midrib, equals responsibility . . . ,
> equals sacrifice, equals the theory of "German democracy" . . . , equals

love (with the masses as feminine), equals idealism, equals obedience
to nature, equals race, nation. (PLF 207)

With the "many voices of the dispersion," Burke sees that Hitler
equates " 'Babylon,' Vienna as the city of poverty, prostitution, immorality, coalitions, half-measures, incest, democracy . . . , death, in-
ternationalism, [and] seduction" (PLF 200).

In addition to the "equals" concept, Burke finds that he needs a
"becomes" concept. He observes that "the two main symbols for the
charting of structural relationships would be the sign for "equals"
and "some such sign as the arrow" (PLF 75). "Since literature is a
progressive form," Burke writes, "the matter of 'equations' always
verges on the matter of the arrow." Burke offers the analogy of a
musical chord and an arpeggio. " 'Equations' . . . cause us to collapse into a single chord a series of events that, by the nature of
the literary medium, must be strung out in arpeggio" (PLF 75).

Since the discussion has led to the types of shorthand that Burke
employs, it is expedient to mention here that Burke's polar nota-
tion, which designates the "compensatory relationship in equations," is "vs." and his shorthand for "a compensatory sequence" is
an "arrow with a slanting line (/) drawn across it" (PLF 77). Since
there is an "arrow" concept, a "from what to what" idea, there is a
middle step that Burke observes that can be quite revealing. He
states, "Along with the distinction between opposing principles we
should note the development from what through what to what"
(PLF 70–71). As examples of this middle step, Burke offers: "the
'laying of the cornerstone,' the 'watershed moment,' and the 'val-
edictory,' or 'funeral wreath' " (PLF 71). In Revelation, the question might be asked, for example, "Through what" does John move
in his vision of chapter 4 with God alone being worthy of praise to
arrive in chapter 5 with both God and the Lamb being worthy of
praise? Perhaps the answer will have equations that may be linked
to similar exaltation steps for the "144,000."

Burke's statistical method, with its "objective citation" proviso,
amounts to an inductive method that may be used "to note what
the . . . equational structure is. This is a statement about its form"
(PLF 101). By tying Burke's statistical method to his theory of form,
Burke has led back from one of those "labyrinthine" "side streets"
in the "city" of his "terminology" to reconnect with the main "ave-
nue" of entelechy (ATH vi).

Summary

Burkean method (as a way of viewing the symbolic action in a given work) tracks down the implications of the terminology in a work. Since "a book is a replica of the human mind," Burkean method may also be used to track down the implications of the terminology of a given symbol-user. The terminology of a given symbol-user in his/her creation of a Symbol, or literary work, may be expected to adhere to principles of consistency. To avoid charges of "intuition" and "idiosyncracy," Burke makes his method inductive by requiring "objective citation" of all terms and equational links. In order to chart the equational structure, Burke employs the equal sign, the arrow, the abbreviation "vs.," and the slashed arrow.

Although the charting of the equational structure or symbol system of a given work or a given symbol-user is itself an entelechial process for the individual performing the analysis, it does not suffice as entelechial criticism. The point of "knowing" the equational structure of a given terminology is to "know" the form (or underlying pattern) that is implicit in a given process of symbolic action. Charting is the first step toward becoming enlightened as to the implications of a given terminology's equational structure. The question that entelechial criticism would address is, in what respect(s) is a symbol-user moved by "a kind of 'terministic compulsion' to carry out the implications of [his/her] terminology" (LSA 19)?

4

Synecdoche and John's Representative Anecdote

Synecdoche is one of the most significant terms in the Burkean system. Burke associates synecdoche with representation, and hence with representative anecdotes. With synecdoche Burke contrasts metonymy, which he associates with reduction. This contrast is an important key for enlightening the imagery of Revelation.

Kaleidoscopes, Metonymy, and Synecdoche

In line with Burke's distinction between the tropes synecdoche and metonymy, emphasizing the representative nature of synecdoche and the reductionist nature of metonymy, in this chapter I propose a replacement for G. B. Caird's kaleidoscopic model for understanding the mutability of Revelation imagery. I contend that the kaleidoscopic model is metonymic, not synecdochic, and that John's imagery (being in the realm of symbolic action) is better represented by a synecdochic model with which John appears to be familiar, i.e., the stream of fire from which (rabbinic literature informs us) angels arise and to which they return. In rabbinic literature, this stream is a highly symbolic and synecdochic concept. Using this stream-of-fire model, with magma as a key term, John's representative anecdote is presented here. Then, the synecdochic relationships between the terms of John's imagery in line with the two major magmas (equals Burkean clusters of the previous chapter of this book) of his representative anecdote are delineated.

G. B. Caird's term "kaleidoscopic" as a description of the imagery in Revelation is a useful metaphor. It is very panoramic. The difficulties involved in visualizing, "e.g., living creatures full of eyes inside and out (iv. 8)," Caird suggests, will be reduced as we "become familiar with the kaleidoscopic quality of dream imagery."[1] While the matter of interpreting "dream imagery" is best left to the psychologists, it seems indisputable that John's symbols seem to be constantly shifting in meaning in much the way that the shifting crystals of a kaleidoscope produce new visual images. Caird observes, regarding chapter 15 of Revelation: "By a slight shift of the kaleidoscope the *ocean of blood* through which the martyrs have passed in the *great vintage* now becomes a *heavenly Red Sea,* poised after the passage of the true Israel to engulf Israel's persecutors" (emphasis mine).[2]

This specific instance of a change in imagery seems to be a remote or minor concern. There are far more central images in Revelation that shift constantly. There is a woman in chapter 12 who shifts without warning from a sign in heaven—to a pregnant woman giving birth—to a group of people who must be protected—to 144,000 virgins (and/or a harlot?)—to a bride—to a city, New Jerusalem, described in terms of a bride. There is a dragon with seven heads that shifts without warning to a serpent, and thence to the Devil or Satan. But this dragon also appears to be the voice speaking through a beast that has arisen from the land, whose job it is to make the inhabitants of the land worship another beast, which remarkably resembles the dragon. Even the seven heads of this beast shift from being seven to eight and back to seven because the eighth represents one of the seven which has suffered a fatal blow. Furthermore, they do not even remain heads. They shift from heads to kings and then to hills.

Is this shifting of imagery purely random and accidental, as might be the case with the images produced by the shifting crystals of a kaleidoscope? Not even Caird claims that much for his metaphor. He observes, "John's faculty for kaleidoscopic changes of metaphor *stops short of sheer incoherence*" (emphases mine).[3] Stopping "short of sheer incoherence" is not even close to a fair description of what John is doing with his imagery. There is method to John's imagery. His consistency may even be implicit in one of Caird's "kaleidoscopic" references. Caird states:

> It is important for our understanding of John's kaleidoscopic imagery to notice that the seven stars do not mean in this letter [to Sardis] what they meant in the letter to Ephesus. There they were the angels of the churches, here they are the sevenfold Spirit of God; and since the Spirit, in speaking to the churches, addresses the angels of the churches, the two are clearly not to be identified. The one symbol does double service.[4]

Caird makes a good point, although his "sevenfold Spirit of God" terminology should be examined more closely. It appears that John is defining the seven stars as the seven spirits of God in the letter to Sardis, whereas they were angels of the seven churches earlier. Furthermore, again present is that troublesome term, "spirit ... say[ing]" things to the churches. How does one resolve such a difficult imagistic tangle? The kaleidoscope metaphor may help, but the kaleidoscopic answer is little more than a rationalization for John's accidental abuse of his imagery. What if there were an artistic explanation that makes of John not an accidental abuser, but a master craftsman? Such an artistic approach was available to John in the first century.

George Kennedy credits Stoic grammatical studies for producing "the theory of tropes, which is first expressly mentioned in a rhetorical treatise by Cicero (*Brutus* 69)."[5] Burke, in his theorizing, narrows the list of tropes from the eight of the grammatical treatises to four master tropes—metaphor, metonymy, synecdoche, and irony (GM 503). Giambattista Vico, as well as historiographers Hayden White and Geoffrey Hartman, likewise emphasize these four tropes.[6] Of these four, Burke shows a marked preference for synecdoche.

Burke claims that synecdoche is the key trope for handling matters of representation, while metonymy is the trope of reduction.[7] Burke complains that often the terminologies that scholars employ to describe phenomena are not representative, but are instead reductionist. He cites, for example, the behaviorists who study animals in order to understand human phenomena. Burke objects to the use of this perspective, "because animals lack that property of linguistic rationalization which is so typical of human motives" (GM 59). Animal behavior cannot represent human action. Viewing human action as animal behavior reduces humans from language-using animals to mere animals. For similar reasons, he also rejects the notion that "people are but chemicals" (GM 59). Burke instead holds "that an anecdote, to be truly representative, must be synecdochic rather than metonymic; or in other words, it must be a *part for the whole* rather than a *reduction of the mental to the physical*" (GM 326, emphasis Burke's).

For this reason, a Burkean must ultimately reject Caird's kaleidoscopic perspective for viewing Revelation imagery. In Burke's terminology, kaleidoscopic is metonymic—not synecdochic! A kaleidoscope is purely "physical." The "mental" of John's imagery cannot be reduced to the "physical" accident of the ways in which crystals might randomly fall. Even if John is not to be viewed as *consciously and deliberately* using a synecdochic art, by the time John wrote, synecdoche was an explicit trope used by rhetoricians. It may have been either an intuitive or a deliberate form of language use for John.[8] Certainly, Jews of John's time thought of God's word (a linguistic, not physical concept) from a synecdochic perspective.

G. F. Moore links the terms of Caird's conundrum of the "seven stars" together quite easily. In his chapter entitled, "The Word of God. The Spirit," Moore states, "God's will is made known or effectuated in the world not only through personal agents (*angels*), but directly by his *word* or by his *spirit*" (emphases mine).[9] Here all three terms of Caird's puzzle fit neatly together. If the seven stars represent angels, then angels are a part of the whole. If the stars represent spirits of God, then spirits are a part of the whole. If "the spirit" is "say[ing]" things to the churches, then what "the spirit says" (or in other words, the word) is a part of the whole.

For John, as for other Jews of his generation, a concept of a whole from which parts spring up and to which they return is the concept of the *Nehar di-Nur* (the stream of fire). Louis Ginzberg states: "Thus there are angels who spring up daily out of the stream Dinur ('stream of fire'; comp. Dan. 7:10); they praise God, and then disappear. Out of every word uttered by God angels are created"[10] Ginzberg says that the rabbis further connected this stream with at least one star: "The stream of fire in which the sun bathes, is identical with the *Nehar di-Nur*."[11] An easy connection would be to see other heavenly lights, such as stars, bathing in and arising out of the stream of fire, as well.

Is John familiar with the stream of fire? He does not mention this stream, but he describes a lake of fire into which the Devil and his angels are thrown. I believe that not only is John familiar with the stream of fire, he even adds a twist to the concept: a stream keeps on flowing, but a lake is the end of the line. Later Jewish writers speak of souls passing through the river of fire where the wicked are judged.[12] Whether these Jewish writers originated the idea of a river of fiery judgment or picked up on John's "lake of fire" is uncertain, but their concept does seem to demonstrate the ease with which fiery judgment and the stream of fire may be connected. This is a synecdochic move.

The purpose of mentioning such a concept is to propose the stream of fire as a synecdochic model to replace Caird's metonymic model of a kaleidoscope as a means of providing enlightenment to John's imagery. The stream of fire is a magma anecdote—the whole in which God's words exist in their "essential" nature before and after becoming angels (-parts). But this chapter is not about angels and the *Nehar di-Nur*. It is about two streams of magma that represent John's imagery. Herein are presented two levels in which John employs synecdoche in the imagery of Revelation.

John's first-level use of synecdoche is to be found in his choice of a primary representative anecdote, the Eve vs. serpent anecdote of Genesis. This anecdote, with the help of a plot twist from John, provides the story that John dramatizes. John's second-level use of synecdoche is evident in the synecdochic fashion in which his specific heroes and villains are brought forth from the magma of his two major streams, only to melt back into the magma and reemerge later as different entities, which hold synecdochic relationships with the earlier entities. This second-level employment of synecdoche requires a more extensive explanation. The former use can be set forth rather succinctly.

THE REPRESENTATIVE ANECDOTE

Burke stipulates the starting point of his inductive procedure: "First: We should watch for the dramatic alignment. What is vs. what" (PLF 69). Some interpreters of Revelation consider the informing anecdote of the book to be the conflict between God and Satan.[13] This perceived conflict is a vestige of Judaism's contact with Persian religion. Martin Hengel discounts such "iranische Dualismus" in accounting for the scene that, for example, produced the "fallen angel" stories in the centuries preceding the New Testament period.[14] In perusing John's Revelation, examples of a direct rivalry between God and Satan cannot be found. While allusions are made to fallen angels in Revelation, it is not clear that they are typical of the fallen angel stories of the centuries preceding the Christian Era.[15] A conflict that pits Jesus against Satan is another option. Certainly Jesus' conquest is discussed in Revelation, but this archetype is not the primal archetype.

Eve versus the Serpent

John appears to be lucidly aware of the dramatic alignment upon which he builds. It is the archetypal conflict between the "woman" (at the point of the woman vs. serpent encounter, she is not yet named "Eve") and the "serpent" in Eden, although it is curious that commentators have not clearly identified the connection. J. M. Ford does note that it "is strange for the dragon" to be referred to as having "stood" before the woman. She suggests, "One may compare the serpent in Gen. 3:14."[16] F. F. Bruce states that the dragon "is identified with the serpent of Eden and with Satan (verse 9)."[17] If Jesus' conflict with Satan is an adjunct to the anecdote, its significance might be found in the language of Genesis 3:15: "I will put enmity between you [the serpent] and the woman and between your seed and her seed. He will bruise your head and you shall bruise his heel." The original significance of the Genesis material need not be discussed here. The question is not whether Genesis 3:15 actually implies a "gospel" prophecy. The only pertinent question is, how did John view the material? That a "protogospel" interpretation of Genesis 3:15—of some sort—existed in Christian circles in the New Testament period is evidenced by Paul's comment in Romans 16:20: "And the God of peace will bruise Satan under your feet shortly." Foerster agrees, "Paul is alluding to Gn. 3:15."[18]

John rather clearly (for John) states his agon in chapter 12. He speaks of two signs (*sêmeia*), in Heaven—a woman (12:1) and a dragon (12:3). John further identifies his dragon in 12:9: "the old serpent, being called the Devil and Satan." Such an equation directs the reader immediately to the Genesis 3:15 story. The conflict between woman and serpent from Genesis 3 informs John's major imagery. The Genesis story is the synecdochic or representative plot of John's drama. Certainly, woman vs. dragon/serpent/Devil/Satan informs much of John's narrative. Yet, the Genesis story would be in a sense a reduction of John's contemporary drama. In that sense, it would be metonymic. However, if this reduction is allowed to stand representatively as the part for the whole, we have in John's representative anecdote the sense of synecdoche.

The Woman Magma

Not only does John employ synecdoche in representing the agon of his drama as the archetypal agon of woman vs. serpent, but he also employs synecdoche in relating the various dramatis personae of his drama to the two antagonists, woman and dragon. The characters composing the woman magma are readily identifiable. The woman changes back and forth from Eve to woman to Israel/Zion in fairly simple ways. John makes the woman into Israel/Zion on the strength of the number twelve. He describes the woman in 12:1 as having "on her head a crown of twelve stars." F. F. Bruce observes the reference to Genesis 37:9, where Israel is "twelve stars" in a dream.[19]

For John, twelve almost always equals Israel. In 7:5–8, he uses the term "twelve" twelve times in calculating his 144,000 heroes—twelve thousand from each of the twelve tribes of Israel. In 21:12, New Jerusalem has twelve gates, manned by twelve angels, and having the inscriptions of the twelve tribes of the sons of Israel. These twelve gates are mentioned once again in 21:21. In 22:2, the tree of life produces twelve fruits, corresponding to the months of the year. It might appear that this twelve has nothing to do with Israel, except for the strange shift from "fruits" to "leaves" in John's statement: "And the leaves of the tree (are) for the healing of the nations." The Greek word for "leaves" is *phulla*. There would appear to be a play on words, what classicists call *paronomasia*, if John had intended the word to be a pun on the word "tribes" (*phulai*). In the Old Testament, the twelve tribes are presented as being capable of healing of the nations, and 1 Enoch 25:4 speaks of the tree of life growing again in Jerusalem. But that "side street" of the "labyrinth" will not be followed yet.[20]

Another link by which John changes from Eve to Israel might be the term "seed" (*sperma* = Hebrew *zerah*), which John uses only once and in the context of the conflict between the woman and the dragon: "And the dragon was enraged over the woman and went away to make war with the rest of her *seed*, those keeping the commandments of God, and having the testimony of Jesus Christ" (12:17, emphasis mine). What does John mean by "the rest" of her seed? Is there some implied seed that is not mentioned before, thus making this newly designated seed "the rest" of her seed? If John does in fact view the Genesis 3:15 passage as both an informing anecdote and a "protogospel," then the term "seed" is implicit in the plot. Woman's "seed" plays an important role in the plot of Genesis. If John further links similar promises to Abraham's seed— "And in your seed shall all the nations of the earth be blessed" (Gen. 22:18)—there is a link between the "tribes"/*phulai* of Israel and the "leaves"/*phulla*, which are "for the healing of the nations." The two concepts of blessing and healing the nations are nearly equivalent. This, however, is but a hypothetical sketch of the manner in which John's "woman" sign may have changed from Eve to Israel/Zion. Perhaps to the Jewish audience it was even unnecessary to provide a link. Israel was the metaphorical wife of God. Hence, Israel assumes the metaphorical Eve role. Thus, she has an archetypal conflict with the serpent.

Regardless of the logic by which John moves from language that appears to indicate the archetypal serpent-woman animosity to language that appears to indicate the Israel/Zion connotation, the connection is in tact. The equation (woman=Eve=Israel/Zion) seems to exist. And that is the important matter. The question is not a question of Old Testament exegesis or even of rabbinic midrash. The question is, what is the symbol system of John? The "woman" magma, thus far, looks like this: the "woman" sign in heaven (with respect to her conflict with the dragon=serpent=Devil=Satan) represents Eve. But the "woman" sign (with respect to the crown of twelve stars) represents Israel/Zion. Add the fact that John presents this woman as being "pregnant," and ready to deliver a "son who will rule the world with a rod of iron" (a clear messianic reference from Psalm 2:9), and she represents the mother of the Messiah (12:2 and 5).

Here is a clear example of the second level of synecdoche. The woman has melted from a part (the specific identity of Eve) into a synecdochic whole (of the people of Israel/Zion), and now has possibly reemerged as a part (Mary, the mother of Jesus), only to melt once again into another whole, in the sense that Jewish imagery can allow for the nation to be pregnant with the Messiah. The motif of the travail of Zion/Jerusalem in bringing forth a "male child" is found in Isaiah 66:7. The Qumran community (those who produced the Dead Sea Scrolls in the years preceding John's writing of Revelation) perhaps combined the sense of Isaiah 66:7 with Isaiah 9:6 in the picture in one of their hymns of "the faithful community as a woman enduring birth-pangs until she brings to birth a man child, a wonder of a counsellor."[21]

As was pointed out earlier, one of the favorite messianic psalms of the early church (Psalm 2) provides the language of ruling the "nations [*ethnê* = Hebrew *goiim* = Gentiles] with a rod of iron." Allusion is made to this psalm in Acts 4:25–26; 13:33; Matthew 3: 17, Hebrews 1:5; 5:5; 7:28; and 2 Peter 1:17. However, John (in Revelation) alludes to it more than does any other New Testament writer, alluding to it in 2:26; 11:15,17,18 and 19:15,19, in addition to 12:5. This psalm surely helped to shape John's messianic view. If John's application of the sense of this psalm is along the line of that recorded in Acts 4, attributed to the apostles Peter and John, John, the author of Revelation, may have viewed the strange alliance of the "heathen" (*ethnesi*) and the "peoples of Israel" (Acts 4: 27) as being responsible for Jesus' death. The context in which Luke places such an accusation is following an unpleasant encounter with "the chief priests and elders" (Acts 4:23). John (in Revelation) makes no such explicit association, but just as Paul saw Israel/Jerusalem as two women (in a positive sense and a negative sense) in Galatians 4:25–26, John seems to split the "woman" here into "virgin" and "harlot."

After the woman has become the "mother of the messiah" (12: 5), John reports that the woman flees "into the wilderness, where she has a place, having been prepared for her from God where (they?) may nourish her a thousand two hundred sixty days" (12: 6). John picks up the same language in 12:14 where she is "nourished" in the "wilderness," but the time period phraseology has been changed to (the equivalent?) "time, times, and half a time" (= 3½ years = 1260 days). John gives the mode of transportation, "two wings of the great eagle," which, at first glance (thinking of the Roman eagle possibility) might produce a connective with Rome in the mind of the reader. However, the more likely reference is to Exodus 19:4: "You have seen what I did to Egypt, and I bore you on wings of eagles, and brought you to me." This Exodus allusion not only serves to corroborate the identification of the woman with Israel, but also appeals as a symbol to assist her in leaving the city of her persecution (CS 154).[22]

The purpose for mentioning the connectives at this point is to identify the woman at this stage. She has now become the Church. This stage in the development in the identity of the woman is the one to which R. H. Charles alludes when he comments that Christ's "mother, i.e. the Church, is preserved from the attacks of the Dragon (5c–6)."[23] It is also the stage to which Caird appeals when he states: "The woman is the mother of the Messiah, not Mary, but the messianic community. This John makes abundantly clear now by a verbal echo of a prophecy about mother Zion (Isa. lxvi.7–9), and later by speaking of the members of the church as 'the rest of her children.' "[24] Here, Caird supports nearly all of the elements in the "woman" magma—"woman" is sometimes Zion, sometimes Mary, sometimes the messianic community, sometimes the church. The various identities of the woman are synecdochic. The church represents Israel/Zion.[25] Mary represents Eve, etc.

Once woman represents Israel/Zion, and Israel/Zion represents the mother of the messiah, the dragon targets "the rest of her seed" (12:17).[26] Clearly, this verse refers to Christians, "those having the testimony of Jesus Christ." It is less clear that it includes Gentiles. "Those keeping the commandments of God" may be exclusively Jewish Christians. The 144,000 of Revelation chapter 7 are described as the tribes of Israel. Gentiles may be included in the "great crowd which no one was able to number" (7:9), but the qualification that these are from all "nations, tribes, peoples, and tongues," if it is intended to specifically include Gentiles, would then by contrast exclude Gentiles from the 144,000. This is a question that must remain unanswered, for now. However, the 144,000 probably represent the "rest of her seed," in which case, they are "virgins" (14: 4).[27] The change from "virgins" to "bride" is accomplished finally in chapter 19 of Revelation.

The Dragon Magma

The first difficulty in detailing the dragon magma is deciding with which archetype to begin. The literary motif of a dragon who pursues a woman is known to many cultures. Of this fact, John may well be aware. Kiddle claims: "John's picture of the Evil One is as syncretistic as the pagan religions of Asia Minor."[28] As shown later, there appears to be some symbolic value in presenting the archetypal (*archaios*, cf. 12:9, 20:2) enemy as the ultimate syncretistic being. Caird reports:

> In Greece it is the dragon Python who attempts to kill the new-born son of Zeus and is foiled by the escape of the mother, Leto, to the island of Delos; there Apollo is born, and he subsequently returns to Parnassus and kills the dragon in its Delphic cave. In Egypt it is Set, the red dragon, who pursues Isis and is later killed by her son Horus.[29]

John wants his audience to know, however, that this dragon, if it is a symbol for Python or Set or Draco or Serpens or the "many-headed Hydra," or, as Caird prefers, "a combination of all three [immediately preceding],"[30] still it is represented by the serpent of Genesis 3, whom John considers to be Satan. Perhaps there is even more synecdochic representation at work here, whereby all dragon vs. woman stories are represented by the serpent vs. Eve story. For whatever reason John may have wanted to allude to the mythology of multiple cultures, he wants his audience to clearly understand that the dragon that he mentions as his archetypal villain is a villain known to those who know the Old Testament.

Here again is encountered John's synecdochic imagery. The ideological "scene" in which John's drama takes place (i.e., the ideology of his audience) may be vast and multicultural. Greeks, Egyptians, Babylonians, Romans, and Persians may all see John's drama against their own ideological backdrop. But one thing is clear. John is applying his own scene as the synecdochic whole whereby all other partial scenes are interpreted. The biblical dragon(s) and serpent are the archetypes. Even the woman is described in imagery reminiscent of a sun-goddess, but again, John subjects the imagery to the interpretive screen of Old Testament archetypes. However, use of the interpretive screen of Old Testament archetypes does not completely solve the problem. There are two major Old Testament archetypes that may be adduced for the dragon metaphor—Leviathan and the serpent of Eden. To these two dragons must be added identifications of Satan, in order to locate the final mixture.

To the mixture that John produces, perhaps the closest parallel in the New Testament is the temptation of Jesus recorded in Matthew 4:8–11 (cf. also Lk. 4:5–8). There, Matthew identifies as the Devil the one whom Jesus addresses as Satan. Satan has assumed the tempter role, associated with the serpent of Eden, and his specific temptation appears to be the offer to make Jesus some type of world ruler. Like John, Matthew uses the terminology "Devil" and "Satan." The denotation of the Hebrew word "satan" is prosecuting attorney or accuser, which John acknowledges in Revelation 12:10. That the satan has a place in Heaven is best understood by considering Job 1:6. This place Satan lost, in Revelation 12:8. Satan's authority to raise up world rulers, while expressed conversationally in Matthew, is expressed symbolically in Revelation in the Leviathan imagery. Actually, the idea that Satan is the "ruler of this world/earth" is an idea that permeates the New Testament (cf. Eph. 6:11–12; 2 Cor. 4:4; John 12:31; 14:30–31; Heb. 2:14; 1 Cor. 2:6–8; 15:22–28; and a textual variant, Mark 16:14b).

The seven heads of John's dragon refer most likely to the ancient mythical sea monster of chaos, Leviathan, to whom Ugaritic texts (ancient Semitic texts at least as old as the earliest biblical Hebrew texts) refer as "the accursed one of seven heads." Psalm 74 utilizes this myth to poetically describe how God drowned the "monster of the waters" (Egyptians) at the parting of the Red Sea, and "broke the heads of Leviathan in pieces." Isaiah 51:9–10 refers to this same literary use of the Leviathan myth, but calls Leviathan by its alias, Rahab. Isaiah 27:1 identifies Leviathan as a "serpent" (*nachash*), the same term used to identify the serpent of Eden. Apparently, John

uses these references to connect the role of the raiser of world
rulers (especially Egypt) to the other roles of tempter and accuser
for the archetypal villain, the serpent of Eden. All of these elements
John is mixing into the magma of the dragon. The dragon is the
synecdochic whole of which each of these elements is a representative part.

What is somewhat surprising is that John wants to interject into
his drama a fallen angel story, as a step in the gradual defeat of
this dragon. This is surprising precisely because the fallen angel
stories are understood by New Testament times to be dangerously
syncretistic (the term syncretistic being an epithet that might best
describe a kind of composite magma, with villainous connotations,
in John's drama, the harlot/*porneia* magma). As Bamberger points
out, "the Talmud never speaks of fallen or rebel angels. This is no
accident; nor were the rabbis ignorant of the legend. They knew it
and suppressed it."[31]

John has borrowed a few strands from the fallen angel traditions.
The first strand is the opposition of angels (specifically, the Devil)
to humanity.[32] This important rivalry explains the agon of the representative anecdote of Revelation. The conflict is not between the
dragon/serpent and God, as some have assumed. It is between the
dragon and a human foe, the woman. A second strand that John
borrows from the fallen angel traditions is the ascending and de-
scending national guardian angels (princes) motif. According to
this strand, every nation has a guardian angel, which may at some
point in history be called upon to ascend the ladder that leads to
heaven (Jacob's ladder). While the national guardian angel (of, for
example, Babylon or Persia or Greece or Rome) is in an ascended
position, the specific nation that the angel (synecdochically) represents rules the world. When he descends, another nation's angel
might ascend to take his place. This strand John readily links with
his Leviathan/dragon imagery and the dragon becomes not the
prince of any specific nationality, but the prince of this world who
raises world empires. In this role, it is about to change synecdochically into the beast, who is the current villain for John's audience.

There are explicit overt links whereby the beast represents the
dragon. Both the beast and the dragon have seven heads and ten
horns (12:3; 13:1).[33] The beast has been identified, nearly unani-
mously among scholars, as the Roman Empire. For purposes of this
chapter, it is not necessary to identify it more specifically—i.e., to
identify a specific emperor as the beast—because the beast is able
to change back and forth synecdochically from the Roman Empire

to a specific emperor (who commands that his image be erected in the Jewish temple) to another emperor (who dies) to another emperor who represents that dead emperor. Furthermore the heads of the beast synecdochically change from Leviathan associations to kings to mountains, and change in number from seven to eight to seven, with ease.

The difficulty that interpreters have experienced for two thousand years—trying to keep up with the various identifications of the beast—are eased, if as Burke recommends, the synecdochic relationships between terms be viewed more as "clusters of what goes with what." To quote Burke:

> It should be understandable by now why we consider synecdoche to be the basic process of representation, as approached from the standpoint of "equations" or "clusters of what goes with what." To say that one can substitute part for whole, whole for part, container for the thing contained, thing contained for the container, cause for effect, or effect for cause, is simply to say that both members of these pairs belong in the same associational cluster. (PLF 77)

Sifting through John's symbol system is frustrating, unless the assumption is made that synecdoche is operative. Utilizing Burke's premise, it is possible to look at the various elements of John's description of the beast with the objective of finding what terms (and possible referents) might fit into the cluster, rather than sorting through referents and debating identities.

Certainly, Nero is the referent of some terms in Revelation. Caird concludes that the character of the beast as "waging war on God's people" would best fit the character of Nero.[34] While the sometimes suggested persecution of Christians by Domitian just prior to A.D. 100 has no real substantiation by secular history, Nero's persecution in A.D. 64–68 is more verifiable. Beginning with the burning of Rome in A.D. 64, which Nero blamed on the Christians whom the classical sources call "a hated" people, Nero appears to have begun a persecution of Christians. The deadly wound, for Caird, is Nero's suicide in A.D. 68. Bruce sees in references to the Euphrates the implicit belief that Nero had gone into hiding in the east and would return with an army of Parthians.[35] Ford cites the Sibylline Oracles 4:119–27 2, corroborating Bruce, that "from Italy a great king . . . shall flee . . . over . . . the Euphrates . . . beyond the Parthian land. And a Roman leader (Titus) shall . . . burn down Solyma's tem-

ple."[36] An Aramaic or Hebrew spelling of Nero Caesar would equal
the notorious number 666.[37]

Caird sees in Vespasian the beast (Nero) coming back to life.[38]
R. H. Charles cites Erbes and Spitta who hold that Caligula is the
beast.[39] There is evidence that Caligula made an impact on the
author and audience of Revelation. He shocked the whole Jewish
world by commanding that his statue be set up in the Temple at
Jerusalem in A.D. 40. Perhaps John's discussion of the image of the
beast alludes to this command. The statue was never constructed,
however. Caligula's untimely assasination was the only thing that
prevented his command from being carried out. Some suggest that
Caligula is therefore a candidate for the head that received a fatal
blow, possibly revived in Nero.

What has preceded is a very brief overview of some connections
that interpreters have made toward identifying specific emperors in
the beast imagery. The virtually certain conclusion, however, is best
stated: the beast is always in some respect the Roman Empire. Synecdochically, then, John maneuvers back and forth from the
whole to a specific part, etc.

The Composite (Magma?)

Kiddle claims that John's dragon is "as syncretistic as the pagan religions of Asia Minor."[40] Perhaps ironically, John's polemic against
fornication/*porneia* both in the church (Jezebel, Balaam, and the
Nicolaitans) and in Judaism (Babylon) is probably a polemic against
syncretism.[41] Technically, the harlot situation that is confronted in
Revelation is one in which there is a fusion of the heroine with the
villain. The harlot is a woman who commits adultery with the horns
of the beast. She is a woman who is seated on the beast. In this
respect, the composite magma is not a separate magma at all. It
belongs in the dragon magma. The harlot is synecdochically the
first Eve who, unlike the virgins in the woman magma, does not
resist the serpent. On the contrary, she joins the serpent in warring
against the virgin Eve. She has, in a Hebrew sense, become one
flesh with the serpent (through the serpent's synecdochic representative, the beast).

Syncretistic tendencies have been identified by Revelation scholars as the *porneia* (fornication) of which John accuses Jezebel and
Babylon. Perhaps syncretistic tendencies are an important rationale
in John's choosing "Babylon" as the name of the harlot. John appears to be greatly influenced by the Book of Daniel. The heroes

of Daniel are the young men who resist syncretism, once they have been carried away into "Babylon." They refuse to eat Babylonian food (Dan. 1:8) on the grounds that they would be defiled (*summolunô* in LXX an early Greek translation of the Hebrew Bible) by (the syncretistic? act of) eating the king's food. This is possibly the verse that John has in mind when he speaks in 14:4 of the "virgins" who were not defiled. John uses the cognate *molunô* (defiled).

The Babylonians attempt to assimilate the young men into their religion by renaming the young men with Babylonian names, often associated with Babylonian deities. Hananiah, Mishael, and Azariah are renamed respectively Shadrach, Meshach, and Aved Nego (Abednego). Daniel is renamed Belteshazzar.[42] Daniel is determined to resist the law outlawing prayer to his God, even if it means incarceration with lions. The other three young heroes are determined to resist pagan worship, even if it means death in a fiery furnace. These heroes are models of antisyncretism. Even John's literary style in many ways imitates this thoroughly antisyncretistic book.

"Why," John's favorite psalm (the 2nd) asks, "do the heathen [Gentiles/*goiim*] rage?" "They have plotted together against the Lord and his Messiah," it answers. All other nationalities are expected to oppose the Lord and his Messiah. Therefore, syncretism does not matter for the heathen. They are all united against the Lord and his Messiah, anyway. Any alliance with these heathen is *porneia*, for John. The dragon is not in the important sense syncretistic, because the union of heathen gods, religions, and cultures is not *porneia*. Only when Jews or Christians are united with heathen elements is there the type of syncretism that is equivalent to *porneia*. The Old Testament harlot, Israel/Zion, is guilty of harlotry only to the extent she seduces and enters into alliances with her heathen neighbors. The specific identity of the neighbor is insignificant— so long as it is heathen. Therefore, John, in guarding against *porneia*, is interested only in this type of syncretism—Jewish (and Christian) alliances with heathen.

An important connector in John's symbol system is the phrase, "kings of the earth." The phrase is a key identification of the villains of Psalm 2:2. The phrase represents an entity that does not appear to be identical to Babylon (because Babylon commits *porneia* with the "kings of the earth"). The assumption, therefore, should be that the phrase refers to the heathen side of the conspiracy, and that, hence, Babylon implicitly would be on the people/Israel side.

If John is familiar with the type of Christian interpretation employed in Acts 4, he knows that one Christianized version of Psalm 2 is:

> And the *peoples* [Gk. *laoi*] think vain things. The *kings of the earth* and the *rulers* [Gk. *archontês*] were assembled on the same (day?) against the Lord and against his Christ. For indeed both Herod and Pontius Pilate, with the heathen and the *peoples* [Gk. *laoi*] of Israel were gathered together against your holy child, Jesus, whom you anointed. (Acts 4:25–27, emphases mine)

Furthermore, Acts connects the term "rulers" with the antagonists of Acts 4. In Acts 4:5, the rulers were gathered along with the elders and scribes. Specifically, verse 6 reports that this group included "Annas the high priest, and Caiaphas, and John, and Alexander, and as many as were of *high-priestly family*" (emphasis mine). Peter addresses the group in verse 8 as "*rulers* [*archontês*] of the *people* [*laos*] and elders of Israel" (emphasis mine). In some authoritative Christian exegesis, then, this psalm is interpreted as a syncretistic alliance between the rulers of the people (the priestly family?) and the kings of the earth (Herod and Pontius Pilate, specifically).

Does John use the phrase "kings of the earth" in a similar fashion? John mentions the "kings of the earth" in Revelation 1:5; 6: 15; 17:2,18; 18:3,9; 19:19; and 21:24. In Revelation 1:5, Jesus the Christ is called the ruler (*archon*) of the kings of the earth, in a conceptualization reminiscent of Psalm 2:8, "[God] will give nations [heathen/*goiim*] as [his Son's] inheritance." In Revelation 6:15, the kings of the earth are among those who hide from the great day of wrath. This may be the wrath of God directed against the kings of the earth in Psalm 2:5. In Revelation 17:2 and in 18:3 and 9, the harlot Babylon commits *porneia* with the kings of the earth. In Revelation 17:18, the harlot Babylon is the city that has "kingship" over the kings of the earth. In Revelation 19:19, the kings of the earth assemble for war with the Messiah, after the harlot has been destroyed, and the beast is at that point thrown into the lake of fire. The kings of the earth (at least some of them?) appear to have survived for in Revelation 21:24, the kings of the earth bring their glory and honor into the New Jerusalem, along with the glory and honor of the "nations" of those who are "saved."[43]

Nevertheless, a connection between the beast and the "inhabitants of the earth/land" is John's next development. John speaks of a syncretistic-looking "another beast" in Revelation 13:11ff., which this time arises not from the sea, but from the "earth/land."

This (second) beast resembles "the beast" in the clear sense that he is categorized as a "beast." He resembles Christ, or perhaps the Jewish sacrificial system, in that he has two horns, like a lamb. But his words are directly from the archetypal villain. He speaks like a dragon. He serves "the beast" by causing the "inhabitants of the earth/land" to worship "the beast" (13:12) and its image (13:15), which he forces the inhabitants to make. Who is this second beast? Ford understands the second beast to be a native (Judean) product, citing "Ramsay (pp. 103–4)" that "whatever comes from the land is a native product," as opposed to the beast which comes from the sea (understood Mediterranean), which would be "an empire born on the Mediterranean."[44]

According to Kiddle, the second beast is "known always, everywhere as 'the false prophet' (xvi.13, xix.20, xx.10)."[45] R. H. Charles elaborates:

> The *pseudoprophetês* [false prophet] was originally a Jewish or Christian Antichrist. That he was the former may be reasonably concluded from xiii.16b, seeing that the Antichrist there requires his worshipers to place his mark on their right hand and brow—an antichristian travesty of the practice of orthodox Judaism, which required the faithful to wear it on the left hand and forehead.[46]

According to Charles, Wellhausen further identifies the image: "The *eikon* [image] is the alter ego of the empire just as Jesus was called the *eikon* of God."[47] Similarly, Ford embarks upon some antithetical associations—"The dragon is the antithesis of God, but the sea beast is the antithesis of the Lamb"; however, she stops short of supplying the antithesis for this second beast.[48]

There are some interesting antithetical possibilities. Since this beast is also called a false prophet, a true prophet might be the antithesis. John, himself, is thus a candidate (1:3; 10:11; 22: 7,10,18,19), as are John's "brothers—those having the testimony [*marturia*] of Jesus—for the testimony of Jesus is the spirit of prophecy" (19:10). If the earth/land is interpreted as being the whole earth (or Asia Minor), John (and his brothers?) might be the antithesis. If the earth/land is interpreted as being Palestine, a third candidate—the two witnesses (*martusi*) who prophecied for three and one-half years, and then lay dead for three and one-half days on the street of the great city where their lord was crucified—might be implied (11:3,6).

There are additional parallels between the second beast and the two witnesses. They all performed miracles. The two witnesses had "the authority to shut up the heaven that no rain" may fall. They also had "authority over the waters to turn them to blood and to strike the earth/land with every plague" (11:6). By contrast, the second beast "was given" signs, such as "to give spirit to the image of the beast, so that even the image of the beast might speak" (13: 15). The two witnesses had "fire" coming "out of their mouth" (11: 5) but the second beast "causes fire to come down out of heaven onto the earth/land before men" (13:13). The causing of "fire" to come from heaven is peculiarly associated with "the sacrificial system" for the Jew. Throughout the Old Testament, God's acceptance of sacrifices was signified by his sending fire from heaven to consume them (Genesis 15:17; Leviticus 9:24; Judges 13:19–20; 2 Chronicles 7:1; 1 Kings 18:38). The "lamb," which the second beast resembled, is also associated with the sacrificial Passover lamb (also, to the exodus; possibly also to Jesus' "wolves in sheeps clothing" Matthew 7:15). If John is using these symbols as allusions to the sacrificial system, then the measuring of the Temple and the altar that directly preceded the witnesses may be a further parallel. The greatest contrast appears to be the source of their messages. The second beast "spoke like a dragon" (13:11), while the two are called by God "my two witnesses" (11:3).

The exact identity of the two witnesses may be less important than their synecdochic identity. One might see in the literary allusions that like Elijah, they "shut up the heaven so that no rain" may fall, and like Moses, they "turned the waters into blood, and struck the earth/land with every plague." Therefore, the two witnesses might be Moses and Elijah, or, synecdochically, their works— the Law and Prophets. The proposal that "to devout Jews shut up in the temple during the siege of Jerusalem . . . an unknown prophet . . . assuring those holding out . . . that they would be divinely protected, though Jerusalem itself would be destroyed," is another possibility. Kiddle rejected this view, on the grounds that it would have been meaningless to Christians in Domitian's reign.[49]

By describing the two witnesses as two lampstands and two olive trees (11:4), John directs his audience to Zechariah chapter 4, where Zechariah had a vision of a lampstand and two olive trees (Zechariah 4:2–3). The olive trees referred (synecdochically) to the oil (of anointing), as Zechariah is informed in 4:14: "These are my two sons of fresh oil who stand by the Lord of the whole earth." If these two witnesses hold "messianic" (in the sense of "anointed") offices, they would be either prophet(s), or priest(s), or king(s).

Since allusion has already been made to Elijah, and since they wore sackcloth (11:3), the rough garments of hair traditionally associated with Elijah (2 Kings 1:8) and other prophets (Zechariah 13:4), and since they have been explicitly called prophets (11:3,6,10), perhaps the proposal of an unknown prophet or two in Jerusalem has merit. However, allusion has also been made to Moses, who could hold either the title of prophet (Deuteronomy 34:10) or lawgiver, almost in the sense of a king. The fact that Moses' brother, Aaron, assisted Moses in most of his work, and that Aaron was called both a prophet (Exodus 7:1) and a priest (Exodus 31:10), further broadens John's possible meanings.

Indeed, does John try to separate the specific offices or, synecdochically, does the messianic office equal all three? In other words, John might have in mind, not prophet or priest or king, but prophet = priest = king. After all, he is willing to make those brothers of John who have the testimony/ *marturia* of Jesus = prophets (19: 10) into a "kingdom, priests to God" in 1:6 and "kings and priests to God" in 5:10 and "priests of God and Christ" who will reign (*basileuô*) in 20:6. Therefore, Zechariah's specific referent, Joshua the high priest, discussed in chapter 3, might be a type, or synecdochically his office might be implied, or his namesake, Jesus = Joshua, might be intended. Thus, Jesus and John the Baptist might be candidates for the two witnesses—except that it would have been too easy for John to have made the "kings of the earth" (specifically, Herod and Pilate) the ones who killed them rather than "the beast" (11:7). Furthermore, John would be very careless to be thinking of Jesus' death, when he speaks in 11:8 of the city where "their lord was crucified."

Peter and Paul have also been mentioned as candidates for the two witnesses, by elaborately making the great city where their lord was crucified somehow mean Rome, and by further speculating that they were both martyr victims of Nero's persecution, the entire interpretive process of which appears to be rather tentative. But, again, is it really necessary to specifically identify these witnesses, or logologically could it not be perfectly acceptable to simply ascertain their significance? That significance is probably best illustrated in the dictum of Zechariah 4:6: "Not by might, nor by power, but by My Spirit, says the Lord of hosts."

These witnesses understood something that the second beast apparently did not—that what appears to be conquering/ *nikaô* by might and power (as when, in 11:7, the beast "conquers" and kills the witnesses) is not true conquest, for in 11:11, the "spirit" of life from God reenters the witnesses and they ascend to Him. The second beast, however, having the "spirit" of a dragon (spoke like one), deceives (13:14), kills (13:15), and exercises economic power (13:17). This second beast, since he is a "false prophet," might be the antithesis to the true "prophets," who are probably the two witnesses in Jerusalem. Synecdochically, the false prophet may be a priest, if John allows the connection through the messianic (anointed) office (since prophets, priests, and kings were all anointed).[50]

The second beast can be understood to synecdochically represent "the beast" as thoroughly as the "image" that the second beast causes to be created (13:14) represents "the beast." It is highly probable that John, with his term "image," is making allusion to the proposed statue of Caligula that would have been placed in the temple in A.D. 40, had Caligula not been assasinated. If, as Wellhausen claims, "[t]he *eikôn* [image] is the alter ego of the empire just as Jesus was called the *eikôn* of God" (cf. 2 Corinthians 4:4 and Colossians 1:15), then a living human being serves as the "image" of the beast, just as the human, Jesus, serves as the "image" of God. Where exactly Wellhausen derives his information that Jesus is the *eikôn* of God, Charles does not indicate; and the explicit statement is found nowhere in Revelation. However, the *Vita Adae et Evae* 13–14 passage clearly calls Adam the "image" of God, and Ginzberg sees in early Christian midrash (Hebrews 1:6) the link that makes Jesus a second Adam in the fashion of *Vita*, hence making him worthy of worship.[51] Thus, intertestamental literature with which John could easily be familiar has a human serving as an "image," and therefore receiving "worship."

If John is making the "image" of God (Jesus) in Revelation 5 "worthy of praise," then, in antithetical fashion, he could be making the "image" of the beast (the high priest) in Revelation 13 the object of (unworthy) antichristian worship. In this way, John could be saying that ironically the abomination that the Jews had felt that they had avoided in the assassination of Caligula happened anyway! Instead of an image of stone, the Jews had in the middle of their temple an amazing sign—an image that could "speak" (13:15)! He was the voice of the empire in the midst of the Temple.

According to Jewish historian Louis Finkelstein, ever since the Seleucid-Ptolemaic period:

> The intermediary between the royal government and the Jews was the High Priest, appointed by the king. Practically, the office was hereditary and was held for life. The high priests, responsible pri-

marily for the tribute, also became accustomed under Egyptian domination to farm the other taxes. In this way, the High Priest became the political head of the nation as well.[52]

When Rome overthrew Jerusalem, "Pompey announced his terms: Aristobulus was a prisoner; Hyrcanus was to be recognized as High Priest."[53] According to Jewish historian Solomon Zeitlin, when Herod the Great was king of Judea: "Herod himself, not being of the priestly family, could not succeed Antigonus as high priest. He felt it to be politically dangerous to appoint a member of the Hasmonean family to a position of such great prominence . . . therefore, . . . he appointed Ananel (Hananel), a priest from the Babylonian Diaspora."[54]

This "Babylonian" priestly family then was the one who ruled Judea and the Temple cult until the destruction of Jerusalem in A.D. 70. It is precisely this high priestly family that the gospel accounts present as engineering the crucifixion of Jesus. While emperor worship was not conducted by the high priestly family, the temple was semiabominated with a golden eagle, the symbol of Rome.[55] A common activity was to offer up sacrifices and prayers on behalf of the emperor in temple services. Perhaps even the "image" of Caesar (Mark 12:16 and parallels), on the coinage that was exchanged in the temple currency exchange system, which Jesus battled, was one further identification between the second beast (priesthood) and the "image" of the beast. John 19:14–15 records a comment made by the priesthood to Pilate that may have been typical of the attitude of the priesthood toward Rome. Pilate "said to the Jews, 'Behold your king!' . . . The chief priests answered, 'We have no king except Caesar!' " Referents for the second beast and the image may be found, if they are identified with the priestly family in Jerusalem. The high priestly party could easily have been understood to be the talking "image" of the beast who compelled people to worship Rome. Zeitlin observes:

On the 28th of Tebeth, the beginning of January 66, a great assembly was convened in the temple for the purpose of establishing a government to carry out the necessary preparations for the war. It chose as head of the government the High Priest Ananus, a Sadducee who inherently was for peace. . . . This government turned out tragically for the State of Judea. It played a double role. It thought it would achieve its goal by shrewdness. Speaking openly for war, inwardly it was for peace. It wanted to disarm the extremists so that it should have all power concentrated in its hands and thus be allowed to make peace with Rome. It failed utterly.[56]

The elements of the dragon magma are as follows: serpent, dragon, and beast. Additionally, the following composite or syncretistic elements might be added to this dragon magma: second beast, false prophet, image of the beast, and harlot. Since the second beast makes the inhabitants of the earth/land worship the beast, these inhabitants are present at the orgy in which the kings of the earth/land commit *porneia* (syncretism) with Babylon, the harlot. In fact, they are drunk with the wine of her *porneia* (17:2). The harlot Babylon is the woman villain who is the dragon's ally.

A few more points should be made about the harlot:

- Revelation 16:1 says that the bowls (of the seven last plagues) will be poured out upon the earth/land. After the sea and the rivers were turned to blood, an angel proclaims, "Since they poured out the blood of the saints and the prophets, You gave them blood to drink" (16.6). Revelation 17:6 identifies Babylon as being "drunk from the blood of the saints and from the witnesses [*martus*] of Jesus." Revelation 18:24 claims that "in her was found the blood of the prophets and of the saints, and of all those having been slain on the earth/land." The only specific city accused elsewhere in the New Testament of "killing the prophets" is Jerusalem (Matthew 23:29–39; Luke. 11:47–51; 13:33–34). Charles claims that John is certainly familiar with Matthew and probably familiar with Luke.[57] In the Old Testament, Ezekiel 22:2ff. calls Jerusalem the "city of bloodshed" who "brings on herself doom by shedding blood."
- Ezekiel 16:13 calls Jerusalem "a queen." In Revelation 18:7, Babylon calls herself a "queen." Both are actually harlots, according to their respective "prophets."
- Isaiah 50:1 and Jeremiah 3:8 speak of God giving Jerusalem/Israel/Judah a certificate of divorce. Ford sees the scroll with seven seals as a specific type of bill of divorce (Ford, 92–94).
- In Ezekiel 16:29, Jerusalem increased her harlotry to "Babylonia, a land of merchants." In Revelation 18:3, the kings of the earth/land commit *porneia* with Babylon and the merchants of the earth became rich with her.
- Jeremiah 4:16 speaks of armies coming to destroy Jerusalem. Jeremiah 6:1 urges people to "Flee from Jerusalem." In Revelation 18:4, God's people are warned to "come out of her."

- Ezekiel 16:37ff. warns Jerusalem the harlot that all of her lovers will gather against her and strip her naked. Revelation 17:16 reports that the ten horns of the beast "will hate the harlot and will make her desolated [*erêmoô*] and naked and will eat her flesh and will burn her with fire."
- Not only will Babylon be left desolated in the previous verse, but also in 18:16 and 19. likewise, the LXX of Daniel 9:27 leaves Jerusalem "desolated," and Matthew 24:15, predicting the destruction of Jerusalem, refers to Daniel's abomination of desolation, at which point Jesus urges those in Judea to "flee."

The most problematic passage in identifying Babylon as Jerusalem is Revelation 17:9, which says that the seven heads of the beast are seven mountains upon which the woman sits. This has been taken almost universally as a reference to Rome's origin on seven hills. While topographically Jerusalem might be divided into seven hills, utilizing important "mounts" that are inside and outside of the city walls, it would sound contrived. The seven hills almost certainly signify Rome.

In Revelation, "sitting" is a term that is used almost exclusively as either sitting on a throne or sitting on a horse. Both senses are possible here. But, 17:3 has already pictured the harlot as sitting on a scarlet beast. If Babylon is Rome, it seems strange to think of her as sitting on the emperor. The sense of sitting on a throne would, it seems, have called for language that has the beast (emperor) sitting upon the woman (as if the city were the throne), rather than the woman sitting on the beast, unless the intent was primarily to show the two entities as somehow united and the easiest metaphor was to have her sitting on the beast in the same way riders are united with their horses. Revelation 17:1 has the harlot sitting on "many waters." Revelation 17:15 identifies these "waters" as "peoples, and crowds, and nations, and tongues." This is of little help. In 18:7, she claims to "sit as a queen." Sitting/ruling over many nations and tongues would be as natural a description for God's queen (Ezekiel 16:13) as it would for Rome or for Rome's queen.

The ten horns of the beast are "ten kings who have not yet received a kingdom but will receive authority as kings one hour along with the beast" (17:12). If they are identified as the "kings of the earth/land" (meaning Palestine), they enter into the equation, in the sense that they would then be understood to have committed *porneia* with Babylon, and therefore this would explain the parallel references to the ten horns of Revelation leaving her naked (17:

16) and Ezekiel 16:37, where it is Jerusalem's lovers who leave her naked. Thus, these "kings" would have an explicit link with Rome (since they are the horns of the beast), although that link is implicit. But these ten horns are described in language that links them philosophically with the second beast. Revelation 17:17 says, "For God gave into their [the horns'] hearts to do His mind and to act in one mind and to give their [plural!] kingdom [singular!] to the beast." The independent Jewish government of A.D. 66 (headed by the high priest Ananus) was similarly described by Zeitlin: "This government . . . played a double role. . . . Inwardly it was for peace. It wanted to disarm the extremists so that it should have all power concentrated in its hands and thus be allowed to make peace with Rome."[58]

How many rulers did this government have? Ten, give or take one or two. Quoting Josephus (emphases and numbers mine):

> They . . . appointed a great many generals for the war. *Joseph* [1] also, the son of Gorion, and *Ananus* [2] the High priest, were chosen as governors of all affairs within the city. . . . They also chose other generals for Idumea; *Jesus*[3], the son of Sapphias, one of the high priests and *Eleazar* (4), the son of Ananias, the high priest. . . . Nor did they neglect the care of the other parts of the country, but *Joseph* [5] the son of Simon was sent as general to Jericho, as was *Manasseh* [6] to Perea, and *John* [7], the Essene, to the toparchy of Thamma; Lydda was also added to his portion, and Joppa and Emmaus. But *John* [8], the son of Matthias, was made the governor of the toparchies of Gophnitica and Acrabastene; as was *Josephus* [9], the son of Matthias, of both the Galilees.[59]

Candidates for number ten might be "Niger, the then governor of Idumea," who as Josephus relates was "obedient" to the named commanders, or "Eleazar the son of Simon," who had possession of all the booty the Jews had taken in their defeat of Cestius. Eleazar used this monetary leverage and some subtle tricks to see that all the people "submitted themselves to his authority in all public affairs" in Jerusalem.[60]

Such "kings of the earth/land" are not heathen. Nevertheless, Herod considers himself almost Jewish. And, if Zeitlin is taken at face value, they act in favor of the "heathen" rule of Rome. These "kings" are specifically "kings of the land," meaning the "land" of Palestine. They actually rule for a short period "along with the beast." While they are (plural) kings, they share a (singular) kingdom. And they do in fact work in league with the beast to destroy Jerusalem. Zeitlin observes:

> This government . . . was greatly responsible for turning a revolution into a civil war." The civil war was the instrument, perhaps more than the Roman siege, which destroyed Jerusalem. The various parties in the war ravaged the citizenry, confiscated and wasted precious food and ammunition. Vespasian, himself, waited for the Jewish civil strife to complete much of the work of destroying the Jewish nation before he pressed the siege. Jewish writers of later years blame those internal struggles for the destruction of Jerusalem.[61]

In terms of the representative anecdote, the harlot is sinful Eve all over again. She is the woman, who instead of recognizing the danger of listening to the serpent, chooses to be his ally.

CONCLUSION

The kaleidoscope model of G. B. Caird is inadequate for explaining the mutability of Revelation imagery. It is not only metonymic (as it reduces symbolic action to physical motion), the invention of the kaleidoscope in A.D. 1815 makes it anachronistic, as well. The magma of the stream-of-fire model is neither metonymic nor anachronistic. Both the trope synecdoche and the stream-of-fire concept of a word "magma" were known in John's milieu. What was (at the turn of the twentieth century) explained by scholars as confusion caused by multiple sources and unskilled editors (which conclusion, we might add, was rejected by subsequent scholars on linguistic and structural grounds), can be better explained by the trope synecdoche.

If the reader of Revelation finds himself/herself in a vicious cycle, not knowing how to distinguish the beast from its heads from the second beast from the image from Babylon, then the reader might, with John, think synecdochically. Just as the various elements of the dragon magma change with each new verse, the syncretistic villain is an intertwining network of synecdochic representation. The beast is not only the creature on which the harlot sits, but also, through its horns, is the harlot's lover, which could even synecdochically be understood to have become "one flesh with" her (cf. 1 Corinthians 6:16). So intertwined synecdochically are Babylon, beast, horns, kings of the earth/land, second beast, image, false prophet, and harlot that they have become one magma.

The imagery of Revelation is better understood by viewing the two (or three) magmas through the plot of the representative anecdote. The good woman magma is in a conflict with the dragon magma, just as Eve (along with her seed) is in perpetual conflict with the serpent. The two (or three) magmas of Revelation are, in Burkean terms, "clusters." And as Burke argues, "[W]ould it not follow that if there are, let us say, seven ingredients composing a cluster, any one of them could be treated as 'representing' the rest?" (PLF 27). The harlot of John's drama is the old Eve who was not only misled by the serpent; she now becomes the serpent's ally. The bride is the new Eve who is no longer misled by the serpent; she now resists the serpent's temptations/coercions even to the point of death. Her former failure has become her new conquest.

5

The Poetics of Revelation

In this book, the book of revelation is viewed from four per-spectives—poetics, psychological, sociopolitical, and rhetorical. This chapter considers the first perspective. As Burke suggests, a work may be considered, if enough evidence exists to do so, from a psychological perspective (by examining the context of the pri-mary audience to determine what expectations might be aroused by the use of specific forms) and from a sociopolitical perspective (by examining the social order in which the work was produced to determine what reinforcements and/or changes of the status quo the author might be recommending). Both the psychological and sociopolitical perspectives, however, require going beyond the text. Hence, Burke recommends beginning with the poetics perspective, by ascertaining what is internal—that which exists if the work exists. Specifically, the arguments in this chapter are twofold: (1) that John employs mirror-image symmetry to perfect a plot for his hu-man drama, and (2) that he tracks down the implications of his two primary characters (woman and serpent) to perfect the dra-matis personae of his human drama.

What would constitute the "perfect" example of biblical litera-ture? Burke claims in CS that "[e]nough has been said to demon-strate that 'perfection' as applied to literature is a meaningless term" (CS 178). The problem, as Burke sees it, is that "[u]niversal and permanent perfection could exist only if th[e] entire range of experiences were identical for all [humans] forever" (CS 179). Fun-damentally, Burke is ruing the fact that literature is an art form that is constructed out of a cooperative material/*hulê*. No two individ-uals share completely the same symbol system. Hence: "To have 'perfection,' we should need a 'perfect reader' to whom such per-fection could be referred" (CS 179). And since no two readers to-tally share the same symbol system, even if someone could produce some "perfect work for people with six toes, this spring," the "con-cept of perfection" would be "of no critical value" (CS 181).

Since finding a "perfect reader" would be "of no critical value," Burke begins with the poetics perspective. He places "perfection" in poetics, not in the mind of the reader or auditor, but in the mind of the poet. The following equation applies here: "Art for art's sake" implicitly has an Art-for-the-artist's-sake aspect. As Harold Bloom observes, "Burke . . . taught us to ask always: What was the writer trying to do for herself or himself as a person, by writing this poem, play, or story?"[1] Says Burke: "But in studying the full nature of a symbolic act you are entitled, if the material is available, to disclose also the things that the act is doing for the poet and no one else" (PLF 25). Burke notes that "[m]any of the things that a poet's work does for him[/her] are not the things that the same work does for us [the readers]" (PLF 73). Yet, "some of them are." And Burke's position is as follows:

> That if we try to discover what the poem is doing for the poet, we may discover a set of generalizations as to what poems do for everybody. With these in mind, we have cues for analyzing the sort of eventfulness that the poem contains. And in analyzing this eventfulness, we shall make basic discoveries about the structure of the work itself. (PLF 73)

Regarding the dramatis personae, Burke writes: "It's an aesthetic or poetic fact that a fiction might put stress upon a stress seeking character because such a character helps keep a plot going. . . ."[2] The various characters in a drama are "terms" in the symbol system of the poet (ATH 312). The perfection principle at work in drama is the poet's entelechial tracking down of the implications of his/her various "terms." Hence, before considering the relationship of a piece of literature to its audience (the psychological perspective), or its sociopolitical circumstances, I seek to locate the entelechial principle in the symbol system of the artist. As Burke advises, "It is necessary to begin with a consideration of the work in its internality, before [we consider] . . . psychological and sociological motives."[3]

So, then, if perfection is viewed from the perspective of a single individual—the artist—the concept of perfection in literature is no longer meaningless. Burke can persist in speaking of a " 'perfection' principle" in drama (LSA 54). He can claim that "drama is the *culminative* form of action" (LSA 54, emphasis mine). Burke states that Richard McKeon's reference to "deep-seated [human] cravings for generality and universality" designates a phenomenon that is " 'entelechially' grounded in the *culminative* possibilities of

language itself" (emphasis mine).[4] Burke's terms—"perfect," "entelechial," and "culminative"—are all in the same equational cluster
in Burke's symbol system. Therefore, Burke's comments may be
interpreted as suggesting that drama is the perfect form of action.
In what respect would that be true?

Burke states: "By entelechy, I refer to such use of symbolic resources that potentialities can be said to attain their perfect fulfillment" (DD 39). Burke sees in Aristotle's term "entelechy" an
application to all symbolic action. He asserts: "[W]e are confining
our use of the principle [of entelechy] to the realm of symbolic
action" (LSA 17). Whenever a human acts, s/he possesses a *telos*
within herself/himself. That *telos* is the perfect culmination for that
act—perfect, at least, in the mind of the actor. Unfortunately, while
each action implicitly contains its perfect *telos*, in actual human experience, the perfect *telos* is seldom if ever attained. Yet, in drama,
the poet has the opportunity to perfect the action. The poet is not
limited to chance conclusions. In drama, the poet can provide a
glimpse into his/her symbol system. S/he can indicate, according to
his/her own symbol system (or at least the symbol system by which
the poet is operating in terms of the drama), what would be the perfect culmination of the action that is represented in the drama. The
poet already possesses the *telos* within his/her own mind.

I may therefore ask, what action does John see as culminating in
Revelation? Nothing less than the entirety of all human action!
John's drama is the human drama! He alludes to the archetype of
human action—Eve's free choice concerning which of two actions
she would take, in light of the serpent's proposal. Indeed, John
makes this paradigm of action the representative anecdote of his
drama.

PERFECTING THE DRAMATIS PERSONAE OF REVELATION

With his choice of a representative anecdote, John has implicitly
chosen the two key "terms" (or "characters") of his apocalyptic symbol system. All other characters in the Apocalypse must now owe
their significance to these two terms—woman and serpent—due to
the "paradox of substance." Burke explains: "A character cannot"
be himself[/herself] "unless many others among the *dramatis personae* contribute to this end, so that the very essence of a character's

nature is in a large measure defined, or determined, by the other characters who variously assist or oppose him[/her]" (LSA 84).

According to Burke:

> A total drama, as the agon, is analytically subdivided into competing principles, of protagonist and antagonist. Their competition sums up to one over-all cooperative act. . . . Also, each of the "principles" possesses satellites, or adjuncts, some strongly identified with one or another of the principles . . . ; whereas other characters shade off into a general overlapping background. . . . Such a set of "mediating" characters is necessary, as a common ground of persons through which the cooperation of the competing principles can take place. Hence, no matter which of the three the dramatist begins with (agon, protagonist, or antagonist) he[/she] cannot give us a full drama unless he[/she] imaginatively encompasses the other two. . . .
>
> But there is obviously a philosophic sense in which agon, protagonist, and antagonist can each be said to exist implicitly in the others. (PLF 76–77)

In the "agon" that is decribed in chapter 4 of this book—the ongoing battle between woman and serpent can be seen the implicit existence of each of the two "principles" (the "antagonist" serpent and the "protagonist" woman) in the opposing character of each. Furthermore, the "satellite" characters of the serpent (the beast, its horns, its image, its false prophet, etc.), as well as the "satellite" characters of the woman (Israel/Zion, the Messiah, the 144,000 virgins, the New Jerusalem, etc.), which are "identified with one or another of the principles," serve as "a common ground of persons through which the cooperation of the competing principles can take place" (PLF 76).

Therefore, all characters in a "perfect" drama, in a sense, imply each other. Whether friend or foe, there must be consistency among all of the terms of a symbol system (i.e., among all characters of a drama). Burke confirms this: "A theoretically perfect Symbol would, in all its ramifications, reveal the underlying pattern of experience. . . . [A] wholly consistent . . . pattern is observable in such minute particles as the single word" (CS 158).

Whenever any one word of a drama thus implicitly represents the entire drama, synecdoche is present. Burke observes:

> The more I examine both the structure of poetry and the structure of human relations outside poetry, the more I become convinced that

this [synecdoche] is the "basic" figure of speech, and that it occurs in many modes besides that of the formal trope. I feel it to be no mere accident of language that we use the same word for sensory, artistic, and political representation. (PLF 26)

As synecdoche relates to characters, Burke maintains: "There are ways whereby, owing to the nature of synecdoche, any member of this family may come to do vicarious service for any other member, or for the family as a whole" (PLF xxi–xxii).

The negatively synecdochic relationship. For Burke, there is even synecdoche in opposing characters:

A dissociate part might be called negatively synecdochic (as the villain is a negative representation of the hero). As an angel, Lucifer [by this term, Burke means the Devil] is in synecdochic relationship with God (i.e., he is a "messenger"). As a rebel [Burke's understanding], he is in negatively synecdochic relationship. (PLF 60)

Negatively synecdochically, then, the tempter implies the tempted. Eve represents the serpent in terms of one of his/her (i.e., the serpent's) aspects, for the very "essence" of the serpent requires that an Eve exist. The whole of Eve represents a part of the "essence" of the serpent. In citing Coleridge's favorite proverb, "Extremes meet," Burke comments: "[W]e often have trouble drawing a sharp line between the consistent and the compensatory" (PLF 76). Burke reiterates: "We are continually coming upon those points where the consistent and compensatory merge" (PLF 77). Burke says "that among the functions of synecdoche is the substitution of cause for effect and effect for cause" (PLF 28). Such is the "labyrinthine" nature of a drama. In Burke's words, even a few terms can suggest "a whole labyrinth of vaguely glimpsed possibilities, or implications."[5]

Tracking down the "implications" of terms (= characters, in this instance) is entelechial! Perfection in poetics is the "fulfillment" by the poet of all synecdochic possibilities! Specifically, regarding the key character(s) in tragedy, when Burke uses the term entelechy, he has in mind something like Aristotle's *Poetics* with its perfect tragic victim: "When the sufferings involve those who are near and dear to one another, when for example brother kills brother, son father, mother son, or son mother, or if such a deed is contemplated, or something else of the kind is actually done, then we have a situation of the kind to be aimed at."[6]

Not only does the perfecting of a drama involve tracking down the synecdochic interrelationships among the dramatis personae, it also involves tracking down the synecdochic interrelations among the various events in the plot. Burke articulates the point:

> The synecdochic function may also be revealed in the form of a poem, from the purely technical angle. If event 2, for instance, follows from event 1 and leads into event 3, each of these events may synecdochically represent the others (the interwovenness often being revealed objectively in such processes as "foreshadowing"). (PLF 28)

In his original draft of "Form and Persecution in the *Oresteia*," Burke says, "the matters considered . . . were immediately preceded by . . . a section designed to show that . . . mimesis" is best understood "through [Aristotle's] concept of the entelechy, with its peculiar stress upon 'fulfillment' " (LSA 125). Specifically, Burke not only understands Aristotle's concept of tragedy to involve the perfect victims (or characters—i.e., intimates), but he also understands tragedy to involve a perfect plot. There must be a "fulfillment" (*entelecheia?*) of the potentialities (*dunamis*) of action (*kinêsis*) available to each character or term. While, for Aristotle, art is an "imitation" (*mimêsis*) of nature, still art (like nature) must have a *telos*—it must have a perfect end toward which the action moves. Just as the "fulfillment" of the potentialities of a kernel of corn would be the growth of that kernel into a stalk, leaves, ears, and new seeds, so mimetic entelechy must also experience "fulfillment." The action must move toward an end.

Where better to look for the end of Revelation than at the end of Revelation! Where is the human action of Revelation headed? Toward a new creation. The final two chapters of Revelation describe a new "heaven" and a new "earth," along with a "New Jerusalem" to inhabit the new heaven and earth. As mentioned earlier, "Jerusalem" (whose other name is "Mt. Zion") is a synecdochic representative for Eve. And, although neither the name Eve nor the name Adam are employed in John's work, the "New Jerusalem" is described as "a bride, having been adorned for her Husband" (21:2). John confirms the identity of her husband in 21:9–10: "Come, I will show you the bride, the wife of the Lamb . . . the great city, holy Jerusalem." The implicit new Adam who, along with his bride, the "New Jerusalem," inhabits the "new heaven" and "new earth," is the Lamb.

CHIASMUS: THE PERFECT STRUCTURE

As early as Homer, poets attempted to give their sentences and even their entire poetic works structural symmetry. In a passage from the *Iliad* that is significant to students of rhetoric, in that Homer uses the term *rhêtêr* in a highly suggestive fashion, the archaic hero is described as a "speaker of words and a doer of deeds." However, this English translation obscures a very symmetric sentence structure in the Greek: *muthôn te rhêtêr emenai, prêktêra te wergôn.* The first word *muthôn* (words) and the last word *wergôn* (deeds) mirror each other. The second and the next-to-last words are both *te.* The third word *rhêtêr* (speaker), and the third-from-last word *prêktêra* (doer), mirror each other. The middle word is the copula *emenai* (to be). Thus, the sentence is symmetrical, a mirror-image.[7]

George A. Kennedy cites Nils Wilhelm Lund's work, *Chiasmus in the New Testament,* as claiming that "[i]f rhetorical criticism is to be valid, it must be practiced with some awareness of the traditions of Jewish speech, of which *chiasmus* is one." Kennedy defines chiasmus as "the reversal of the order in corresponding words or phrases."[8] Kennedy offers chiasmus as an example of rhetorical "devices commonly found in ancient texts and given labels by modern critics [that] are not identified at all in handbooks of the classical period."[9] He explains that the term "chiasmus" "appears first in Pseudo-Hermogenes, *On Invention* . . . a work perhaps of the fourth century of the Christian era." Furthermore, he notes: "Yet as a figure it is not uncommon in classical Greek literature."[10] As a New Testament example, Kennedy offers Mark 2:27: "The Sabbath was made for man, not man for the Sabbath." Another example is found in John 1:1: "In the beginning-was-the word-and-the word-was-with God."

Kennedy continues:

In the Old Testament whole passages are often composed chiastically, with the parts arranged in a sequence A, B, C, . . . C', B', A'. This elaborated chiasmus can also be found as a compositional technique in Greek as early as Homer . . . but it is ignored by classical rhetoricians and literary critics alike.[11]

Kennedy's student John T. Kirby, in his essay "The 'Great Triangle' in Early Greek Rhetoric and Poetics," states:

The peitho/bia axis is at the base of some of our most ancient literary and rhetorical formulations. It determines Homer's overall structural poetics in the *Iliad*; the trajectory of the story-line as a whole is a kind of arc from bia to peitho, and books 1 and 24 represent the opposite extremities of this arc. . . .

Within this arc there are other recognizable points, in somewhat symmetrical arrangement. Book 9 . . . is balanced further by its mirror-book, 16.[12]

Elizabeth Schüssler Fiorenza proposes a structure for Revelation that is a "concentric ABCDC'B'A' pattern"[13] along the lines discussed above, but I am not convinced by her proposal. It appears to me that what is in Revelation is more closely related to what Kirby calls the "mirror-images" between Homer's *Iliad* and *Odyssey*. Kirby claims that it is a "fact that rhetorically . . . [the] plot-trajectories [of the *Iliad* and the *Odyssey*] are mirror-images of one another."[14] If Homer could produce works that are mirror-images of one another, then John could produce a work that is the mirror-image of an entire corpus of literature—the Judeo-Christian scriptures. I believe that this is precisely what John does in Revelation.

To take the rhetorical device of chiasmus to "the end of the line," a book may be written that is the mirror-image of all previous sacred literature. If the prior literature details the history of humankind, then John's book might in mirror-image account for the remainder of human history by going "back to the future," so to speak:

1. If Genesis begins with the words, "God created the heavens and the earth," John can close with a description of God's "new heaven" and "new earth" (Revelation 21–22).
2. If the first human "action" was the anecdote of a "fall" in the battle of woman vs. the serpent, John can penultimately describe the "conquest" of the bride, the "new Jerusalem" over the dragon (Revelation 19–20).
3. If the second book of the Old Testament, Exodus, describes the "plagues" upon Egypt that propelled Israel to the "Promised Land," John's antepenultimate act can be the "plagues" upon the "land" (of Israel?) that propelled the Jewish church from Palestine (Revelation 15–18).
4. If the Jewish prophets (Isaiah, Jeremiah, Ezekiel, and Hosea) present Israel/Zion as the wife of God who played the "harlot" and who therefore was threatened with "divorce," John might precede his "plagues" with the *telos* of this threat—the "di-

vorce" scroll with seven seals, as seen by J. Massyngberde Ford (Revelation 6–11).[15]

5. If the Gospels present a mortal Jesus who is the servant of God, John might precede his "divorce" of Israel/Zion with a picture of the exaltation of the Lamb in Heaven (Revelation 4–5).
6. If the church in dispersion (to whom John is writing) was informed largely through the "epistles" of Paul and others, John might begin his book exactly where the church is, with "epistles/letters to the seven churches in Asia Minor" (Revelation 1–3).

That "middle" section (Revelation 12–14) omitted in the foregoing sequence may give evidence of a somewhat symmetrical form internal to Revelation as well. It is in this section that John spells out his representative anecdote and builds his two major equational clusters. I have not attempted to be overly precise in these divisions, but it is fascinating that the structure that falls into place is a "seven" structure, surely a very plausible structure for a man who thinks consistently in terms of the number "seven." The structure adumbrated is only preliminary, however. The most compelling argument on its behalf is John's obsession with "beginning" and "end." God and the Lamb are both referred to as the "alpha and omega," the "first and the last," the "beginning and the end." It is "qualitatively" significant that John ends his book with a "new" creation. If the "end" is thus a "mirror-image" of the "beginning," the chiastic impulse must be examined to see if it is operative in Revelation.

The internal structure of Revelation is probably closer to the structure of the Greek drama. Fiorenza comments: "It is especially interesting to note the affinity of the structure of Revelation to that of the Greek drama. According to the compositional rules of tragedy, the climax falls near the center of the action and the denoument comes near the end."[16] This is the type of "symmetry" or "balanced structure ABCDC'B'A' " that Fiorenza sees in Revelation, rather than a mirror-image emplottment.[17] Fiorenza does not, in the essay cited here, employ the term chiasmus or its cognates.

But, there may be a sense in which even her comparison with Greek drama may be seen better as John's attempt to view the entire human drama. Genesis presents the agon, the dramatic struggle between "woman" and "serpent" wherein woman loses the first battle (in Eden). Yet, even in the curse that is placed upon the "woman" and the "serpent" in Genesis, there is the promise (fore-

shadowing?) of a continued agon between the two: "I will put enmity between you [the serpent] and the woman, and between your
seed and her seed. He [the woman's seed] will bruise your head
and you shall bruise his heel" (3:15). As discussed in chapter 4 of
this book, John may also see in this verse an ultimate victory of the
"seed of woman" over the "seed of the serpent."

Perhaps, as in the first century A.D. Jewish school of Rabbi Elias,
John structures the human drama in terms of primarily three stages.
(Actually, the school of Elias sees a seven structure that is, practically speaking, compressed into three stages.) Based on Psalm 90:
4, which implies that a "day" in the Lord's timetable is equal to one
thousand years, Elias's school propounds the theory that the history
of mankind is equal to one week. The first two days (= 2000 years),
mankind is without the Law. This might correspond in Revelation
to the era of the "woman" Eve. The second two days (= 2000 years),
mankind has the Law. This might correspond to the era of the
"woman" Israel/Zion. The third two days (= 2000 years), mankind
lives under the reign of the Messiah. This might correspond to the
era of the church, as the bride of the Lamb. The final day, for the
school of Elias, is the Sabbath, the day of ultimate "rest." So, in
terms of human action considerations, it is not included in the
human drama. Thus, the school of Elias provides a three-stage (albeit six-day) structure for human action.[18]

If Revelation is read from the perspective of the school of Elias,
John's use of the "thousand years" terminology in Revelation 20
provides some corroboration of a trilogy reading. Following the
defeat of the beast and the false prophet, John's drama has the
dragon (= Satan = Devil) being bound for a thousand years (20:
3), and shut up and sealed in the abyss so as not to "mislead the
nations any longer until the thousand years are ended [*teleô*]" (20:
3). But, then, there appears to be a continuing human history for
some period of time, after the thousand years are ended. John predicts: "And when the thousand years are fulfilled [*teleô*], Satan will
be loosed out of his prison and he will go out to mislead the
nations" (20:7–8). Assuming that, as John contends, the reign of
the Messiah never ends (11:15) and that human history continues
for some period of time following the thousand years imprisonment
of Satan, a messianic reign of two thousand years is not excluded.
Thus, the plot of Revelation can be made to coincide with the theory of the school of Elias.

If John uses the theory of the school of Elias to emplot Revelation, where would John place himself and his primary audience in

terms of this three-stage plot? Certainly not in the very middle of the human drama, nor apparently at the very end. John might be providing an account of the transition from the second stage to the third stage. In his possibly describing the "divorce" of Israel/Zion as preparation for the "wedding feast of the Lamb" and his "bride, New Jerusalem," John can be read as unfolding the drama from the vantage point of the end of "act 2." Other than the allusions to the woman and the serpent, John says virtually nothing about act 1. Act 3 would begin in chapter 19 with the "wedding feast of the Lamb" and continue through chapter 20 with the "thousand year" imprisonment of the dragon, followed by his release to "mislead the nations." The final section of Revelation (chapters 21 and 22) would describe that cosmic "Sabbath" that the school of Elias predicted as an epilogue to the three-stage structure of the human drama.

John's primary interest in Revelation might lie neither in the far distant past nor (to any large extent) in the distant future. He spends no more than (and arguably fewer than) four of his twenty-two chapters on these time periods. Instead, John is claiming that he and his primary audience are living in (entelechially) significant times. He states that the "time" (*kairos*) is "near" (1:3; 22:10). Jesus is "coming quickly [*tachu*]" (2:16; 3:11, 11:14?; 22:7; 12, 20). God has shown "to his servant [John] what must happen soon [*tachos*]" (1:1, 22:6). As seen from the *kairos* and *tachos* references, John is using some mirror-imaging in encompassing his narrative with immediacy comments. So, the bulk of what John describes should be understood as relating to the lifetime of his primary audience. Although John describes contemporary events as mirror-images of the days of the Old Testament prophets (the divorce scroll), or the Exodus (plagues), he is writing concerning predominantly contemporary events. Is it possible, then, to combine the tripartite schema of the Elias school with the structure of Greek drama, all the while remaining conscious of chiastic structure? Yes. Furthermore, if John is trying to do just that, further evidence of entelechy from the poetics perspective is present.

What is John doing for John? What does any author do for himself/herself when s/he attempts to perfectly "fulfill" the "expectations" of a "conventional form"? S/he satisfies an entelechial appetite. S/he fulfills an entelechial tendency. S/he consummates an entelechial drive. In demonstrating that chiasmus as a form was known to John's milieu, chiasmus for John's milieu may be categorized as a "conventional form." Likewise, with the tripartite schema of the school of Elias may be categorized as a conventional form. And, as Fiorenza claims: "Interpreters have not merely acknowledged the dramatic character of the book but have maintained that Revelation is patterned after the Greek drama, since it has *dramatis personae,* stage props, chorus, a plot, and a tragic-comic ending."[19] John may be attempting to perfect three (or more!) possible "conventional forms" at once. Other "conventional forms" that John may have in mind are apocalyptic, prophetic, and epistolary. But the three that I have been considering are more "culminative," more entelechial. Burke notes the " 'perfection' principle" in drama," claiming that "drama is the culminative form of action" (LSA 54). John may not consider himself to be at the end of the human drama, but by placing himself at a key transitional point in the human drama, and by chiastically tracking down the "end" of the human drama as a mirror-image of the "beginning" of the human drama, John "dramatically" culminates the action of all humanity. He gives himself the satisfaction that one feels when one writes (or reads) the final sentence of the final chapter of the novel. He gives his (and all other human) life a *telos.*

Greek tragedies traditionally are composed as trilogies. The *Oresteia* is an example of such a trilogy. There is some correspondence between such trilogies and the tripartite schema of the school of Elias. Billerbeck calls the schema of the school of Elias a *Weltwochenschema* or "cosmic week" which consists of three double-days of human action followed by a *Weltensabbat,* or "cosmic sabbath."[20] Is it possible that the school of Elias would have envisioned human history in terms of a Greek trilogy? Burke reports "that traditionally a [Greek] tragic trilogy was in turn completed by a satyr play, a fourth play, turning the trilogy into a tetralogy. Burke notes that the satyr play "burlesques . . . the very characters who were treated solemnly in the tragedies" (LSA 137–38). Burke opines: "Such an arrangement would be very civilized. It would complete the completing" (LSA 138). While it would be a sacrilege to equate the *Weltensabbat* of the Elias school with the obscenity that is implicit in Greek satyr plays, Henry Fischel contends:

It is fortunate that at this stage of scholarship no further defense has to be made for the assumption that Greco-Roman situations were well-known to the creators of the Midrash, i.e., the literature that modifies the word and world of Scripture by interpretation, explicitly or implicitly. Rather the problem is how far this knowledge went, *how much of Greco-Roman academic procedure and* philosophical quest *was*

used [emphases mine] in that on-going process, in which the culmi-
nation of the tannaitic culture, c. 200 A.D. (the codification of the
Mishnah) and that of Palestinian amoraic culture, c. 400 (Jerusalem
Talmud) were important stages.[21]

In answering Fischel's question in this instance, I would hazard a
guess that at least this "much of Gre[ek] ... procedure ... was
used": the school of Elias accepts the conventional trilogy form for
drama, and finds it easy to turn the trilogy into a tetralogy, due to
the nature of Jewish conventional form, which revolves around a
concept of six days (or six years) of action followed by one day (or
one year) of "rest." Furthermore, while the *Weltensabbat* is in no way
libertine or licentious (as the satyr play is), it serves a similar purpose. While Burke says that Greeks could "sum up the analysis of
'tragic dignification' by a satyr play, that is to say, a burlesque of
the solemnities that have preceded it,"[22] by a parallel euphoric celebration, the *Weltensabbat* can "sum up" and/or transcend the "solemnities" of the human drama. Laughter is a release from the
tensions of tragic drama, and similarly "sabbath" rest is a release
from the tensions of human drama. Sabbath release is not along
the lines of tearful catharsis. Sabbath release is in the comic category, as is the satyr play.

PERFECTING THE CYCLE

Burke asserts that "Greek tragedy was 'cathartically' designed" for
"the ad interim resolving" of "civic tensions ... by poetic means"
(LSA 125). Tragedy was never intended to bring about "permanent" resolution of "civic tensions." "Hence," writes Burke, "tragic
purges, twice a year" (DD 15). Burke claims, "Thomson puts us on
the track of symbolic devices whereby tragedy ... can symbolically
transcend modes of civic conflict that ... are never actually re-
solved" (DD 14).

Burke takes catharsis to be a "purgation by symbolic victimage,"
wherein the audience "identifies" with an imaginary victim who represents a "superior" class of humans which the audience—"the *hoi
polloi*"—"cannot love." Identification is accomplished, not through
the perfect "identification" of "love," but through what Burke considers to be a "surrogate for love," namely "pity." The tragic "plea-
sure" would then take place when the one whom the audience has
"pitied" is "killed." Since "identification" has produced consubstan-

tiality between the audience and the victim, it is as if in a sense the audience has died symbolically, and thus is free to take on a new identity, since the old, fearful identity has been "purged." This new identity would be the (perfected?) identity which the audience member has sought. Thus the tragedy has gratified entelechy—a sense of perfection (*telos*) within the audience (DD 12–15).

In his essay, "Form and Persecution in the *Oresteia*," once again, Burke observes that "Greek tragedy was 'cathartically' designed" for the purpose of relieving "civic tensions" (LSA 125). He again discusses how fear is transformed to pity (as a surrogate for love). He develops at length his choice of " 'pride' as the third major motive involved in tragic catharsis," to modify/explain "Aristotle's famous formula . . .'pity, fear, and like emotions' " (LSA 125). He equates these three in Freudian fashion with the "three privy functions of the 'Demonic Trinity' " (LSA 126). He once again demonstrates that his concept of entelechy is indebted to the "principle of expectancy we had called 'form.' " He reviews: "Years ago, in Counter-Statement, we had analyzed form as the arousing and fulfilling of expectations" (LSA 127).

"Fulfillment" is equated by Burke with *telos* and entelechy (LSA 125), and is linked to the *Oresteia*:

> I would at least restore a reference to the fatal formula that Clytemnaestra utters just before leaving to murder her husband: "Zeus, Zeus, that fulfillest, fulfill these my prayers. / To thee be the care of that thou wouldst fulfill." Here the notable word *telos* appears three times in two lines . . . *teleie, telei, telein.* (LSA 125)

This equational link in Burke's symbol system reconfirms that the "fulfillment of expectation" is an entelechial formula.

What Burke does with the *Oresteia*, in addition to what he does elsewhere with tragedy in general, is to point out the cyclical nature of tragic entelechy. Burke is intrigued by beginnings and ends and how they are linked together. Here, Burke leaves no doubt of the link that he sees between firsts and lasts. Burke offers (as a key term for the cyclical nature of tragic entelechy in the *Oresteia*) the term "*Amphisbaena*: from *amphis*, both ways; and *bainein*, to go. [*Amphisbaena*] is a serpent, in ancient mythology, beginning or ending at both head and tail alike" (LSA 135). This term is "uttered by Cassandra (who, as prophetess is sure to state the motivational essence) when she is trying to decide what the murderous Clytemnaestra should be called" (LSA 135). Burke sees the term in the *Oresteia* trilogy as similar to the image of "a snake with its own tail in its mouth" (LSA 132). More precisely, the cyclical snake is elsewhere identified by Burke as "the mythic design of the serpent *Ouroboros* with his own tail in his mouth" (LSA 406). In this image is the cyclical concept of each ending turning into a new beginning. The killers of the first two plays, Clytemnaestra and Orestes, are both considered "serpents" by their victims. Burke seems to view this amphisbaenal serpent as the paradigm of the successive kills.

The arousing of cyclical expectations is found in the *Oresteia* by virtue of the nature of the "original sin," as Burke sees it. Burke points out the bloodguilt, of the variety "that curses the house of Atreus." Atreus "slew the children of his brother, Thyestes, and served them to Thyestes at a banquet that was supposedly to celebrate the brothers' reconciliation" (LSA 129). This bloodguilt brings with it that cyclical avenging-killing that promises death after death after death. Says Burke, "this kind of form encourages a plot to proceed like a row of falling dominoes, each knocking down the next" (LSA 131). He alludes to mathematical "wave theories" (LSA 131), whereby an infinite parade of deaths following each upon the prior one is expected.

With each tragic death, the civic tensions are purged. Yet the conclusion of each of the first two plays is unsatisfactory. Such is the problem with civic tensions as well. In ziggurat-fashion, each step of the "social pyramid" (LSA 137) that might be ascended moves the ascender to the "top" of the prior stage which is a simultaneous "bottom" of the stage immediately above it. Here, "top" and "bottom" are merged in the way that Burke's entelechy merges first and last, and in such a way that the amphisbaenal serpent may represent the confusion/consubstantiality of head and tail.

The third cycle of the trilogy moves to this higher step in an entelechial ziggurat of social cooperation: "The purely social kind of 'justice' which is finally celebrated in the third play's pageantry, having to do with the mythic founding of the Acropolis, is in the last analysis a dialectical 'transcending'" (LSA 135). Instead of avenging the death of Clytemnaestra by seeing Orestes (her killer) killed, the third play of the trilogy kills "killing." Burke observes, "the playwright must somewhere depict the ultimate slaying" (LSA 136):

Here, even the slain mother must stand for something beyond herself. And Cassandra tells us what; namely: the *amphisbaena*, which we take to be the mythic representation of the ultimate, vegetatively, non-verbally dreaming worm, circling back upon itself in enwrapt self-engrossment (somewhat as with the self-love of Aristotle's God, and likewise of many later theologians' Gods). (LSA 136)

Is this an enigma? Of course! The second play creates the knot of a report, "The dead are killing the living," which enigmatically can be translated, "The living kills the dead" (LSA 136). Burke applies this to the *lex talionis*: "We are killed by treachery, even as we killed" (LSA 136). Burke is claiming that the *lex talionis* is that cyclical snake, that *amphisbaena*, which starting at its tail eats itself into non-existence. Circling back upon itself, the doctrine of blood vengeance (= God?) devours itself. The new order that is instituted in the third play killed blood vengeance, in favor of a judicial system.

Burke, of course, is not satisfied with this new solution, but entelechially desires (as was routine for the Greeks) the fourth play, turning the trilogy into a tetralogy. He wants a satyr play that "burlesques . . . the very characters who were treated solemnly in the tragedies" (LSA 137–138). Says Burke, "Such an arrangement would be very civilized. It would complete the completing" (LSA 138).

Whether one opts for a plot structure resembling the chiastic mirror-imaging of Revelation to the Judeo-Christian scriptures or for a plot structure which builds upon the *Weltwochenschema* of the Elias school or for an entirely different plot structure, the end of the Book of Revelation demands a "cyclical" interpretation of some sort. The "new heavens and new earth" of chapter 21 lead into a new era of human existence. This new era is qualitatively different from all eras that go before it, in much the same way that a satyr play is for the Greeks an example of "qualitative progressive form" (CS 124–25). John does not even begin to predict what type of emplottment might go with the "new" cycle. He is content to simply characterize the qualitative shift.

Clearly, there is a cyclical plot in John's description of the reign of the Messiah. The messianic reign begins on the heels of a battle (Armaggedon) in which a woman (the harlot Babylon) is destroyed (16:16ff.), and it ends with a battle (of Gog and Magog) that the New Jerusalem wins. It begins with a preliminary defeat of the dragon, with his being imprisoned in the abyss (20:3), and ends with the ultimate defeat of the dragon, his being cast into the lake of fire (20:10).

Just as Burke appears to see in the third cycle of the *Oresteia* trilogy, an ultimate slaying (the slaying of "killing," in the sense of the *lex talionis*), so John appears to locate an even more ultimate slaying in the messianic (third?) cycle of his human drama. At the end of this cycle, not only does John see the ultimate defeat of the dragon, he sees "DEATH" itself "thrown into the lake of fire," which is "the second death" (20:14). Thus, John has put an end to ends. He has transcended the death of Eve in Genesis, plus the death of Israel/Zion (both the positive deaths of the "virgins [= martyrs]" and the negative death of the "harlot"), with the death of death!

There are several cyclical elements in John's treatment of Israel/Zion. There is possibly the implicit marriage-divorce cycle. There is the implicit cycle that begins with "plagues" upon Egypt and ends with "plagues" upon the "land" (of Israel?). There are the "birth" cycles in chapter 12 that imply a woman (= Israel) who gives birth to the Messiah (the next generation).

While Aristotle's seed entelechy does not emphasize death in the cyclical rebirth of the entelechial process, death is implicit. As the perennial cycle of "corn" or grain unfolds, there is the paradigm of birth, growth, maturity, reproduction (of new seeds), and death. This process is followed cyclically, year after year. The Gospel of Mark attributes a parable to Jesus which refers to this cycle:

> A man scatters seed on the ground. Night and day, whether he sleeps or gets up, the seed sprouts and grows, though he does not know how. All by itself the soil produces grain—first the stalk, then the head, then the full kernel in the head. As soon as the grain is ripe, he puts the sickle to it, because the harvest has come. (Mark 4:26–29)

And the Gospel of John attributes to Jesus the "death and rebirth" element implicit in the "seed" analogy: "[U]nless a kernel of wheat falls to the ground and dies, it remains only a single seed. But if it dies, it produces many seeds" (John 12:24). Here, what Aristotle views as merely a chronological cycle, the Gospel of John presents as a "transcending" cycle. Instead of viewing the consecutive cycles of seed entelechies as first this entelechy, then that entelechy, then another entelechy, *ad infinitum,* the Gospel of John presents a quantitative (and hence a qualitative?) transcendence in the death of one seed to "produce many seeds."

For Burke, "rituals of rebirth" are extremely significant. He teaches: "They are magical incantations whereby the poet effects a change of identity, killing some portion of himself[/herself] . . . for membership in a new situation" (ATH 17). He notes that "Wagner's Tristan und Isolde . . . transcendentally puts life and death together" as "Tantris dies for Isolde and is reborn as Tristan" (ATH 89). Burke advises: "The trend of the whole plot . . . may show us . . . a crucial point in a ritual of rebirth by which the author is able to 'transcend' some previous conflict" (ATH 191–92). Burke describes "rituals of rebirth" as "changes of identity" that are tied to " 'climacteric stages' of one sort or another" (ATH 317). In this respect, Burke is more closely allied with the seed analogy of the Gospel of John than he is with the seed analogy of Aristotle. Aristotle's seeds are sequential; Burke's and the Gospel of John's are transcendental, in the sense that they represent "climacteric stages."

Burke ties together the terms "dying," "reborn," and "fulfilment" (note the spelling!) in ATH 87. Later, he notes:

> For there is a sense in which both time and thought continually hurry to their "death," and yet are continually "reborn," since the death of one moment is incorporated in the moment that arises out of it, and the early stages of a thought process are embedded in its fulfillment [note the spelling!]. (LSA 210)

In *Implicit Rhetoric: Kenneth Burke's Extension of Aristotle's Concept of Entelechy*, I demonstrate the link that I see between Burke's use of the terms "fulfilment/fulfillment" and "entelechy."[23] Put simply, I find that Burke's inconsistency in spelling "fulfilment/fulfillment" sometimes with two l's and sometimes with three l's, betrays his reliance upon an English translation of *entelecheia* in Aristotle which uses two l's in translating *entelecheia* as "fulfilment." Hence, by equating "death" and "rebirth" with "fulfilment/fulfillment," I see Burke's "rituals of rebirth" as part of his entelechial theory.

One approach to purgation by symbolic victimage is seen in the concept of the "scapegoat," wherein all that is negative in the society is identified and becomes consubstantial with some perfectly villainous alter ego. The symbolic destruction (or in Hitler's case, the literal murder) of the scapegoat thus purges society of all that is negative in it. Again, a new (perfected?) identity emerges. In terms of the scapegoat, Burke comments:

> Thus, the principle of drama is implicit in the idea of action, and the principle of victimage is implicit in the nature of drama. The negative helps radically to define the elements to be victimized. And inasmuch as substitution is a prime resource of symbol systems, the conditions are set for catharsis by scapegoat (including the "natural" invitation

to "project" upon the enemy any troublesome traits of our own that we would negate). (LSA 18)

In Revelation, external killing (the destruction of the wicked woman, the harlot Babylon) clears the way for reidentification as the good woman—New Jerusalem, the bride of the Lamb. John seems to sense the importance of developing consubstantiality between his heroes and his scapegoats, in order to make the scapegoat technique function. He accomplishes his goal by the employment of the woman metaphor, as borrowed from the Old Testament prophets. The prophets used the woman metaphor to indicate the "relationship between God and his people (or Zion)."[24] Hosea indicates that Israel is "an adulterous wife" (1:2). He continues the metaphor throughout. Isaiah 54:6 calls Jerusalem = Zion = the holy city (52:1) "a wife deserted" whom God will redeem. Isaiah 50:1 speaks of the "bill of divorce" that God had given Israel. Jeremiah 2–6 describes Jerusalem/Israel/Judah as a "bride" (2:2) who was constantly unfaithful, and behaved as a "prostitute" (2:20, et al.), has committed adultery (3:6), was given a "certificate of Divorce" by God (3:8), and is warned that armies will come to destroy Jerusalem (4:16). In Jeremiah 6:1, for safety's sake, people are urged to "Flee from Jerusalem!" Ezekiel 16 likewise speaks of Jerusalem as a female child who was exposed in an attempt to kill her at birth, but whom God saved, and married. He made her into a "queen" (16:13) and showered her with luxuries. She became a "prostitute" (16:15) and increased her promiscuity to include Egypt (16:26) and "Babylonia, a land of merchants" (16:29). She is warned that all of her lovers will gather against her and strip her naked (16:37ff.). She will be treated like her sister, Sodom (16:49ff.). Ezekiel renews his diatribe against the prostitute Jerusalem in chapter 23, after calling her in 22:2 the "city of bloodshed," who "brings on herself doom by shedding blood" (22:3ff.).

J. M. Ford notices that John is employing the prophetic dissociation between those people who have maintained a positive relationship with God and those who have not. She understands the "harlot" Babylon to be "faithless Jerusalem."[25] Clearly the "bride," New Jerusalem, is the Church. Thus, John makes the heroine and the villainess logologically "intimates," prior to the catharsis by scapegoat. The troublesome traits that John negates for the Church are "projected" upon "faithless Jerusalem." If the woman metaphor throughout Revelation refers to Israel/Zion, then an entelechially purgative scapegoat mechanism is present. The "woman clothed

with the sun . . . and [having] a crown of twelve stars on her head"
(12:1) is Israel who is about to give birth to the "son . . . who will
rule all the nations" (13:5). But this woman has a good inclination
(Hebrew: *yezer ha-tov*) and an evil inclination (*yezer ha-ra*). She splits
into two women: a good woman = bride = virgin whom God pro-
tects, and a wicked woman = Babylon = harlot, whom God de-
stroys. Entelechially, then, the harlot, with whom the bride can have
"identified" and have had at one time "consubstantiality," is
"purged" in Revelation, as the harlot, Babylon, is destroyed. The
bride and the harlot are "intimates" in Burke's, Aristotle's, and possibly even Freud's sense of equivalent terms. The bride is either the
sister or the daughter of the harlot. Either way, the old identity is
purged. "Reidentification" can then take place as the "New Jerusalem," the "bride," can at last be joined with the Lamb at the
"wedding feast" of Revelation, chapter 19.

Sacrifice, the positive purge, is seen clearly in Revelation as the
heroes of the book (the "martyrs") unselfishly offer up their lives.
Note that while "martyr" is always a positive, unselfish term for John,
Burke usually views the term "martyrdom" negatively. He advises
"revolutionaries" to recognize "the ways in which the tragic mechanism may lead to a deliberate courting of martyrdom" (PC 246).
However, Burke observes in DD that a cause may be recommended
in "two quite different ways." The first way is quite pragmatic: "You
may recommend a cause by listing the advantages which will be
gained by its triumph." The second way relates to the "sacrificial"
motive: "You can recommend the cause by depicting admirable persons who are willing to sacrifice themselves for the good of that
cause" (DD 21). Elsewhere, Burke calls this second method of rec-
ommendation "tragic dignification." By this terminology, he refers
to "the rhetorical fact that one can dignify a cause by depicting
serious people who are willing to undergo sacrifices in behalf of
that cause." These people are " 'bearing witness'—that is, in etymological literalness, being 'martyr[s].' "[26]

Despite John's account of the death of a scapegoat, the harlot
Babylon, John is recommending his cause primarily in the second
way described in the previous paragraph. With the "Lamb who was
slain" (Revelation 5:6,12) as the perfect prototype of a "conqueror"
(Revelation 5:5), John proceeds to perfect his audience by recommending perfect conquest. Revelation scholars are not incorrect in
seeing "martyr" as the perfect fulfillment of the meaning of the
word *ho nikôn*—the conqueror, the hero of each of the letters to
the seven churches, "whose martyr's death is his victory, just as the

Cross was the victory of Christ."[27] Indeed, the archetypal martyrdom of the Lamb would be the perfect fulfillment.

It does not even matter, entelechially, that some scholars are not willing to go so far as to suggest that the literal martyrs are the only conquerors. Aristotle added to his list of tragic killings the language, "or if such a deed is contemplated, or something else of the kind is actually done, then we have a situation of the kind to be aimed at" (*Poetics* 50). Thus, a Burkean interpretation that entelechy is present, so long as the "willingness" to sacrifice is present can be derived. Abraham, therefore, possesses entelechy/perfection in his pious willingness to sacrifice his son, Isaac, even though the actual sacrifice does not take place. Just so, those scholars who believe that total Christian martyrdom is not the intent of John's Revelation can be considered logologically to be in agreement with those scholars who believe it is. Christians who are willing to be martyrs might be classified as conquerors whether or not their martyrdom ever occurs. Hence, in a sense, they become entelechial martyrs whether or not they ever become literal martyrs.

SUMMARY

So, what does Revelation do for John? This is the question that an entelechial critic from a poetics perspective should ask. The answer is twofold:

1. Revelation provides a "perfect" plot for human action. By using mirror-image symmetry, John tracks down (from a Judeo-Christian perspective) what a perfectly symmetrical end to the human drama might look like. He incorporates the chiastic conventional form of Judaism, and perhaps something of the Elias school's *Weltwochenschema*, along with the trilogy-tetralogy form of classical Greek tragedy in emplotting his human drama. He develops this plot, using a tripartite identification of "woman" (Eve, Israel/Zion, New Jerusalem) in the prototypal agon of human action—the woman vs. serpent anecdote.
2. Revelation tracks down the perfections implicit in John's "characters," his dramatis personae. The perfection of Eve is a "dissociation" between the two "inclinations" that the first "woman" possessed when she took the first action. She had a "good inclination"—not to bite—which is perfected by John into a "virgin" "bride" role that remains "undefiled" and in-

herits "life." She had an "evil inclination"—to eat from the
forbidden fruit—which is perfected by John into a "harlot"
role that inherits not just physical death, but the second death,
the lake of fire. The perfection of the serpent/dragon results
in a "climacteric progression" from world ruler to fallen to
imprisoned to destroyed in the lake of fire.

The various satellite characters are synecdochically interrelated
to these two principal characters in entelechially synecdochic fashion. The "terms" of John's Apocalypse are "consistent." Hence,
from the perspective of the "symbol system" of the author, entelechy is detected in the poetics of Revelation.

6

The Psychology of Revelation

THIS CHAPTER TURNS FROM A CONSIDERATION OF THE PERSPECTIVE of the author of Revelation to a consideration of the perspective of the readers that comprise the primary audience of Revelation. Such a move necessitates going beyond the text. Materials exist that make such a move possible. Judeo-Christian scriptures, which were formative for John's primary audience, emphasize the expectations implicit in the "seven" structure, the creation-week archetype, which this chapter considers as an example of entelechial criticism from a psychological perspective.

The term that, in Burkean criticism, transcends the division between poetics and psychology is "pragmatic." Burke clarifies:

> The general approach to the poem might be called "pragmatic" in this sense: It assumes that a poem's structure is to be described most accurately by thinking always of the poem's function. It assumes that the poem is designed to "do something" for the poet and his[/her] readers, and that we can make the most relevant observations about its design by considering the poem as the embodiment of this act. In the poet, we might say, the poetizing existed as a physiological function. The poem is its corresponding anatomic structure. And the reader, in participating in the poem, breathes into this anatomic structure a new physiological vitality that resembles, though with a difference, the act of its maker, the resemblance being in the overlap between writer's and reader's situation, the difference being in the fact that these two situations are far from identical.
>
> The justification for this pragmatic view of the poem resides in the kind of observation that a functional perspective leads us to select, from among an infinite number of possible observations about poetic structure. (PLF 89–90)

Hence, the genus to which both poetics criticism and psychological criticism belong, in the Burkean system, is "function" or "prag-

matic." The differentia for psychological criticism is to be found in
the shift of standpoint from the poet's to the auditor's. The question addressed in this chapter is, what is Revelation doing for John's
audience? Burke is confident that there is some "overlap" between
the "situation" of the poet and the "situation" of the reader. Earlier,
Burke's notion that "some of" the "things that a poet's work does
for" the poet are "the things that the same work does for" the readers is discussed (PLF 73).

Many of the observations made in the previous chapter could be
repeated in support of this notion of Burke's. Certainly, the symmetrical and cyclical "forms" of the human drama that John presents do
things for the readers as well as for the writer. Even presenting the
human condition in terms of a "drama" with a beginning and an
end does things for the readers. But, this chapter is focused more
directly on one specific example of Burke's psychology of form.
Attention here is concentrated upon the strength of the very first
psychological form presented in the book of Genesis, the archetypal
week.

Archetype, Entelechy, and Eschatology

In DD, Burke guards against "the 'temporizing of essence' "
whereby the term " 'archetype' gets tied up with notions of a quasi-
historical past" and the "concept of the 'entelechy' . . . take[s] on
quasi-futuristic assumptions . . . of a predestined era still to come"
(DD 57). On the other hand, John's world view and that of his
audience would, no doubt, accept the Edenic archetype of Genesis
and the futuristic millennium as being literal periods. But, one goal
of this chapter is to consider the nontemporal aspects of the terms
"archetype" and "entelechy."

This might, at first glance, appear to be particularly difficult to
manage since cognates of both of these terms are closely linked by
John with a cognate of the term "eschatology," a term that is nearly
always applied to a consideration of the end of time. The term
"*eschatos*" John uses in a parallelism that equates it and "*prôtos*"
(first) with "*archê*" and "*telos*" (cognates of archetype and entelechy). Revelation 22:13 quotes Jesus as saying "I am the first [*prôtos*]
and the last [*eschatos*], the beginning [*archê*] and the end [*telos*]."
Since *telos* and *eschatos* are equated by John, and since entelechy is
the *telos* within, viewing what John might see as the eschaton within
would seem consistent with Burke's thinking on entelechy. Inter-

estingly, John does not seem to emphasize the temporal aspects of a term ("*eschatos*") that has almost universally been considered in terms of its temporal sense.

Of the six times John uses the term "*eschatos*," three times (1:17; 2:8; 22:13) are in the formula mentioned above ("I am the first and the last, the beginning and the end"). Twice (15:1 and 21:9) it refers to the seven "last" plagues. Once, in 2:19, the church at Thyatira is commended because its last (or most recent) works are better than its first (or earlier) works. In the 2:19 passage, there seems to be a sense of maturing (or perfecting) in what the Thyatiran Christians have been doing, but there does not seem to be any deep theological teaching about the (futuristic) "end." The formula passages do not contain that futuristic end-time sense either. If anything, they appear to identify Jesus as the "summarizing principle." This is a Burkean-style use. John is neither interested in tracing Jesus' prehistory nor is he fixated on some future Jesus. The Jesus who is the "first and the last" is the Jesus who is present (right then and there), to help the saint become the "conqueror" by serving as both the archetypal and the entelechial principle of conquest. Perhaps the closest instance of temporality is the reference to the seven "last" plagues. However, even there, the significance is noted by John in 15:1: "Because in them the wrath of God is perfected [*teleô*]." The point of having "last [*eschatos*] plagues," then, would not be to predict the future so much as it would be to psychologically complete some incomplete aspect of the drama.

Rather than searching through Revelation for indicators of a chronological progression toward the end of time, a more fruitful search would be for what Burke would call the entelechial principle, and what John might call the *telos/eschatos* principle (*archê*). The beginnings of a Burkean-style cluster have already been shown to exist, as demonstrated by the formula passages: *eschatos* = *telos* = *archê* = *prôtos* = Jesus. The cluster may now be expanded by tracing each one of these terms throughout Revelation. What becomes evident in such an investigation is that John considers some terms to have (already) achieved perfection/*telos*. (Some other terms will achieve *telos* in the distant future.) This use of *telos* is the summarizing principle variety. Jesus, God, the dragon (Satan), and the beast (Roman Empire) are the primary symbols already infused with a sense of perfection—clearly, with some terms having positive, and others negative, perfection. Discussions of the new heaven and new earth in the distant future are also summarizing principles of perfection—the type at which to be aimed.

Of those terms that have (already) achieved *telos*, "Jesus" has already been indicated. Not only is he known as "the first and the last, the beginning and the end," in 3:14, he is called "the *archê* of the creation of God." (Similarly, 1:5 calls him the "first-born [*prôtotokos*] from the dead.") In 22:13, John provides another formula describing Jesus as *archê* and *telos*: "I am the alpha and the omega." Jesus, as "the Lamb who was slain" (5:6,12) would serve as the archetype for John's concept of human *telos*/perfection. Given the preponderance of archetypal and perfectionist language (just cited) that John has connected with Jesus, his life has certainly become the "summarizing principle" for that entelechial impulse that John would have operative in every Christian in his audience. Jesus as the archetypal "Lamb who was slain" can stand synecdochically for all perfect conquerors (martyrs). Hence, while he is technically no longer involved in the major agon of Revelation (the Church vs. the Roman Empire), he represents the proper response to Rome for every Christian. Jesus is never referred to as *pantokratôr* (the Almighty) or as the one "who was and who is and who is coming." However, John connects the phrase "*prôtos kai eschatos* [the first and the last]" with Jesus in language about his being "dead" and now being "alive" (a similar notion) in 1:17–18 and 2:8. Other than in the formula "*prôtos kai eschatos*," the term "*prôtos*" does not seem to hold the type of summarizing significance for John that the term "*archê*" holds. Rather, it seems to indicate sequence.

Not unexpectedly, "God" is also linked with such perfectionist language. In 21:6, apparently God is the self-designated "alpha and the omega, the *archê* and the *telos*." And in 1:8, the phrase just quoted is applied to God along with another equal phrase: "who was and who is and who is coming," plus the entelechial epithet, "the Almighty [*pantokratôr*]." Likewise, 1:4 identifies God as the one "who was and who is and who is coming." Revelation 4:8 and 11:17 repeat this identification of God and include *pantokratôr*. Other verses that identify God as *pantokratôr* include 15:3; 16:7,14; 19:6,15; and 21:22.

John likes to contrast his villains and his heroes in terms of their similarities. Like God "who was and who is and who is coming," the beast "once was, now is not, and yet will come" (17:8). Using Burke's polar contrasts, such language may be cited as evidence that John sees the beast as being the perfect villain. Like the Lamb who "was dead" but is "alive forever" (1:18), the beast "seemed to have a fatal wound, but the fatal wound had been healed" (13:3).

This contrast may indicate the summarizing principle in terms of the perfectly negative.

In archetypal language, John calls the dragon the "ancient [*archaios*] serpent" once in 12:9, and twice in 20:2. As shown later, his (archetypal) "seven heads" also connote perfection. The number seven indicates perfection. The seven spirits, lampstands, and stars are perfections aligned with the positive cluster. The seven heads of the dragon and beast, and the seven crowns on the dragon's heads may be *telos* symbols, aligning the dragon and the beast as perfect villains. The seven mountains on which the harlot sits might align her with perfect villainy, as well.

An examination of the term "*telos*" and, more frequently, its cognate verb, "*teleô*," proves especially revealing. In addition to the earlier mentioned formula, the term "*telos*" is used just once in Revelation (2:26). Here, the Thyatirans are told that the "conquerors and those keeping [Jesus'] works until *telos*" will be given "authority over the nations." Hence, whatever *telos* signifies (and it seems to be parallel to "until I come" in the preceding verse), this situation refers to a category different from the previous discussion. Whereas, the prior discussion focuses on those terms that have already achieved *telos*, this verse focuses on a *telos* that is not yet.

This second category of *telos*/eschaton of which John speaks would clearly be in the distant future from John's perspective. This point is observed in forms of the verb *teleô* found in chapter 20, verses 3, 5, and 7. Here, John speaks of events that will happen when the thousand year prison sentence of the dragon has been completed [*teleô*]. G. B. Caird sees a "serious problem" in "John's double eschatology." He recounts that scholars such as R. H. Charles have had trouble with the millennium discussed in chapter 20. But, Caird believes that "the dual fulfillment, with the intervening millennium, is a vital part of John's theology." He states: "The seventh bowl, which completes the wrath of God and brings about the collapse of Babylon is the end of an epoch, but it is in a different category from the dissolution of the physical cosmos which accompanies the final judgement (xvi.17–21; cf. xx.11)." Caird writes: "We return therefore to the question raised by the very first sentence of the Revelation. What did John think was 'bound to happen soon'? Certainly not the End, which was at least a millennium away."[1] These ends point toward what Burke calls a "theological translation into terms of a final destiny in an afterlife." Burke continues, "A sheerly logological explanation must leave such doctrinally stimulated hunger unappeased" (RR 300). Burke is not interested in discussing "millennarian" futurist aspects of entelechy.

However, most significant terms could be said to be (in John's mind) in a third category of *telos*—on the brink of *telos*, hence still in the process of entelechy. Being on the brink of *telos* would indicate that the perfection is still unrealized, an implicit goal within the human being. Nevertheless, glimpses of Jesus as "*archê* and *telos*" remind the Christians of their entelechial destinies.

THE ARCHETYPAL "SEVEN" FORM

Returning to the seven last/*eschatos* plagues concerning which the significance is noted by John in 15:1—"Because in them the wrath of God is *perfected* [*teleô*]" (emphasis mine)—the verb "*teleô*" fits the connotation of perfecting more than ending. Interpreters should ask the question, in what respect(s) are the seven eschato(logical) plagues a perfect demonstration of the wrath of God? The answer may be related to the necessity of destroying/purging the Babylon the harlot identity from Israel, so that the New Jerusalem—the bride reidentification—may result.

The Seven Trumpets

In another group of seven, John states that "in the days" of the "seventh" trumpet, the "mystery of God" will be "perfected [*teleô*]," which God "announced to . . . the prophets" (10:6–7). What is this "mystery" that God announced to the prophets? Revelation 17:5–7 points once again to the harlot. John possibly had in mind the harlot imagery of the Old Testament prophets. Therein was a discussion of God's marriage to Israel/Zion, the ensuing harlotry of the wife, and the promised divorce and destruction of the harlot. If the sounding of the seventh trumpet fulfills/completes a divorce threat between God and Israel as foretold by the prophets, such an event would be entelechial. Just such a possibility exists.

The Seven Seals—Extended

The seven trumpets appear to be an expanded explanation of what occurred in the breaking of the seventh seal (8:1ff.). Thus the seven trumpets might be the analog of what parents do when they tell their children that they will give them until the count of three. Upon counting one and two, the parents might count 2½, 2¾, 2⅞, etc. This tactic does not nullify the threat of the ominous number three. Instead, it intensifies the threat by dramatically emphasizing the brink number, two. Similarly, in his number seven threat, John emphasizes the brink number, six! However, upon reaching the seventh trumpet of the seventh seal, John hears the angel say in effect: We're out of time (10:7). With the seventh trumpet the mystery (divorce?) will be perfected.

J. Massyngberde Ford observes:

> The Hebrew document which resembles the apocalyptic scroll most closely is the get *mequssar*, the tied (folded and sealed) deed.
> . . . .
>
> It is said that the folded get originated with priests who wished to divorce their wives, as in *Baba Bathra* 160b (Epstein):
> What is the reason why the Rabbis instituted a folded (deed)?—
> They were [in] a place [inhabited] by priests, who were very hot-tempered and they divorced their wives (for the slightest provocation). Consequently the Rabbis made [this] provision, so that in the meantime they might cool down.
> . . . .
>
> While this explanation of the origin of the folded get may be questioned, the fact that it was used in divorce cases is interesting. . . . [T]he Lamb's *biblion* . . . might easily be a bill of divorce. . . .
> *Biblion* is used for a bill of divorce in LXX Deut 24:1,3, Isa 50: 1, Jer 3:8, Mark 10:4, Matt 19:7. . . . Although the Greek *biblion* is usually qualified by *apostasion*, the Semitic word *get* is often used without qualification when it means "bill of divorce."[2]

The Greek of John is idiosyncratic and Semitic. Possibly, John's *biblion* equals the Semitic *get*. If the reference to the "mystery of God," which He "announced to . . . the prophets" (10:6–7), is taken to mean the "words of God" that will "be perfected" (17:17), the latter passage may also refer to the divorce or destruction of the harlot, described above.

These two instances of the seven plagues and the seven trumpets have in common the distinctive (for John) number seven; they are an introduction to John's most powerful psychological use of entelechial motivation. He is subtly "arousing and fulfilling expectations" in the minds of his auditors. The number seven is noticed by virtually everyone who has read John's Apocalypse. It is without doubt a key term in John's symbol system. The preceding discussion has already associated the number with entelechial considerations. Elizabeth Schüssler Fiorenza observes:

> The number seven for example was already integrated by Jewish apocalypticism into Jewish beliefs and was the number of divine [and, in line with Burke's insight, I would add satanic] *perfection* [emphasis mine] and holiness. In Revelation it characterizes not only the churches, their angels, and the spirits of God but functions also as a basic structural component in the composition of the book. The four septets (the letters, the seals, the trumpets, and the bowls) decisively structure Revelation.[3]

Fiorenza proposes a seven-part "surface structure" resembling "the golden candelabra which appears on the arch of Titus in Rome" and defends her structure by pointing out: "The pattern is a widely employed pattern in the literature of antiquity."[4] Whether or not one agrees with Fiorenza's "surface structure" proposal, one is obliged to admit readily to her observation that the four septets decisively structure Revelation. Structure is equivalent to "form" and hence, the seven-fold structure of each septet would, in Burkean terms, arouse and fulfill expectations. What type of expectations? Fiorenza has answered: perfection-related. Not accidentally, forms of *teleô* appear at the "seventh" trumpet and at the "seventh" plague. By the time the "seventh" aspect has been reached, the *telos* has arrived.

THE NUMBER SIX

What is instructive in the light of Caird's query—"What did John think was 'bound to happen soon?' "[5]—is to look instead for the number six. The supreme archetype with entelechial implications in the entire book of Genesis is the creation week. When day number seven arrives, *telos* has already been achieved. Creation has been completed (perfected) by the end of day six. The word "sabbath" even carries the perfected denotation of "rest" in Hebrew. Since John (intuitively) knows that his seven structure has aroused an expectation of *telos* in the number seven for his audience, John consistently places himself and his audience at the number six, thus indicating almost by the sheer weight of form that he and his readers are on the brink of *telos*—but they are still in the process of entelechy (*telos* has not yet come).

The Sixth Emperor

The most poignant verses in the book for those looking for internal evidence of the date of Revelation are 17:10–11. Scholars have agreed that the "seven heads = seven kings" refer to Roman emperors. Hence, calculations ensue in an effort to determine the emperor's reign under which the book is being written. While the answer to the calculation is of vast importance, the psychologically entelechial significance of the verses has been missed. John states that "five fell, one is, and the other has not yet come." That places John and his audience precisely in the reign of emperor number six. They are on the brink of *telos*.

The Number 666

Additionally, the number of the beast "who has the wound of the sword and lived" (13:14) is the infamous number 666. Along the line of reasoning advanced earlier in my "parents counting to three analogy," this infamous number seems to signify the last brink of the last brink of the last brink of *telos*. Gematria is the technical term for the activity of codifying someone's name into a number, a very popular practice in the first century. Unlike English, which uses an alphabet for letters and an arabic number system, ancient languages such as Hebrew, Aramaic, Greek, and Latin made the alphabet serve a dual purpose. The use of roman numerals in English today illustrates such a dual use of letters. A type of coin circulated in the province of Asia, on which the abbreviated style of Domitian in Greek appears (Emperor Caesar Domitian Augustus Germanicus) yields the total of 666 in the value of the Greek letters. An Aramaic document of Nero's reign from the Wadi Murabba'at, in Jordan, contains the required spelling for Nero Caesar, which would equal 666 in either Aramaic or Hebrew. But the formal— the psychologically entelechial—significance comes not from identifying the individual to whom the number referred (John's primary audience surely knew!). The sense of being on the ultimate brink of *telos* comes from the sheer archetypal entelechial form— the "expectation" that number seven (*telos*) is almost on the scene.

The Sixth Seal and Sixth Trumpet

This use of the number six is similar, formally, to the positioning of the interlude between the sixth and seventh trumpets, in which John hears the seven thunders, but does not write the messages down; he eats the scroll that was sweet in his mouth but bitter in his stomach (i.e., he must prophesy); he measures the temple; and the two witnesses prophesy. Since the seven trumpets are an expansion of the seventh seal, John and his audience (at this point, chronologically and logologically) are on the last brink of the last brink of *telos.* An interlude of eating a scroll and hearing seven thunders does not tell much about the temporal standpoint of John and his audience. There are some clues in the measuring of the temple and in the prophecy of the two witnesses. If it is the Jerusalem Temple that John is told to measure, the date should probably not be placed much (if at all) later than A.D. 70, the year in which the temple was destroyed.

Daniel and the Entelechial Seven Structure

The language in Revelation 11:2–3, related to the "forty-two months" = "a thousand two hundred sixty days" (= three and one half years) corresponds to Daniel 9 and the times of the destruction of Jerusalem and the temple. In fact, the "three and one-half years" of the testimony of the witnesses (11:3) and the "three and one half years" of the trampling of the city by the Gentiles (11:2) have overwhelming entelechial significance themselves. They appear to be either one or both halves of the "last week of years" described by Daniel in chapter 9. Daniel 9:24–27 speaks of seventy (entelechially significant!) weeks (entelechially significant!) of years. During the first sixty-nine (the brink) weeks of years, Jerusalem—including its walls—would be rebuilt (9:25) and the Messiah prince would be "cut off" (9:26). In (9:27) the last week of years (entelechially, tremendously significant!), "a desolator on the wing of abominations" would come—a figure that Mark 13:14 identifies with Jesus' prediction of the fall of Jerusalem within a generation (Mark 13:30). In the "middle" of that last week (another brink), the desolator(?) "shall cause the offering and sacrifice to cease" (Daniel 9:27). Dividing the final seven years in the "middle" leaves two periods of "three and one-half years" each—one before the cessation of sacrifice and one following the cessation of sacrifice. Daniel concludes in 12:11 with the words: "And from the time the daily [sacrifice] shall be taken away, and the abomination that makes desolate set up, a thousand two hundred ninety days [= roughly, three and one-half years]," after which will come *qeytz* (a word which means "end" but is easily associated, for plays on words, with the verb "to awaken," cf. Ezekiel 7:6). Perhaps the Semitic play on the words "end" and "awaken" has Burke's "reidentification" sense, as well.

The various interpretations of Daniel by Old Testament scholars need not be traced in this instance. The early church clearly interpreted Daniel in terms of the fall of Jerusalem. Thus, the reference to something happening in the middle of the last week of the seventy weeks of years is tantamount, entelechially, to the ultimate brink of *telos*. If the "great city which is spiritually called Sodom and Egypt, where also their lord was crucified" (Revelation 11:8) is an unmistakable reference to Jerusalem, as several scholars believe,[6] the identification of the significance of Jerusalem's doom for John's audience is supported.

Euphrates References in the Sixth Plague and Sixth Trumpet

Further clues may be noted in the sixth plague and the sixth trumpet. In some respects, these two "sixes" are equivalent. In the sixth plague, the "angel poured out his bowl onto the great river Euphrates and its water was dried up so that the way of the kings from the rising sun might be prepared" (16:12). In the sixth trumpet, "the four angels bound at the great river Euphrates" were released (9:14). These are the only two passages in the entire New Testament where the Euphrates is mentioned.

Ford sees a possible reference to Jeremiah 51:59–64, where Jeremiah's book is thrown into the Euphrates with the warning, "So shall Babylon sink."[7] Another Euphrates-related prophecy is directed against Jerusalem in Jeremiah 13:1–14, with God promising to "ruin the pride of Judah and the great pride of Jerusalem" (13:9). These are the only two times Euphrates is used as a prophetic symbol in the Old Testament.

Some scholars have thought that the Euphrates points to the Parthian menace to Rome. F. F. Bruce invokes the Nero myths as an explanation of the Parthian/Euphrates significance. Nero had committed suicide on 9 June, A.D. 68, and Bruce states:

When Nero, deposed by the senate in A.D. 68, committed suicide to escape the ignominious death to which that body had condemned him, many of his eastern subjects (among whom he had enjoyed great popularity) refused to believe that he was really dead. For some twenty years after his death, therefore, the belief persisted that he had not really died but gone into hiding, probably beyond the Euphrates, and that he would return one day at the head of an army of Parthians . . . and rule once more as emperor. . . . After 88, . . . the belief that Nero was still alive was generally given up; but it was replaced by the belief that one day Nero would return from the dead. . . . This later belief in a Nero Redivivus . . . can be traced . . . almost to the end of the second century.[8]

Caird rejects, however, the idea of John being concerned "with the possibility of a literal Parthian invasion," in favor of an interpretation related to the Gog and Magog pattern (Israel's symbolic enemy).[9]

If (regardless of the rationale) doom for Jerusalem (Babylon) is intended, the historical indication that Jerusalem is on the brink of destruction might signify that John's audience is on the brink of *telos*. This would be in line with the Mark 13 apocalypse. The fall of Jerusalem and *telos* (Mark 13:7) are discussed in conjunction with each other.

The Weltwochenschema

There may be one other entelechial "six" to which John might be alluding. It is referred to in the introduction—that difficult millennial issue of Revelation chapter 20. Paul Billerbeck, in the important German work by Herman Strack and himself, *Kommentar zum Neuen Testament aus Talmud und Midrasch*, provides the background information regarding the popular belief among the Jews of the time that the messianic reign would last for one thousand years.[10] His findings may be summarized as follows:

- Rabbi Eli'ezer ben Hyrkanus (c. A.D. 90) taught that it would last 1000 years, based on Psalm 90:15.
- Rabbi Yehoschua (c. A.D. 90), taught "2000 years," based on the same text.
- Rabbi El'azar ben Azarja (c. A.D. 100 taught "70 years," based on Joshua 23:15.
- Rabbi Akiba (c. A.D. 135) taught "40 years," based on Deuteronomy 8:3 and Psalm 90:15, or on Micah 7:15 and Psalm 95:10.
- Other proposals by rabbinic sources were: 60 years, 600 years,

400 years, 100 years, 365 years, 365,000 years, 354 years, 4000 years, and 7000 years. They all used scripture texts to support their various views.

Sanhedrin 97a is quoted by Billerbeck, who states that in the school of Elias, it is taught that the world will stand for six thousand years: two thousand years without the Law, two thousand years with the Law, and two thousand years with the Messiah. The final thousand years of this *Weltwochenschema* will be the *Weltensabbat,* as Billerbeck interprets.[11]

If, by speaking of a thousand year imprisonment of the dragon, John is implying *Weltwochenschema,* then the sixth millenium might be entelechial in John's view, also, with Billerbeck's *Weltensabbat* (sabbath of the cosmic week) being the *telos* of the entire human drama for John. Certainly, the end of each millennium in the Christian era has brought with it apocalyptic expectations. The end of the second Christian millennium in the year 2000 produced such a psychology among true believers. Barry Brummett comments:

> One motivation for increased attention to apocalyptic discourse is the impending close of the second millennium, with anticipated attendant awakening of millennial fever among many. The extermination of David Koresh's explicitly apocalyptic Branch Davidian group at Waco, Texas, in 1993 is but one example of this expected intensified millennialism.[12]

CONCLUSION

This chapter has focused upon "what [Revelation] does for" its readers. Surely there are many more insights to be offered from an entelechial critique from the psychological perspective than those presented here. However, John's use of the archetypal form "seven" is one extremely powerful example of what Burke means by the "arousing and fulfilling of expectations"; for John and his primary audience, it is doubtful that any structure could be more entelechial than a "seven" structure. Burke's statistical method recommends that studies be "term-guided." If they are term-guided, the "objective citation" of the specific terms that a given writer uses must be paramount. What words are at war with what other words? What words are the allies of the words on each side of the conflict? What words stand for victory, perfection, defeat?

In this chapter, Burke's method of being guided by John's words themselves has been followed. The attempt was made not to force meanings and equations upon terms, but, by citation, to allow the terms to disclose themselves. Each individual builds his/her own symbol system, and John is not different. Any symbol system is, however, a cooperative effort. No one builds a symbol system in a vacuum. One builds it out of situations, forms, patterns of experience, symbols, and terms that have "overlaps" of meanings in one's society. Hence, dictionaries and lexica may be employed to find socially cooperative meanings. The extension of the dictionary is the literature with which the author was likely to have come in contact. Therein may be found meanings and equational links for patterns, forms, symbols, and terms. Accordingly, this chapter has traced the network of equations in John's symbol system related to how John viewed perfection. Although John's view of perfection is definitely temporal at times, the nontemporal implications of his symbol system are every bit as fascinating as the temporal.

Revelation is replete with perfectionist expectations—entelechial, Burke would say. When in 11:7, John describes the two witnesses in terms of "perfecting [*teleô*] their witness [*marturia*]" (an entelechial concept) the beast comes up and kills them. Being slain has little to do with futuristic eschatology, but it is both chronological and logological for the individual. As each witness/martyr views his/her possibly impending death, s/he is on the ultimate brink of *telos*. S/he is on the brink of becoming, in John's terms, a conqueror. When in 2:25–26, John quotes Jesus urging Thyatirans, "Hold until I come . . . until the *telos* of my works," he wishes his readers to sense that they are on the brink. The *telos*, whether personal (death) or futuristic (Jesus' coming) is "near" (1:3; 22:10). Things will happen "soon" (1:1; 22:6). "Behold I come quickly" (2:16; 3:11, 22:7, 12, 20). John has his readers poised at number six. Number seven is nearly here. Psychologically, John places his readers on the brink— infused with a principle of *telos* within, entelechy.

7

The Sociopolitics of Revelation

CRITICISM FROM A POETICS PERSPECTIVE (BEING PRIMARILY INTERNAL) requires little extratextual material to perform. Criticism from a psychological perspective requires a knowledge of the formal expectations of the audience. Criticism from a sociopolitical perspective requires significantly greater access to extratextual material. Furthermore, sociopolitical criticism requires a precise assessment of the sociopolitical context in which the literary work is produced. This chapter posits an intra-Jewish sociopolitical context prior to the fall of Jerusalem in A.D. 70 for Revelation. Following Leland Griffin's adaptation of Burkean theory into a social movements model, first-century Christianity is presented as a social movement within Judaism. Revelation is then placed within this intra-Jewish sociopolitical context and an entelechial critique from a sociopolitical perspective is provided.

What is the sociopolitical problem which the Apocalypse of John addresses? Elisabeth Schüssler Fiorenza claims: "New Testament scholars generally agree that . . . Rev[elation] . . . depict[s] the . . . political struggles of the churches in Asia Minor at the end of the first century."[1] According to this context, the sociopolitical struggle would be between Christianity and the Roman Empire. Revelation's negative reference to Jews would open John to a charge of anti-Semitism. While Fiorenza's claim that "New Testament scholars generally agree" concerning this is true, the general agreement is not necessarily correct. Fiorenza notes: "After reviewing scholarly efforts to arrive at a definite interpretation of Rev[elation], [E. Lohmeyer] concludes that the proposed interpretations are so diverse that the true meaning of Rev[elation] still remains hidden."[2] If two or three good alternative interpretations exist for a given text, the text should be considered open to new ideas and further exploration.

As was Luke T. Johnson, I personally am indebted to Henry Fischel, who, as he did for Johnson, "introduced me to the Talmud and whose pioneering work on Judaism as part of the Hellenistic world is a model."[3] Hence, I have a sensitivity to the anti-Semitism that has unfortunately been at least a part of the history of Christianity throughout the past two millennia. Like Johnson, I have no desire to support anti-Semitism in any form. Johnson's explanation of what has been called "anti-Jewish slander" in the New Testament refers to the rhetorical climate that was a part of the Greco-Roman milieu, in line with the basic methodological tenets that Fischel taught. Johnson suggests "that the slander of the N[ew] T[estament] is typical of that found among Jews as among other Hellenists."[4] According to Johnson, the problem with many approaches to the "anti-Jewish" issue is that "they isolate 'Christianity' over against 'Judaism' as though each was [sic] a well-defined entity when the polemic was written."[5] Johnson argues that Christianity was merely one of a number of rival Jewish groups: "So-called normative Judaism was not normative in the period of the N[ew] T[estament]. The question Who is a real Jew? was then an open question, debated fiercely and even violently by rival claimants."[6]

Apparently, this intra-Jewish rivalry is operative in Revelation, as well. R. H. Charles argues and most subsequent scholars agree that the author of Revelation is Jewish.[7] The author holds great respect for the twelve tribes of Israel. He applies the terms Mt. Zion and Jerusalem to his heroes with a healthy respect for such terms. His 144,000 are identified not as Gentiles, but as being from the twelve tribes of Israel (minus Dan). If anything, he is jealous of the Jewish terminology, and unwilling to apply what he considers to be prestigious nomenclature to those whom he considers unworthy to be called "Jews." Yet, it seems clear that at least some of John's villains are Jews. And, as Johnson points out:

> In the first generation, furthermore, the messianists were a persecuted sect. Some non-messianist Jews certainly sought to extirpate the cult. Jesus was executed. Subsequent leaders of the movement were arrested, imprisoned, stoned, killed. Whether this was all the direct work of Jews is irrelevant, because in the eyes of the messianists they were to blame. ... Even if I Thess 2:14–16 is an interpolation, it is early evidence for the messianists' perception of Palestinian and diaspora persecution from Jews. Together with Paul's statements about his own activity (Gal 1:13; Phil 3:6; 1 Cor 15:8; 1 Tim 1: 12–13) and experience (2 Cor 11:23–29), and the evidence of Acts (5:17–18; 6: 12–13; 7:58; 8:3; 9:1–2; 13:50; 14:19; 17:5; 18:12; 23:12–15), as well as that of Josephus . . . , the simple statement of my text may be allowed

to stand as historically accurate. . . . The fact of such persecution is also acknowledged by D. R. A. Hare.[8]

EARLY CHRISTIANITY AS SOCIAL MOVEMENT

Assuming that Johnson is correct in proclaiming Christianity in the first generation to be one of a number of rival Jewish sects, instead of an institutional religion, Christianity exists definitionally as a "social movement," prior to any religious "institutionalization." According to Stewart, Smith, and Denton, such movements "cease to be social movements if they become part of an established order."[9] First generation Christianity was not an established order, but, instead, a social movement that was less concerned (sociopolitically) with rivalling the Roman Empire than it was with its competition with the top echelon of the Jewish sociopolitical hierarchy, the high priestly party. Revelation should be dated in the context of this Jewish sociopolitical struggle. The sociopolitical *telos* of the book is the replacement of the current Jewish sociopolitical order.

Although there is evidence of cooperation among various leaders in the (Christian) movement, and an implicit agreement that issues of debate are best settled by conference, there appears to be no set power structure in existence as late as the Jerusalem conference described in Acts 15. Here, a procircumcision party from Judea has become embroiled in debate with Paul and Barnabas, arguing that Gentiles must become Jewish proselytes as a prerequisite to being considered "Christians." Paul and Barnabas were commissioned by the church in Antioch to present the anticircumcision position at a meeting with "apostles and elders" in Jerusalem (15:2). At this meeting, the distinguished leader Simon Peter spoke, not as the final arbiter of the issue, but as a witness who concurred with the conclusion drawn by Paul and Barnabas. The final solution—a letter absolving Gentile Christians from most of the requirements of the Jewish law—appeared to be the result of consensus among "apostles and elders, along with the whole church" (15:22), rather than the decree of one or more hierarchical authorities. While this consensus decision permitting uncircumcised gentiles into the Church may have opened the way for Christianity to become an institutional religion, separate from Judaism, it did not result in the immediate distinction between Christianity and Judaism. Instead, as late as the writing of Revelation, Christianity appears to be vying for recognition as the true Jewish religion (Revelation 3:9).

Although the Book of Acts, Josephus's writings, and Paul's various epistles as cited by Johnson earlier in this chapter provide evidence of serious conflict between the first generation Christians and the institutional Jewish Temple cult, the Book of Revelation may actually contain the most vigorous "anti-Jewish" language in the entire body of first generation Christian primary literature. As a post-Holocaust society would avoid the type of racial invective that produced a Hitler, so must be understood the sociopolitical situation that produced the New Testament—the paradigmatic polemic upon which much of historical anti-Semitic polemic is based.

Elisabeth Schüssler Fiorenza and J. Massyngberde Ford provide two important assertions related to what may have been going on sociopolitically in the Book of Revelation. Fiorenza asserts that the book is a unity—the product of a single author.[10] J. Massyngberde Ford asserts that the bulk of internal evidence demands a Jewish milieu, prior to A.D. 70.[11] Of course, Fiorenza and most current scholars disagree with the early date proposed by Ford, favoring instead a date in the last decade of the first century A.D. However, a number of scholars (Charles, Grant, Caird, Bruce, et. al.) would consider a date between A.D. 68 and 70 to be a possibility. The most serious criticism of Ford is related to her dissection of the Revelation text, the type of critical move that had many adherents in the nineteenth century, but since then has been largely dismissed.

Burke, Griffin, and Social Movements

Leland Griffin has already successfully adapted Burkean concepts to the discussion of social movements. Using Griffin's dramatistic model of social movements,[12] the so-called "anti-Jewish" rhetoric of the first generation Christians is analyzed here as an example of a social movement at work. My hope is that a better understanding of such early Christian invective would argue against much of the anti-Semitism that has used the New Testament as a springboard in the past two millennia. The analysis will follow the broad outlines of Griffin's model through the "inception" and "crisis" periods. Griffin understands that virtually all social movements proceed through three periods—the inception period, the crisis period, and the consummation period.

Explaining Griffin's Model

The following is a brief overview of these three periods:

(1) The inception period is marked by indecision and alienation. In this period, participants in the movement are concerned with determining destinations/meccas and devils/evil principles. Griffin divides the period into three phases:

   (a) Phase one is the development of an antimovement, a negation designed to promote doubt, indecision, and division through two strategies:

   (i) The first strategy employed by the movement is one designed to intensify misunderstanding.

   (ii) The second strategy is one designed to provoke conflict. In provoking a countermovement (one that opposes the antimovement mentioned before), the antimovement is provided with a scapegoat (the countermovement) upon which the antimovement may load all guilt.

   (b) Phase two is the phase of conversion and catharsis, which utilizes two strategies:

   (i) The first strategy is to promote decision by converting the estranged, and by convincing prospects for the movement that by "attitude" they are already a part of the movement.

   (ii) The second strategy is to provoke action, since "attitude" is "incipient action." This action would be a negation of the countermovement's negation. The action would kill the kill.

   (c) Phase three is the phase of profusion and intensity wherein three dangers to the movement must be circumvented:

   (i) The first danger is that the countermovement that has been provoked might kill the antimovement. This danger is circumvented by developing eloquence (perfecting the form to the appetites of the hearers), producing commitment, and raising up prophets.

   (ii) The second danger is that the antimovement's rhetors might err in adapting to new exigencies. This danger is circumvented by abandoning ineffective appeals, adapting new modes of arguments, and intensifying the use of available channels.

(iii) The third danger is that the movement might splinter or fail to accomplish merger. This danger is circumvented by promoting solidarity.

(2) The crisis period is marked by mass decision, collective catharsis/purgation, and resolution of public tensions. In this period is transformation that comes by killing something. What is killed may be the old order, whereupon a new social ladder is created. What is killed may be the scapegoat, the countermovement. (What is killed may be the old self, but this "mortification," for Griffin, effectively takes place in the inception period rather than the crisis period.)

(3) In the consummation period, leaders change from being prophetlike to being priest-like. Herein, the movement changes from an antimovement to a pro-movement, having a rhetoric of assent and allegiance rather than dissent. Strategies are employed that arouse and gratify the natural appetite for "obedience," and that strive to actualize the perfecting myth of the movement, utopia. Thus, the consummation period is a tome of mortification and self-sacrifice as all are called to accept this new order—despite the individual's tendency to seek a better order, to negate the present order.

As does Burke, Griffin assesses the nature of humans to be "rotten with perfection." Acceptance of any order seems to represent "pure tension." It is "where the pendulum is at rest, not hanging, but poised exactly above the fulcrum (Santayana)." Griffin's "consummation period" as it applies to Christianity will not be discussed in this study, since that period of Christianity as a social movement is better placed in the early Catholic period of the second century A.D. This study focuses on first generation Christianity.

Prior to the analysis of early Christianity, a brief discussion of the theoretical foundations of Griffin's model in the hierarchal theory of Kenneth Burke is provided. This section of the chapter, then, identifies the specific hierarchy or order that Christianity sought to replace, the specific "logological" developments taking place at each phase and period in the social movement, and the ways in which the so-called "slander" was used to accomplish the social movement's goals.

The logological theory that Griffin borrows from Kenneth Burke follows from Burke's threefold question in PLF: "From what, through what, to what?" (PLF 71). Griffin develops a three-step pattern for examining the development of social movements, paralleling what Burke observes in tragic drama: "*From* Order, Guilt, and the Negative, / *Through* Victimage and Mortification, / *To* Catharsis and Redemption."[13] Griffin recognizes that language is the method by which humans are so moved. "And thus the significance of 'Order, the Secret, and the Kill' "[14] becomes for Griffin the driving force in social movements.

The "secret," for Griffin following Burke, is the "mystery" that "arises at that point where different kinds of beings are in communication" (RM 115).[15] In first generation Christianity, the secret refers to the "mystery" that arises when the upper class priests of the Temple cult are in communication with (what could only be understood as) the lower-class Christian leaders. Several such points of communication are documented from the Christian perspective throughout the New Testament. A sense of order is implicit.

With respect to the kill that produces tragic catharsis, Burke prefers the perfect tragic victim(s) of Aristotle's *Poetics*—intimates. Burke understands that there are family tensions in human patterns of experience that might best be perfected in the tragic "father-kill." He sees Freud's interest in Oedipus as evidence that Freud considers these family tensions to be primal. The order to which Freud responds would be the "patriarchal" order of the family. By having a son (lower class) kill a father (upper class), there would be purgation, catharsis, and redemption. The son would then be in a position of voting in a "new order," with himself at the top of the hierarchy. Some type of "kill" is required to expunge the old order and institute the new. Griffin subdivides the kill into the positive kill, mortification, and the negative kill, victimage. A term that Griffin uses as a synonym for the negative kill is "scapegoating."

Applying Griffin's Model

Turning now from theory to application, Griffin's model is directed to the three periods of a social movement. Rather than a historiographic approach, this application pursues a textual approach. This application utilizes the perception of the events from the perspective of the Christian movement and its texts—the books of the New Testament. (These books, it should be noted, were not written until phase three of the inception period.) The point of this application is to provide some broad outlines of the way in which Griffin's model may be employed to discuss the Christian social movement from its own authoritative perspective.

Griffin states: "Movements begin when some pivotal individual or group—suffering attitudes of alienation in a given social system . . . gives voice to a No."[16] For the Christian movement, the pivotal individual who gave voice to the "no" was Jesus of Nazareth. Jesus was apparently a man of lower-class origins. Born of questionable circumstances, he was raised as a carpenter. He could stake no claim to priestly lineage. While at least two attempts (Matthew 1 and Luke 3) were made to trace his ancestry back to King David, there is no indication that such an ancestry gave him any rank in the established Jewish order. Although Luke 2:46–47 provides an account of a brief opportunity for Jesus at age twelve to listen to and ask questions of Jewish scholars in the Temple, there is no evidence that he studied systematically under any influential Jewish rabbi(s). However, as a popular teacher, he was effective. Crowds of as many as five thousand were reported to have gathered to hear him teach (Mark 6:30–44; Luke 9:10–17). But his frequent clashes with scribes, Pharisees, and Sadducees indicate that the intellectually elite did not accept him as their equal. John 8:48–52 relates a typical assessment of Jesus: "Has any of the rulers or of the Pharisees put his trust in him? No! . . . Look into it, and you will find that a prophet does not come out of Galilee." Ultimately, the most astounding "no" that he voiced would be his Temple invective. In addition to making various predictions of a future destruction of the Temple, Jesus, according to all three synoptic gospels, actually staged a prototypical social movement demonstration in the Temple (Matthew 21:12–17; Mark 11:12–19; Luke 19:45–48). He overturned the currency exchange tables. He charged the Temple authorities (i.e., the high priestly family!) with making a "house of prayer" into a "den of thieves!"

Phase one then began, in Griffin's terms, as "the rhetoric of an anti movement."[17] Jesus was, throughout the Gospels, merely a teacher, albeit with a number of disciples who later forge a social movement in his name. Griffin informs us that the "first strategy [of a social movement in its initial phase] is . . . to permeate the prevailing scene with a sense of the . . . injustice of the existing order."[18] Jesus' attack upon the institutional order of the Temple cult exemplifies this strategy in action. The second strategy outlined by Griffin "is to provoke conflict."[19] Jesus' attack accomplished just that. John 11:45–57 describes a conspiracy by "chief priests and the Pharisees" to capture and kill Jesus. The countermovement, which Griffin calls "vital" because it "provides the movement with . . . a salient Victim, a scapegoat, a Kill—a rhetorical Vile beast to be slain . . . a Negation to be negated,"[20] had begun. Of course, the first phase of the inception period ended with the crucifixion of

Jesus, carried out under the willing auspices of the Roman government, but, in the minds of the Christians, engineered by the Jewish Temple cult authorities.

Griffin states: "The second phase of the period of inception . . . turns to a rhetoric of conversion and catharsis. Its first strategy is to promote decision, to convert the estranged."[21] This phase of the Christian movement had a very precise beginning—the day of Pentecost, seven weeks after Jesus' crucifixion. With a call to "repent and be baptized" (Acts 2:38), Simon Peter implied that all Jews had corporate (or synecdochic) responsibility with the old order in nailing Jesus to the cross (Acts 2:23). The only solution to the dilemma was to kill the old order on an individual, personal basis via "repentance." Since the term "repentance [*metanoia*]" means a "change of attitude/mind," Peter was appealing to fellow Jews (to use Griffin's language), "to convince them that by attitude they are of the movement."[22]

The second strategy of this phase "is to provoke action."[23] Here, Griffin introduces "mortification." While for Burke attitudes are incipient acts, Griffin views the logologically suicidal act of mortification as follows: "In the order of murder, when the converted rise up, in the arena of their minds, and negate the contradictions of the counter-movement . . . they 'see through,' reject, and thus slay them."[24] Fittingly, the first overt "act" Simon Peter required of his converts was baptism, an act that symbolized the "death, burial, and resurrection" of the convert (Romans 6:1–4). Yet this symbolic act was only the prelude to the literal martyrdom that the deacon Stephen suffered at the hands of countermovement Jews (Acts 7:54–60). Approving of his execution was Saul of Tarsus (Acts 8:1), who subsequently became a leader of the countermovement that "dragged off men and women and put them in prison" (Acts 8:3). Saul received his authority to imprison Christians from the high priest (Acts 9:1–2). Although Herod (representing the Roman government rather than the Jewish authorities) was responsible for killing the Apostle James (Acts 12:1–3), he reportedly "saw that this pleased the Jews" and proceeded to arrest Peter, as well. Saul, himself, after his conversion (and thus reidentification as "Paul") faced Jewish countermovement plots on his life in Iconium (Acts 14:5), Lystra (Acts 14:19), Thessalonica (Acts 17:5), and Jerusalem (Acts 21:27–36). Paul's subsequent trial in Jerusalem was handled by the high priest, Ananias, in a reportedly biased fashion (Acts 23:1–2). At this trial Pharisees were openly supportive of Paul, while the Sadducees and priests were antagonistic (Acts 23:9). Contrary to popular belief (no doubt, based on Jesus' debates with the Pharisees), Pharisees do not emerge as the scapegoats of the Christian movement. At most, references to the Pharisees in the context of postcrucifixion accounts of the Church are ambivalent. The most significantly powerful enemy of the Church appears to be the priestly family, leaders of the Temple cult.

The martyrdom that Jesus and the early Christians experienced appears to be continuing even at the time of Revelation. The clear hero(es) of each of the seven churches to which Revelation is addressed is the one who "overcomes" (*ho nikôn*). Scholars agree overwhelmingly that this term refers to "martyr[/s]."[25] It is in Griffin's discussion of the second phase of the inception period that he discusses martyrdom, stating that "of all the modes of dying, none is more eloquent than martyrdom—ultimate Mortification, self-Victimage."[26]

The third phase of the inception period is focused on circumventing three dangers that might abort the movement. The first danger is that the countermovement might kill the movement. Griffin suggests that movements here try to develop eloquence, produce commitment, and raise up prophets. Literal "prophets" were to be found in virtually every church that was established in the New Testament period. Commitment was being produced. Although the New Testament writings discuss matters purported to have occurred as early as 6 B.C., the earliest gospel account was probably not written any earlier than A.D. 58. The Book of Acts, which describes the history of the church, beginning at around A.D. 30 was probably not written before the decade of the 60s. Of the books of the New Testament, Paul's letters are probably the earliest written accounts, some of which could be dated in the 50s. These writings, to use Griffin's terms, would probably be an attempt to "perfect" the form to the "appetites" of the hearers.[27] The prologue to Luke (1:1–4) claims that the book is an attempt to provide an orderly account of the life of Jesus. The random stories and sayings with which the audience may have been familiar were being placed into a coherent narrative.

The second danger is the potential failure of the movement to adapt. In the early stages of Christianity, the movement's leaders used the public forum of the synagogue in each city as a means to disseminate their views. As the countermovement closed these venues, the leaders turned to the Gentiles, and their public meeting places. Even prisons wherein the Christian leaders were incarcerated provided "captive" audiences (cf. Acts 16:16–40, for example). When leaders were arrested and brought up for trial, they used their "defense" speeches as opportunities to try to gain converts among the authorities.

The third danger that might have aborted the movement, according to Griffin, is failure to accomplish merger. By this language, Griffin means that movements, since they have no institutional organization, are susceptible to fragmentation. If no attempt is made to coordinate the efforts of the various elements of the movement, the impact of the movement may be so limited as to abort the movement. This danger for Christianity was circumvented by the use of conferences among the leaders, such as the Jerusalem conference of Acts 15.

Jesus provided the "no" of the antimovement by challenging the legitimacy of the priestly hierarchy of the Temple cult. The priests responded with a countermovement that resulted in the killing of Jesus and some of the early Christian leaders. The movement had its scapegoat, the high priestly family. Through individual conversions and subsequent profusion and intensification, the Christian movement gradually became a rival to the priestly hierarchy. However, as late as the Jewish-Roman war of A.D., 66 to 73, the high priestly family was still firmly entrenched as the hierarchical head of the Jewish people. Jewish historian Solomon Zeitlin observes:

On the 28th of Tebeth, the beginning of January 66, a great assembly was convened in the temple for the purpose of establishing a government to carry out the necessary preparations for the war. It chose as head of the government the High Priest Ananus, a Sadducee who inherently was for peace.[28]

January A.D. 66 was the beginning of the crisis period. Within seven years from the establishment of the government, the Temple cult would be completely annihilated. The Temple itself was destroyed in A.D. 70, as Jerusalem fell to the Romans. A temple cult without a Temple was a virtual impossibility. From the remains of a temple-based, sacrificial Judaism, two religions arose. Rabbinic Judaism, based on the pharisaic teachings contained in the Talmud, became what is often called "normative" Judaism. Christianity, which in its "adaptive" phase had opened its doors fully to Gentile participation, became a Judaism for all nations. The great enemy against whom Christianity had vented its fierce anger in the first generation was not this later, normative Judaism. The great enemy was the Temple cult with its high priest whom Christianity had blamed for the crucifixion of Jesus, the martyrdom of Stephen, and

the many other persecutions that it had endured. From this perspective, the anti-Semitism of the twentieth century (as well as the
anti-Semitism of the past two millennia) has no legitimacy in pred-
icating its slander upon any so-called "slander" in the New Testament. In this crisis period (in which Griffin locates the killing of
the scapegoat), we find the so-called "anti-Jewish slander" of the
Book of Revelation. Here, during the years immediately preceding
the destruction of the Temple, John refers to Jerusalem as "Sodom
and Egypt, where also their Lord was crucified" (Revelation 11:8).
In this period, John writes of "the slander of those who say they are
Jews and are not, but are a synagogue of Satan" (2:9). At this time,
John calls Jerusalem "the harlot Babylon" (as J. M. Ford interprets)
and exults in her gory destruction.

The use of Griffin's model suggests that early Christianity might
best be viewed not as an institutionalized religion at war with another institutionalized religion, Judaism, but rather as a social
movement within Judaism. Early Christianity seems not to have
been a Gentile movement with a racist attitude. Its leaders were
virtually all Jewish. It suffered from persecution by the Temple cult
authorities, the order that it sought to replace. It sought a new
order, wherein the clearly Jewish teachings of its clearly Jewish hero,
Jesus, would have the dignity in the Jewish sociopolitical order that
Christians felt those teachings deserved. Griffin's crisis period corresponds somewhat to what Stewart, Smith, and Denton call the
"Enthusiastic Mobilization" stage of a social movement, wherein
"persuaders must employ harsh rhetoric . . . replete with name calling against the devils."[29] The so-called "slander" that the Christians
employed was a symbolic killing of the scapegoat, the high priestly
family. Throughout the phases of the movement, a logological "kill"
is involved. The kill of Jesus produced a scapegoat. The mortification of the converts prepared them for action. The killing of the
old order in the crisis period paved the way for a new order.

SOCIOPOLITICAL ENTELECHY AND REVELATION

In his autobiographical essay, "The Anaesthetic Revelation of
Herone Liddell," Burke relates the "perfectionist" impulse to the
"socio-political order" (CWO 289). He calls "language" the " 'grace'
that 'perfects' nature" and speaks of "language" as becoming "re-
enforced by a complex socio-political order." He stresses the "ide-

ality of socio-political communities (which are saturated with the genius of language)" (CWO 290). Burke explains:

[The hu]Man's symbolistic genius first exiles him[/her], by putting a symbolic veil between him[/her] and the non-symbolic. Next, it aggravates this state of alienation by making possible the complicated world of social status, the ladder or pyramid or hierarchy of offices, with their various "unnatural" kinds of livelihood. Next, symbolism acts to make amends by dialectical devices—of poetry, philosophy, politics—whereby things otherwise thought disjunct can be said to partake of a single unifying essence that transcends their separateness. (CWO 292)

According to Burke's schema just presented, transcendence is a "unifying" step that follows two dissociative steps. First, there is the dissociation between the "symbolic" and the "non-symbolic." Burke illustrates: " 'Love' begins as a sheerly natural emotion (animal, non-symbolic)" (CWO 293). But when language (for example, the term "love") is applied, there is dissociation. The second dissociative step is taken "once the symbol-using animal has developed complex ideas of property, with . . . corresponding . . . propriety" (CWO 293). Propriety is "profoundly inspirited by the negative (as in the thou-shalt-not's essential to . . . all moral and social codes: justice, etiquette, 'protocol')" (CWO 293). This (hortatory) "negative" is dissociative. By way of illustration, consider a hypothetical young woman. Because she is considered the "property" of her parents, a young man who may have a "natural" (CWO 293) attraction to her may be expected in her culture to ask her father or mother for permission to ask the young woman to marry him. This would be an example of "protocol" that is a symbolic participation in a "social order." There is an implicit hierarchy of ownership in such a situation. Clearly, the young woman is not yet considered the "property" of the young man; nor is she her own "property." She is the "property" of her parents. But at a second level, the fact that the young man is only asking permission from the parents to "ask" the young woman to marry him implies that a secondary title of ownership of the young woman belongs to the young woman herself. Should she consent to marry the young man, a new social order may be established, with the young man now "owning" his fiancée, so that any other suitors would be in violation of this new social order. This brief sketch indicates the possible intricacies of social order.

Should the young woman object to the dissociation in the social order whereby she is deemed the "property" of either her parents or her fiancée, she (and the others) may experience a desire for a "single unifying essence that transcends their separateness." Burke terms such a desire "a motive, a desire to have perfect consistency" (CWO 292). This transcending unification may be accomplished by yet another "symbol"—the term "family." Although the young woman, at various times, assumes various familial hierarchal levels, the young woman may (or may not!) be placated by such a "transcendence" (i.e., pointing out to her that "we are all a 'family' "). Yet, as Burke teaches, dissociation (or division) and unification (or identification) in this example may frequently be dialectically transcended by rhetoric: "But put identification and division ambiguously together, so that you cannot know for certain just where one ends and the other begins, and you have the characteristic invitation to rhetoric" (RM 25). Since transcendence, as a third step that unifies dissociations, is so characteristically rhetorical, the transcendence step will be considered in the next chapter—as Revelation is viewed from the rhetorical standpoint.

As shown, the two steps that precede the unifying step of transcendence are dissociative. While sociopolitical order (as dissociation) would not be the ultimate entelechy of symbol-use in Burke's system, "hierarchy" certainly implies some variety of entelechy. Entelechial criticism from a sociopolitical standpoint would consider not the ways in which unification occurs, but the ultimates implicit in dissociation.

Surprisingly (considering the "priestly" hierarchal order that the early Church sought to supplant in Judaism, as well as the elaborate ecclesiastical structure that soon after developed in the Catholic church), the sociopolitical order that John *proposes* is extremely egalitarian—so much so that Burke probably would have been profoundly skeptical of its feasibility. John employs the term "priest(s) [*hiereus*]" (the etymological root of the term "hierarchy") three times:

1. In Revelation 1:6, John speaks of himself and his primary audience as having been made "a kingdom of priests" to serve God.
2. In 5:9–10, "the Lamb" is praised for having "purchased [persons] for God from every tribe and language and people and nation [*ethnos*]" and for having "made them to be a kingdom and priests to serve our God."

3. In 20:6, all who "have part in the first resurrection . . . will be priests of God and of Christ and will reign with him for a thousand years."

John makes no indication whatsoever that any given priest is sociopolitically superior to any other. A "kingdom of priests" who "serve" God suggests that the role of "priest" in the new order implies not dissociation, but transcendence.

Some might think it strange that John would use the term "priest" three times in Revelation, yet never apply the term to the Jewish priesthood, if (as I have suggested) the book is written before the fall of the Temple and is aimed at supplanting the existing priestly order. Nevertheless, I take John's omission in this regard as evidence of his consistency in refusing to allow his opponents to claim the "nomenclature" of "true Judaism." This feature of John's rhetoric is discussed more fully later. As considered in chapter 4, however, specifically with respect to "priestly" terminology, John's "false prophet" may be a (synecdochic) priestly reference. His description of the "second beast" may be a reference to the priestly family. His "image of the beast" and the name "Babylon" may also be priestly references.

None of the early Catholic offices—*episkopos* (bishop, overseer, episcopate), *poimên* (shepherd, pastor), *diakonos* (deacon), or *presbuteros* (presbyter, elder)—appear to be ecclesiastical offices in John's Revelation. Of these terms, only presbuteros is mentioned as an office, but it refers to a group of twenty-four elders who surround the throne of God in Heaven. This is hardly an earthly hierarchy.

Another hierarchal possibility for John was a hierarchy of "charismatic" offices. Since both John and Paul write to audiences in Asia Minor, the possibility of a "charismatic" hierarchy similar to those described in Paul's epistles should be considered. First Corinthians 12:28 suggests a possible hierarchy of "spiritual gifts" [*pneumatikôn charismatôn*]": "And in the church, God placed first apostles, second prophets, third teachers, then powers, then gifts of healing, supporting, governing, and kinds of tongues." In Romans 12:6–8, Paul repeats the prophetic and teaching offices and adds others. While the Pauline authorship of Ephesians is questioned by some scholars, the tri-level hierarchy of apostles, prophets, and teachers is corroborated in Ephesians 4:11 (with two additional offices). Of all of the roles that Paul(?) lists as charismatic offices, only two are found in Revelation—apostle and prophet.

John mentions "apostles" three times. In 21:14, the twelve foundations of the wall of New Jerusalem have the names of the twelve apostles on them. In 18:20, "saints and apostles and prophets" are told to "Rejoice" concerning the judgment upon Babylon. But there is certainly no elaborate discussion of an "apostolic" hierarchal level. In fact, in 2:2, the church at Ephesus is praised for testing "those who claim to be apostles but are not"!

John uses the term "prophet" in both positive and negative ways. Similar to Revelation's objection to false "apostles" is its objection to the woman "Jezebel, who calls herself a prophetess" (2:20), as well as the "false prophet" of 16:13, 19:20, and 20:10 (who may be the Jewish priesthood). John uses the term "prophet" in a positive sense when referring to the Old Testament "prophets" (10:7, 11:18, 16:6, 18:20,24, and 22:6—admittedly, some of these references could also refer to prophets in the church). Yet, in terms of hierarchal levels, an interesting account is recorded in 22:8–9:

> I, John, am the one who heard and saw these things. And when I had heard and seen them, I fell down to worship at the feet of the angel who had been showing them to me. But he said to me, "Do not do it! I am a fellow servant with you and your brothers/sisters [adelphôn] the prophets and of all who keep the words of this book. Worship God!"

And, in a parallel incident (19:10), John falls down to worship an angel and is told: "Do not do it! I am a fellow servant with you and with your brothers/sisters [adelphôn] who hold to the testimony [marturia] of Jesus. For the testimony [marturia] of Jesus is the spirit of prophecy." Apparently, all who give testimony (marturia) to Jesus can be said to possess the "spirit of prophecy." Is John equating all Christians with the prophets? If all possible "offices"—priest, prophet, saint (and even angel)—are transcended by the term "servant," there appears to be no hierarchy, except that of the two who in Revelation are worthy of worship (God and the Lamb). While John is aware of the (old) priestly sociopolitical hierarchy in Judaism, his new order is patently egalitarian.

The single most important tenet of Judaism is monotheism. "Hear, O Israel, The Lord our God, The Lord is One" (Deuteronomy 6:4). John's audience can easily accept the premise of Revelation chapter 4—that God is worthy of praise and worship. But, in chapter 5, John introduces a new entity who is now also worthy of worship in heaven—the "lion from the tribe of Judah" who is also "the lamb who was slain." Is John proposing a new divine hierarchy? Is John making monotheism into a "trinity" or "duality"? How does John explain his change in the heavenly order? Both God and the Lamb are referred to as "alpha and omega," "the first and the last," "the beginning and the end." Without a doubt, John places them in the same equational cluster. But, the term "*pantokratôr*" (Almighty) is applied by John to God alone. John does not apply the term to the Lamb (or Jesus). Furthermore, the term "God [*theos*]" is never applied to the Lamb (or Jesus), despite the fact that John uses the term *theos* ninety-five times in Revelation!

If John is not making Jesus (a) God, but is making him equally worthy of worship, Burke's formula—"From what, through what, to what?" (PLF 71)—must be recalled to consider what move John is making. Revelation chapter 4 presents the "from what." The situation in Heaven before the change is thoroughly monotheistic. God alone is worthy of praise. Revelation chapter 5 presents the "to what." The situation in Heaven after the change has two entities who are worthy of praise—God and the Lamb. So, the question that remains to be answered is "through what?" Griffin insightfully observes that Burkeans would look for a "kill" in the "through what" stage. He claims that change is "Through Victimage and Mortification."[30] In this instance, "victimage" is inapplicable. There was no entity in Heaven that was victimized in order to elevate the Lamb to his new position. However, there certainly is "mortification," the positive purge. The "Lion from the tribe of Judah" who assumes the new importance in Heaven is "the Lamb that was slain." The Lamb has experienced "mortification."

However, the Lamb is not the only entity in Revelation who is slain. Why are the other "slain" individuals not also "worshipped"? Return to John's "representative anecdote" for the answer. Since the agon of Revelation is the struggle between the "ancient [*archaios*] serpent" and "the woman," there are two other implicit characters in the paradigmatic "scene"—God and Adam. Before "woman" and "serpent" came on the scene, there were God and Adam. Since John speaks of an "image [*eikôn*] of the beast" who receives worship (13:15; 14:9,11; 16:2; 19:20; 20:4), and of God and the Lamb who are worshipped (5:14), the Lamb may be in some sense the "image" of God. Wellhausen sees Jesus as "the *eikôn* of God" just as the *eikôn* of the beast "is the alter ego of the empire." And, of course, Genesis reports that Adam was created in the "image" of God. The *Vita Adae et Evae* understands that, since Adam is the "image" of God, he is worthy of worship. Ginzberg thinks that Hebrews 1:6 makes Jesus a second Adam in the fashion of *Vita*, and thus makes him worthy of worship. Perhaps John is doing precisely the same thing in chapters 4 and 5 of Revelation. But while the first Adam may not have deserved worship, due to his sinfulness, the second Adam is the "entelechial" Adam. Jesus not only takes the Adam role in the "representative anecdote," he "perfects" the role! While the first Adam "deserved" death, the second Adam (through mortification) "paid" off the death-debt incurred by the first Adam. He therefore is worthy of worship, as the first Adam would have been, had he not been sinful.

While the Christian "conquerors" (martyrs) also have experienced "mortification," they are not objects of worship in Revelation. Perhaps this fact relates also to the "representative anecdote." The "conquerors" take the role of "woman" (or Eve) in the representative anecdote. There is no literary foundation (biblical or otherwise) available to John or his primary audience for any worship of Eve. Yet, there is an implicit entelechy for the "conquerors." Their implicit *telos* is to "perfect" the Eve role in the same way that Jesus perfected the Adam role.

Readers may wonder how the new development in the Heavenly hierarchy affects the sociopolitical order in Judaism. The answer is two-fold:

1. With the offering of a "perfect" kill—the slaying of the Lamb—the Temple cult's "priestly" function becomes effectively outmoded. No other blood sacrifice is necessary. The "new song" that is sung to the Lamb says: "You are worthy . . . because you were slain, and with your blood you purchased men for God from every tribe and language and people and nation. You have made them to be a kingdom and priests to serve our God" (5:9–10).
2. With the exaltation of Jesus to such a high position in the heavenly order, Jesus' followers are no longer members of the lower class. They are "a kingdom of priests." The old hierarchal priesthood is gone. The new egalitarian priesthood (with its all-encompassing role—"servants") is installed, although Burke would surely question the possibility of an egalitarian priesthood on this earth.

CONCLUSION

William Rueckert considers Leland Griffin to be one of Burke's best "apologists," and considers Griffin's essay, followed in this chapter, to be "one of the finest syntheses and applications of Burke" with which he is familiar. He suggests that Griffin does for the "rhetoric of movements" what "Duncan did for sociology, . . . Ferguson did for drama, and what [Rueckert] tried to do for literary criticism: to develop a model or abstraction from Burke" for application to a specific discipline.[31] Griffin's model is a useful tool for considering the sociopolitical scene of John's Apocalypse.

At the writing of Revelation, Christianity is a Jewish social movement for John. John seeks to replace the priestly hierarchy of the Temple cult with an egalitarian "kingdom of priests." He holds that this "priesthood" is the sociopolitical *telos* of the exaltation of Jesus/ the Lamb (in the heavenly order). Entelechial motivation in the sociopolitical realm is dissociative. John dissociates Jesus from the rest of Judaism by placing him in the ultimate human position as the "perfect" Adam. All remaining Jews (as well as angels) are on an equal level—his servants and worshippers.

8

The Rhetoric of Revelation

SINCE ARISTOTLE, THE RHETORICAL PERSPECTIVE HAS BEEN CHARAC-
terized by the term "persuasion." Aristotle's definition of rhetoric
conceives of persuasion as a *telos*, a goal for the achievement of
which the available means should be found. In extending Aristotle's
concept, Burke recommends adding the term "identification" as it
relates to congregation and segregation. Identification is one of the
available means of persuasion. This chapter provides an entelechial
critique of Revelation that focuses upon the action that John is
persuading his primary audience to take. The ultimate action—
death as a martyr—is also an ultimate passion. John uses identification and transcendence as two means of persuading his audience
to take the ultimate action.

RHETORIC AND DEATH

The terminology of "death" is important in Burke as is the terminology of "death" and "martyrdom" in Revelation. John is advo-
cating for his primary audience martyrdom or, at least, a willingness
to become a martyr (if necessary). John, however, appropriates the
terminology of the Roman "conquerors" in the process of "transcending" the "conqueror/conquered" dichotomy. John advocates
"being conquered" as the ultimate (or entelechial) form of "conquest." To understand the "dialectical transcendence" John is attempting, Burke's notion of "transcendence" must be considered.

Of the references to the term "entelechy" in RM, Burke's index
points to only one page (14). Here, Burke describes "the Aristotelian entelechy" as a principle "which classifies a thing by conceiving
of its kind according to the perfection (that is, finishedness) of
which that kind is capable." Burke appears to make a transition
from Aristotelian entelechy (which is concerned primarily with the
biological) to Burkean entelechy (which is concerned almost exclu-

sively with the logological) by commenting that "the perfection of humankind is in the order of rationality (an order or finishedness which one would not apply to things incapable of Logos, the Word)." Entelechially, Burke sees two primary means of expression, one time-bound ("narrative") and one timeless ("philosophic").

Burke contrasts "narrative terms" with " 'timeless' ones." Along the lines of his "arpeggio vs. chord" analogy, Burke sees the "fixities" of "philosophic expressions" as "later translations of the earlier narrative [expressions]." He sees no reason why narrative expressions cannot be looked upon as translations of philosophic ones. He says: "By such heuristic reversal, we note how the imagery of death could be a narrative equivalent of the Aristotelian entelechy." Implicitly, Burke recognizes Aristotelian entelechy as a "philosophic expression," or (in terms of Burke's analogy) a "chord" ("narrative" being the "arpeggio"). Since an arpeggio spreads out in "time" what a chord does in an "instant," narrative modes of thought present information "in terms of a history." And the terms "dramatic" and "tragic" come to mind when a "perfection" motive is identified "with a narrative figure whose acts led to some fitting form of death." Burke uses the terms—narrative, dramatic, and tragic—interchangeably as he discusses his "heuristic reversal." He speaks of a "narrative equivalent" and a "tragic equivalent" of Aristotelian entelechy. Five pages later, Burke writes of a "dramatic equivalent for an 'entelechial' pattern of thought" (RM 19).

Throughout the discussion of the narrative (or dramatic or tragic) equivalent of Aristotelian entelechy, Burke constantly returns to the concept of a "fitting form of death" (RM 14). And, in a comment that makes Burke's entelechial-criticism-from-a-rhetorical-perspective directly applicable to the Book of Revelation, Burke comments: "In this respect, the Christian injunction to lead the 'dying life' is itself a formula that translates the Aristotelian entelechy into its tragic equivalent" (RM 14).

RHETORIC AND TRANSCENDENCE

In addition to some understanding of the terminology of "death," in Burke and in Revelation, some understanding of Burke's notion of transcendence is required. *Websters Seventh New Collegiate Dictionary* generally defines "transcendence" as the quality or state of exceeding, surpassing, rising above, or going beyond the limits of something. This concept of transcendence has been employed by rhetorical analysts in the past as a strategy for overcoming a specific rhetorical impasse. Not relying heavily on Kenneth Burke's theory of transcendence,[1] Charles J. Stewart writes: "When operating at the highest level of transcendence, persuaders claim that a goal, group, or right, for instance, is superior to or greater than all other options."[2] He states that, in "a rhetoric of transcendence, persuaders argue that a person, group, goal, thing, right, action, or proposal surpasses, is superior to, or was prior to related choices."[3] This use of the term "transcendence" would certainly fit the dictionary definition, but it is not fully encompassing of Burke's theory.

While Burke certainly retains in his theory the "surpassing" element of transcendence, he uses the term to designate not a mere "comparison" of disparate goals, etc., but, more importantly, a "combination" of disparate matters and even of polar opposites. An example that he offers is "[t]he battlefield, for instance, which permits rival contestants to join in battle." For Burke, "battlefield," therefore, allows the contestants to transcend "their factionalism, being 'superior' to it [their factionalism] and 'neutral' to their motives" (RM 11). Burke's key term for rhetoric is identification (RM xiv). Yet, even in his comments on identification, Burke combines the polar opposites—identification and division—to create the transcendent concept of "rhetoric" (cf. RM 25). Wherever there is ambiguity concerning identification and division, Burke sees a "characteristic invitation to rhetoric."

Transcendence is accomplished, Burke indicates, by a widening of circumference. In a discussion of Dostoevsky's *The Brothers Karamazov*, Burke suggests that the elder brother Mitya was limited by the scene in which he envisioned his actions. He dreamed of a better scene in which he could have a new life. But his younger brother transcended Mitya's scene:

> [T]he mystic Alyosha . . . was in the same scene . . . and . . . for him it had a different circumference. . . . His terms amounted to a migration . . . by a "transcendence," a "higher synthesis," that in effect "negates" the terms of the scene as Mitya interpreted it. For Alyosha's terms implied a wider circumference. (GM 85)

The widening of circumference often involves a Burkean tracing of the fingers back to the hand (GM xxii), to the point where they meet.

Burke distrusts "both 'perfectionist' and 'inverted perfectionist' motivations." His advice is to "feel justified in never taking at its face value any motivational reduction to a 'simple' " (GM 101). Burke assumes that any "motivational simplicity . . . contains a diversity." And yet, states Burke: "We have postulated that the 'ideas' or parts [of a given model of the universe] are motivated by a desire to transcend the limits of their distinctness (and the limited points of view that go with it) and to realize that they are all integrally interrelated aspects of the same position" (GM 102). Transcending "the limits of . . . distinctness" (GM 102) requires the search for a "motivational ground" (GM 41), but not a motivational ground that would negate "the source which it transcends, but as the ultimate completion or fulfillment of" that source (GM 152). Transcendence occurs as a person "learns to take the oppositional motives into account, widening his[/her] terminology accordingly, . . . [thus arriving] at a higher order of understanding" (GM 40).

Burke, in discussing Cardinal Bembo's oration on a transcendent concept of beauty, (from Castiglione) writes of a widening of the circumference of the senses from the purely visual to the eye and the ear, used as receptacles for "intellect." Burke refers to "talk of a transcendent insemination (putting the seeds of virtue into a mind, 'the right engendering and imprinting of beauty in beauty' . . .)" (RM 231). Earlier Burke employs this insemination/seeds language in his discussion of the transcendent principle in Epicurean ethics:

> Epicurean physics is the basis for an ethics. Hence we are dramatistically admonished to look for the "seeds" of an ethical principle in the physical terminology itself. Or otherwise stated, we are admonished to examine this "inclination" of the atoms on the possibility that it is a device for transcending sheer motion, and opening towards the wider realm of action and agenthood. (GM 160)

The clearest (and, possibly "only") dichotomy in the theory of Burke is the "action-motion" dichotomy. The active-passive pair is closely related due to the fact that whatever is not "action" (as in "active") falls into the category of "motion." Hence, while Burke may be moderately interested in such polar combinations as identification vs. division into "rhetoric" and good vs. bad antagonists into "battlefield" and aesthetically pleasing vs. intelligent into pure "beauty," he would likely be fascinated by the strategies whereby humans attempt to transcend the action-motion or the active-passive binaries. Such is the case.

Not only does Burke note the transcendence of the action-

motion pair in Epicurean physics (as noted above), he is impressed
by the "dialectic of tragedy" wherein "the agents' action involves a
corresponding passion and from the sufferance of the passion,
there arises an understanding of the act, an understanding that
transcends the act" (GM 38). Writes Burke, "the tragic hero's action, involving his passion, attains its rest and summation in his
understanding" (GM 41). Thus, "the knowledge derived from the
act is a knowledge of the act's context, or motivational ground"
(GM 41). Burke learns from the Greek proverb "*ta pathemata math-
emata*" (GM 39, 41), the things suffered are the things learned. If
"suffering" is "passive" (and, thus, related etymologically to "passion"), and "learning" is "active," there is a transcendence of this
pair in both tragedy and the Greek proverb.

Burke is particularly intrigued by the fact that most successful
attempts at transcending the active-passive pair involve "killing." He
comments: "Since imagery built about the active, reflexive, and passive forms of death (killing, self-killing, and being killed) so obviously contributes to dramatic intensity, and since thoughts of death
are so basic to human motivation, we usually look no farther to
account for their use" (RM 13). In Coleridge's observation that "no
Cain Injures uninjured," Burke finds "motives interchangeable
which might be considered mutually exclusive" (RM 10). Coleridge
and Burke understand Coleridge's observation to indicate something possibly similar to the parent's preface to spanking the child:
this is going to hurt me more than it hurts you! In the parental
example, the hurter becomes the hurt. Similarly, in Coleridge, Cain
(the injurer) becomes Cain (the injured); the murderer becomes
the murdered in the sense that something inside Cain is killed as
Cain kills Abel. Employing a certain circumference, a human can
see death in terms of rebirth. Burke sees transformation possibilities
in "the imagery of Life and Death, with its variants of being born,
being reborn, dying, killing, and being killed" (RM 12).

Burke sees at least three distinct possibilities of "stylistic transformation (magnification, purification, martyrdom, etc.)" (RM 12).
Thus *Samson Agonistes* provides "the poet's identification with a
blind giant who slew himself in slaying the enemies of the Lord"
(RM 19). Among other things, Burke sees therein an example of
magnification or purification:

> [H]ere the poet presents a motive in an essentially magnified or per-
> fected form, in some way tragically purified or transcended; the im-
> agery of death reduces the motive to ultimate terms, dramatic equiv-

alent for an "entelechial" pattern of thought whereby a thing's nature would be classed according to the fruition, maturing, or ideal fulfillment, proper to its kind. (RM 19)

"Otherwise put, . . . the killing of something is the changing of it" (RM 20).

In the Book of Revelation there is a kind of transcendence as a rhetorical strategy that blurs the distinction that Burke would make "between transformation by victimage (dramatic catharsis) and transformation by dialectical 'transcendence' " (LSA 191). Not only is there a "tragic" formula for transcendence in Revelation, there is a "dialectical" formula as well. "Conquest" is John's term that allows for both transformation by victimage and dialectical transcendence. Burke tells us that "the paradox of the absolute figures grammatically in the dialectic, making for a transcending of one term by its other" (GM 38).

As has been shown by scholars for the last century, the clear hero of each of the seven churches to whom Revelation is addressed is the one who "overcomes"—*ho nikôn.* The hero is mentioned in each of the letters to the seven churches (2:7,11,17,26; 3:5,12,21), as a participle of the verb, *nikaô.* This verb appears to be a favorite in John's vocabulary. He intersperses the term eight more times throughout the balance of the book, thus using it fifteen times altogether. The book of 1 John uses the verb six times and its cognate noun, *hê nikê,* one time. But, other than in Revelation and 1 John, the verb occurs only five times in the rest of the New Testament. It carries the sense of victory, winning, conquest. Translating the participle as "he who overcomes" or, with J. M. Ford, "he who prevails" is adequate. Somehow the translation, "winner," does not carry enough magnitude. Even "victor," while seemingly bolder, more impressive, lacks something—perhaps due to its two syllables—whereas the three-syllabled, "conqueror," as Kiddle and Caird have translated, is more magnificent. Since *ho nikôn* is the hero of the book, this discussion will employ "conqueror" as a translation.

However, cognates of *nikaô* are not always used in Revelation in a positive sense (for Christians). Revelation 11:7 speaks of the beast who comes up from the abyss "conquering" God's two witnesses—i.e., killing them. Frankly, this "killing" connotation is *the* significance of *nikaô* prior to Revelation. Bauernfeind notes that outside the New Testament, the term *nikaô* means "to defeat."[4] He asserts, "It is also generally assumed that a *nikan* or *nikê* is demonstrated by an action, by the overthrow of an opposing force, and that the success is palpable and manifest to all eyes."[5]

John takes the concept of conquest back to its motivational ground—killing—and rather than asking the Socratic question, "Is it better to do wrong, or to be wronged?" John transcends the active term "kill" by what appears to be the passive term "be killed." Except John has made "be killed" into an "active passion." Burke explains how this works:

> Or action and passion may be made simultaneous equivalents, as with the theory of Christian martyrdom, wherein the act of self-sacrifice is identical with the sufferance. . . . [T]he saint has first suffered temptation . . . and the understanding (mathema) derived from the trial equips him[/her] for martyrdom (which is a new level of action-passion in one). (GM 265)

As discussed earlier, scholars are virtually unanimous in identifying the beast of Revelation as Rome. Revelation 13:4 provides a sense of the desperation that Jewish subjects might have felt when considering the prospect of war with Rome (which developed in A.D. 66): "Who is like the beast? Who is able to make war with it?" In 13:7, the beast is reported to have made "war" with the "saints" (i.e., Christians), and "conquered [*nikaô*]" them. This concept of "conquest" is then summarized by John in 13:10: "If anyone captures, into captivity he goes; if anyone kills by the sword, by the sword he must be killed." If defeating (killing) one's enemies is the meaning of "conquest" in John's milieu, how can John speak of the heroes of the churches as "conquerors"? The answer is clear. He employs a strategy of "dialectical transcendence."

So, Caird asks: "Who is the Conqueror? To what battle is he summoned? And by what weapons is he to win his victory? . . . The Conqueror, in other words, is the victim of persecution, whose martyr's death is his victory, just as the Cross was the victory of Christ."[6] Here there is agreement among scholars. Charles states, "But the word *nikan* is not used . . . of every Christian, but only of the martyr."[7] Says Kiddle, "Those who fall in the great martyrdom will gain the conqueror's reward. . . . Some are to be put in prison and they doubtless are those who are to die."[8] Interestingly, Fiorenza, before having written a verse-by-verse commentary on Revelation, finds herself discussing the "persecution and suffering" of the "rhetorical situation" on the page of her book in which she mentions the contribution that an understanding of Kenneth Burke can make toward an understanding of Revelation.[9] My Burkean insights into Revelation are independent of any that Fiorenza has, but I find it gratifying that a Revelation scholar of Fiorenza's caliber recognizes Burke's usefulness in Revelation studies. Elsewhere she clearly states, "The author of Rev[elation] emphasizes the demand for active resistance which results for him in tribulations, persecutions, captivity, and violent death."[10]

J. M. Ford would not disagree that those who were "slain for the word" are among the heroes of Revelation, but she would quibble somewhat with Caird and Charles over which terms and phrases actually refer to such heroes. In her notes on "the blood of the martyrs of Jesus" (17:6), she comments:

> One suspects that this phrase may be an interpolation. First, *martus*, in the sense of one who dies, occurs here only; the usual way martyr is expressed in Revelation is "those slain for the word of God" (6:9). In the rest of the NT *martus* indicates a witness rather than one who dies in order to witness.[11]

She passes over her translation of *ho nikôn* ("he who prevails") without significant comment on the issue. However, she attends to the word "slay [*sphazô*]" of which she says:

> Although "slay" . . . may be used in the sense of an animal sacrifice ritual, the more usual meaning is "to kill a person with violence". . . . In the NT it is never used in the sacrificial sense and only occurs in Revelation and I John. . . . On the whole, martyrdom . . . seems to be the most likely interpretation; it would class the slaughtered lamb with the souls under the altar (6:9) and the saints, and other slain prophets. (18:24)[12]

Since Ford associates the word "slay" with "martyrdom," perhaps the word "slay" in Revelation should be traced to see if it is associated with *nikaô*. The results are interesting. *Sphazô* occurs in Revelation 5:6,9, and 12, referring to the Lamb who was "slain," and who is therefore "worthy" to open the seals. But the Lamb is introduced in 5:5 as the "Lion of the tribe of Judah" who has "conquered [*nikaô*]" and is therefore able to open the seals. There seems to be an association between the first horseman of 6:2 who "conquers [*nikê, nikaô*]" and the second horseman of 6:4 who makes men "slay [*sphazô*]" each other, although both terms have here taken on a sinister (Roman?) connotation. They refer to the villain, as opposed to the hero. *Sphazô* is also associated with *martus* (martyr/witness?) in 6:9, something that was overlooked in the earlier comment by Ford. The only specific hero who was named in letters to the seven churches is Antipas (2:13), who would almost unquestionably be classed as *ho nikôn* (2:17), of whom it is said he was "put to death," and he was called a *martus*.

What is happening here is that a Burkean-style cluster is developing. Even if there remains some argument among scholars as to the exact denotations of each term, there are "approximations" of equations that can be demonstrated as "conqueror" = "martyr" = "put to death" = "slain." Furthermore, Fiorenza has added to this cluster the terms "tribulations" = "persecutions" = "captivity," and Ford has added "blood" = "the Lamb" = "the souls under the altar" = "the saints" = "the prophets."

John is transcending the Roman view of "conquest." Revelation 17:12–14 speaks of an alliance between the beast and "ten kings" of "the land" who will "make war" with the Lamb. But the "Lamb will conquer [*nikaô*] them." Revelation 15:2 refers to the Christians who "have conquered [*nikaô*] the Beast and its image." In 12:11, John provides a paradigm of "conquest." He envisions the fall of Satan from Heaven as a result of a war between the archangel Michael and Satan (probably happening during the lifetime of John's audience). John says, "And they conquered [*nikaô*] him [Satan] because of the blood of the Lamb and because of the word of their [the Christians?] testimony [*marturia*]. And they [the Christian martyrs] did not love their life, even unto death."

So, is the point here that John has simply reversed the meaning of conquest? Is his point merely that "being killed" is qualitatively better than "killing?" No. The conquest by the Christians is juxtaposed against the defeat of the elites of the old Jewish order, which Christianity sought to supplant. Revelation is not so concerned with the "conquest" over the beast as it is with contrasting Christian "conquest" with the "cowardice" displayed by the beast's ally—who is the Jewish high priesthood, as I understand John's view. In the Christians' "conquest" of the beast in the Revelation passages cited above, an ally of the beast is always mentioned whom the Christians have also conquered. In chapter 17, the ally is the "ten kings of the land." In chapter 15, the ally is the "image" of the beast. Throughout this book, I argue that this ally is primarily the Jewish high priesthood. The high priestly family is identified throughout the New Testament as the Jewish entity most responsible for the crucifixion of Jesus (in league with Roman rulers, Pontius Pilate and

Herod), as well as the persecution of the church throughout the Book of Acts. I understand the high priestly family to be the foe of the Christians in the Jewish social order in Revelation.

The clearest indication of the opponents of the Church in Revelation, in John's terminology, seems to be "the inhabitants of the earth." Ford, citing Minear, pp. 261–69, observes that:

> This phrase is used eleven times in four separate visions. He [Minear] feels that "the dwellers on the earth" are probably to be identified with the "beast worshippers." . . . Minear cites 1QH 8:19–36, where the "dwellers on earth" are opposed to the army of the holy ones; p. 262 citing Burrows, *Dead Sea Scrolls*, pp. 404f. "Earth" is a term which is the "common denominator for all antichristic forces," although it has four distinctive uses in this apocalypse: 1) It is used with heaven to denote the range of God's creation. 2) It signifies the sphere where God is making a new creation. 3) Most frequently it is used for that which has been corrupted and destroyed by those opposed to God. 4) It is the area in which God inflicts His punishments (p. 264).[13]

Suggesting a possible locus for the fourth use just listed, one prominent possible interpretation of the word "earth" is found in Jastrow's Dictionary (of rabbinic Hebrew). It was common for the Jews of the first century to refer to Palestine as *eretz yisrael*, the earth (or land) of Israel. Jastrow even lists separately the word for earth with the definite article, *ha-aretz*, with the one word definition: "Palestine."[14] This specific sense is mentioned by Charles in discussing "the inhabitants of the earth":

> The phrase . . . is the equivalent of the Hebrew (yoshve ha-aretz). . . . In the O.T. this phrase can denote either (1) "the inhabitants of the land," i.e. Palestine, Hos. iv.1; Joel i.2,14, ii.1; Jer. vi.12, x.18, etc.; or (2) "the inhabitants of the earth," Isa. xxiv.6, xxvi.21, etc.; I Enoch xxxvii.2,5, xl.6,7, xlviii.5, etc.
>
> Both these O.T. meanings appear in our text. The latter is found in iii.10, viii.13, xiii.8,14, xvii.8, and the former at all events originally in the verse we are now dealing with (11:10). For, as Bousset . . . has rightly urged, it is hard to see what the inhabitants of the earth would have to do with the two prophets who appear in Jerusalem. . . . [15]

Kiddle sees nothing of "Palestine" in the phrase "the inhabitants of the earth." For him, the "dwellers on earth [are] the heathen gentiles as distinct from the Church . . . : by this phrase John always means the whole wide world."[16] Kiddle does not view the term as being villainous as do Ford, Caird, and Minear. Caird agrees with Minear, as cited by Ford. Says Caird, "Here, as elsewhere in his book, John calls the persecutors of the church the inhabitants of earth (cf. iii.10; viii.13; xi.10; xiii.8,12,14; xvii.2,8)."[17]

While scholars generally agree that the "inhabitants of the earth" may be the force opposed to the church, the specific identification of this force varies from "the heathen gentiles" to the "dwellers of the Land of Israel" to the "whole wide world." Ford, citing Minear, is fairly safe in saying that they are "beast worshippers," since the text explicitly states the fact, "All the inhabitants of the earth will worship the beast" (13:8). This fact is confirmed in 13:12: "The earth and its inhabitants worship the first beast." The inhabitants are contrasted with the conquerors in 13:15 wherein all inhabitants of the earth "who refused to worship the image" of the beast were "killed." Hence, there exist the beginnings of another cluster, "the inhabitants of the earth" = "beast worshippers." The charting of equations may follow the texts where either of these two formulas exists:

- in 6:10, the text states that the souls who had been "slain" (= conquerors) ask God to judge the "inhabitants of the earth" and "avenge our blood." Surely this citation adds slayers-of-the-conquerors to the equation;
- in 11:10, the inhabitants "gloat over [the bodies of the two witnesses = prophets who are killed by the beast] because [the villains had been] tormented [by them]." Thus is established the equation: the inhabitants = the enemies of the two witnesses;
- in 13:12, the inhabitants appear to be under the control of the second beast (with two horns) who "made the earth and its inhabitants worship the first beast." Hence, the inhabitants = controlled by the second beast. In 13:14, the inhabitants = deceived by the second beast, and the inhabitants = ordered by the second beast;
- predictably, 17:8 reports that the inhabitants' "names have not been written in the book of life";
- in 17:2, John observes that, while the "kings of the earth committed adultery" with Babylon, the harlot, the inhabitants "were intoxicated with the wine of her immorality [*porneia*]." If this verse is seen as a parallelism, then "the inhabitants of the earth" = "the kings of the earth." More likely, this is not a parallelism;

then "the inhabitants of the earth" are figurative guests at an orgy wherein the kings and the harlot commit immorality, and the inhabitants only celebrate and support the union by getting drunk at the party.

Tracing the "beast worshippers" equation, a term must be added to the equation that represents the formula that the worshippers used in their worship, "Who is like the beast? Who can make war against him?" (13:4). This formula appears to be a concession that the beast cannot be conquered, a concession that obviously John and his "conquerors" would NOT make. Although there is no one term that John uses repeatedly to express this situation, he does use the word "coward" (*deilos*) one time, as the first term of negative contrast with the "conquerors" in 21:7–8. Since Burke would look in a text for "what is vs. what," and since the language of the worship formula suggests the need for a shorthand term that would express the concession/forfeiture idea, and since Burke's statistical method requires "objective citation," the author's own terms should be used, and since the term "coward" seems to best fit as a shorthand term, it will be added to the equation, with the stipulation that it stands for the worship formula: "Who is like the beast? Who can make war against him?"

Not only does the charting of equations for "beast worshippers" point out the "coward" equation, but also, according to 13:14, the "inhabitants" (by order of the second beast) "set up an image" of the "beast" and in verse 15 become "image worshippers" thereafter (14:9,11; 16:2; 19:20). Furthermore, there is an exact equation between those who are "image worshippers" and those who have received the "mark" (*charagma*) of the beast, or his name. The textual citations are identical with those listed above for "image worshippers"—13:15–17; 14:9,11; 16:2; 19:20—as well as 20:4, which corroborates the earlier identification of the heroes as martyrs ("those who had been beheaded because of their testimony [*marturia*]"), and then contrasts these heroes with the villains ("They had not worshiped the beast or his image and had not received his mark on their foreheads or their hands").

Recapitulating, the inhabitants of the earth = beast worshippers = cowards = slayers of the conquerors = enemies of the two witnesses = controlled, deceived, and ordered by the second beast, become image erectors and worshippers = having the mark of the beast = (at least) consenting observers of Babylon's *porneia*.

Returning to the letters to the seven churches, surprisingly, not much of the cluster, thus far developed, appears. John just mentions the "inhabitants of the earth" (3:10), whom he says will be tested when the testing hour comes upon the whole inhabitable world, but he lists his specific villains, in the letters to the seven churches, as "wicked men" (2:2), "false apostles" (2:2), "Nicolaitans" (2:6,15), "those who say they are Jews, but are not" (2:9; 3:9), "synagogue of Satan" (2:9; 3:9), "Balaam" (2:14), and "Jezebel" (2:20).

Perhaps the closest the letters come to the equation developed apart from them is in their use of the term *porneia* (referring to literal or figurative sexual immorality), which is ascribed to "Babylon" (the Harlot/*pornê*) elsewhere and to Jezebel in 2:21. The verb form of *porneia, porneuô,* is applied to Jezebel as she misleads Jesus' servants into this literal or figurative activity in 2:20, and it is applied in a parallel situation to Balaam in 2:14, who taught Balak to entice the sons of Israel into this activity. The Nicolaitans might be brought into this equation, if the reference to Balaam is actually used as an Old Testament type of the Nicolaitans who are actually the ones enticing the Church at Pergamum into the activity, as 2:15 would appear to suggest, since the victims of Balaam are only indicated as the "sons of Israel" (presumably) at the time of Balak (2:14). Thus, Jezebel = Balaam = Nicolaitans = *porneia.*

Fiorenza links "the Nicolaitans" with "the people 'who call themselves apostles' "(2:2), as well as "those who hold the teaching of Balaam" (2:14), and "Jezebel . . . and her friends and followers." She states:

> The phrase "to eat food sacrificed to idols" refers to food which had already been consecrated to an idol as well as to participation in pagan feasts. Likewise *porneusai* (the practice of immorality) should be understood in a literal sense as well as in a metaphorical sense, namely, in reference to syncretistic tendencies and idolatry.[18]

Caird comments: "We may reasonably assume that John's quarrel with the Nicolaitans was over their attitude to pagan society and religion. The . . . teaching of Balaam is merely John's opprobrious name for the teaching of the Nicolaitans."[19] Caird further links Jezebel with the group, but disagrees with Fiorenza that the term *porneia* refers to literal "sexual license." He assumes that as "in every other case except one in which he uses the verb *porneuein* or the noun *porneia* he uses them metaphorically."[20]

Ford, likewise, links the "Nikolaitans" with the "adherents of the teaching of Balaam" and states that "the same heresy may be referred to in" the case of Jezebel,[21] as does Kiddle: "To these 'Balaamites' John gives the more explicit party name of Nicolaitans."[22] Kiddle would also include Jezebel in the group.[23] Charles also sees the equation, Nicolaitans = Balaam = Jezebel.[24]

Ford sees a "play on words" between the Hebrew word "Balaam" (= *bala am* = *balah am*, according to the Talmud Sanhedrin 105a) and the Greek word "Nikolaitan" (= *nika laon*). She credits Charles with pointing it out.[25] Caird also considers the play on words worth mentioning,[26] as does Kiddle.[27] According to Charles:

> Balaam = *bala am* = "he hath consumed the people" . . . while Nikolaos = *nikai laon*. Such a play on the etymology of words is thoroughly Semitic. There is, it is true, no exact equivalent to *nikan* in Hebrew. Hence the above can stand. Furthermore a comparison . . . which shows that the Balaamites and the followers of Jezebel were guilty of exactly the same vices, makes it highly probable that the latter were a branch of the Nicolaitans.[28]

According to the translation of *nikaô* employed in this study, *Nikolaos* would be translated "he has conquered the people." This is a sufficiently close parallel to let Charles's play on words between Balaam and Nicolaitan stand, but it produces an even more interesting observation: there may be a play on words between the hero(es) of Revelation (the conqueror = *ho nikôn*) and the villains (the Nicolaitans).

As observed earlier, the cognates of *nikaô* are applied throughout Revelation to both the heroes and the villains. The hero associations have already been cited, along with two villain associations. If "Nikolaitan" means "he 'conquers = slays' the people," charting John's use of the term "the people" might be interesting. John predominately uses the term in a formula that usually includes "every" and the terms (not necessarily in the same order) "tribe, language, people, and nation" (5:9; 7:9; 10:11; 11:9; 13:7; 14:6; 17:15). But in 18:14 and 21:3, the only other times he uses the word, it means the "people of God."

This usage of *nikaô* in the term Nikolaitan may be an example of what Burke calls "repetitive form." John likes to contrast his villains and his heroes in terms of their similarities. Like the Lamb who "was dead" but is "alive forever" (1:18), the beast "seemed to have a fatal wound, but the fatal wound had been healed" (13:3). He "once was, now is not, and yet will come" (17:8). Like the harlot Babylon, the bride New Jerusalem is a woman and a city. There are first heavens and new heavens. There is first earth and new earth. The 144,000 are sealed with a seal on their foreheads (7:3) whereas the beast worshippers have a mark on their foreheads. There is the "temple" in the "holy city" (11:2) that was measured, resulting in the prophecy and martyrdom of the two witnesses. But the "ark of His covenant"—the surest sign of God's presence—is seen, not there, but in God's "temple" in "heaven" (11:19). The villains "worship" the beast and his image, but the conquerors "worship" God (22:11).

John, however, often disagrees with the nomenclature used by the villains. The *nikaô* issue is a case in point. The villains believe that they "conquer" by "slaying." John claims that real "conquest" comes by "being slain," just as it did for the Lamb. Other examples of John's penchant for disputing the meanings that his opponents might attach to words are as follows: the second beast had two horns like a "lamb"—a positive image for John, certainly—but he spoke like a "dragon" (13:11). Babylon claims, "I sit as a queen . . . I will never mourn" (18:7), but the balance of the chapter is filled with laments, "mourning" the fall of Babylon.

In this context the remaining appellations of John's villains in the letters to the seven churches may be understood. The problem in Sardis is that the Christians there "have a reputation for being alive," but they are "dead" (3:1). Those at Laodicea say "I am rich" but are told that they are actually "poor" (3:17). The "wicked men" of Ephesus are those who "claim to be apostles but are not" (2:2). The villains of Smyrna and Philadelphia are "those who say they are Jews, but are not" (2:9; 3:9). John gives them their correct name—the "synagogue of Satan" (2:9; 3:9).

If John's repetitive form is operative, the interpretation would follow that John is in fact objecting to the nomenclature that the villains have applied to themselves. John does not mention what specific tests were applied to the "false apostles," which they failed, but the villains called themselves "apostles." Similarly, the ones John labels "synagogue of Satan" probably called themselves "Jews."

What is strange in Revelation is that John is not willing to call ANYONE a Jew. The fact that the word Jew is in his vocabulary is evident by two citations (2:9; 3:9), but it occurs nowhere else in Revelation. The word Israel occurs in three locations. In 2:14, Balaam caused the Israelites to sin, but these Israelites were from past ages. In 7:4, the 144,000 saved from the earth are clearly Christians, but are identified as the tribes of Israel. In 21:12, the gates of the city (New) Jerusalem are inscribed with the names of the twelve tribes of Israel. John uses the term "Jerusalem" three times (3:12, 21:2,10), but all three instances refer to the "New Jerusalem," not the old Jerusalem. "Mount Zion" occurs once (14:1), but it refers once again to the 144,000. If, as Ford understands, the harlot Babylon is faithless Jerusalem,[29] John is continuing his rejection of the villains' nomenclature. Thus, he renames "the holy city" (11:2) in which the "Lord was crucified" (11:8) "Sodom and Egypt." If he refers to Jews who dwell in Judea, he calls them the "inhabitants of the land" and leaves off the words "of Israel."

At least some of John's villains are Jews by the weight of the language used in 2:9 and 3:9. In terms of scholarly support for this conclusion, Fiorenza informs us that "It is a debated question whether those who call themselves Jews are actually Jews or whether, as Koester and Newman assume, they are Christians belonging to the group of the Nicolaitans."[30] But she concludes: "Therefore, the so-called Jews and the Nicolaitans should not be identified. The Jews do not seem to represent a Christian group, but the Jewish citizenship of these cities."[31] Kiddle also understands the villains in Smyrna and Philadelphia to be literal Jews.[32] Caird concurs,[33] as does Charles.[34]

Upon concluding that the letters to the seven churches indicate two different types of villains—the Nicolaitans and the Jews—and finding that the villains who are known as the "inhabitants of the land" are in a rather different equational cluster and do not easily appear to be identical with either group in the letters, the question may be raised, what, if anything, do these villains have in common? A return to the term "*porneuô*" with its cognates is necessary for an answer. Fiorenza suggests that "*porneusai*" "should be understood . . . in reference to syncretistic tendencies and idolatry."[35] Caird agrees "that John's quarrel with the Nicolaitans was over their attitude to pagan society and religion."[36] If "*porneuô*" is taken as the glue that ties the disparate villains together, and if it is a code word for "syncretistic tendencies," then referring to Babylon as the harlot (*pornê*) is very enlightening. In this equational cluster, Babylon would be expected somehow to be identified as either a Christian or Jewish entity with "syncretistic tendencies." Identifying Babylon as Rome would make no sense, if Fiorenza is correct in her assessment of the connotation of *porneusai*. Rome could hardly be accused of "syncretistic tendencies" in either a Jewish or a Christian world view. Rome WAS Caird's proverbial "pagan society."

Ford's understanding of Jerusalem as Babylon fits Fiorenza's understanding of *porneusai* much better than Fiorenza's interpretation

of Rome as Babylon. If Jerusalem = Babylon = syncretistic tendencies, then those "who claim to be Jews" in the churches in Asia
Minor are linked equationally with Babylon, and the Nicolaitans are
the "syncretistic" force within the churches.

CONCLUSION

Assuming that Fiorenza's "syncretistic tendencies" observation is
correct, the real question in Revelation is how various terms are
equated with or related to the clearly understood villain term, "the
beast." Apparently, John is positioning his discussion of "conquest"
in a Jewish milieu in which the Roman question was paramount.
The concern for all Jews (both Christian and non-Christian) was,
"What can or should we do about this all-powerful empire who
could easily 'conquer' us?" "Who can war against the beast?" Three
alternative approaches are offered by Jewish groups. They are discussed in chapter 2.

Some Jewish extremist groups such as the Sicarii and the Zealots
felt that with God on the side of the Jews, they could defeat Rome
in actual battle. Their view prompted a declaration of independence from Rome in A.D. 66, followed by the establishment of a
government headed by nine or ten governors (possibly, the "ten
kings" of Revelation).

A second view was held by the high priestly family, who held the
most important positions in this new government. The view of the
high priestly family may be characterized by the words of the high
priest Caiaphas in John 11:50. Upon being confronted with the
words, "If we let [Jesus] go on like this . . . the Romans will come
and take away both our place and our nation," Caiaphas responded,
"it is better for you that one man die for the people than that the
whole nation perish."

John, in Revelation, is not attacking the extremist position that
Jews should fight Rome in battle—unless it is to be understood in
his comment in 13:10: "If anyone captures, into captivity he goes;
if anyone kills by the sword, by the sword he must be killed." But
the extremists did not exist as a countermovement to Christianity.
Instead, John is fighting the view of the high priests—"If you can't
beat them, join them!" He characterizes this view as "cowardice,"
symbolized by the phrase, "Who can war against the Beast?" Effectively, the high priest could then serve in a sense as the "talking"
"image of the beast" who stood in the Temple and commanded the

"inhabitants of the land" to "worship the beast." John knows that Rome cannot be "conquered" by the extremists' approach. And, John feels that an alliance with Rome (as sought by the high priests) is tantamount to *porneia*. His only choice is to show bravery by transcending the Roman concept of "conquest." The Christians will neither kill like the Romans and the extremists; nor will they join the beast, like the high priestly party. John, instead, is intent upon turning the "passive" "motion" of "being slain" into "action." Burke teaches:

> If one happened to stumble over an obstruction, that would be not an act, but a mere motion. However, one could convert even this sheer accident into something of an act if, in the course of falling, one suddenly willed his fall (as a rebuke, for instance, to the negligence of the person who had left the obstruction in the way). "Dramatistically," the basic unit of action would be defined as "the human body in conscious or purposive motion." (GM 14)

So, John takes the "ultimate passive"—being slain—and, by widening the circumference to the point where his primary audience can see that death is but a rebirth into a much more significant realm of existence, he (rhetorically) enjoins his audience to turn "being slain" into the ultimate action! His readers will "conquer" in the way that their master "conquered." They will be "slain" as the "Lamb . . . was slain." They will have a transcending conquest.

9

Conclusion

IN APPLYING BURKEAN ENTELECHIAL THEORY TO THE BOOK OF REVE-
lation, this is an attempt to, as Burke says, "join in" the " 'unending
conversation' that is going on at the point in history when we are
born" (PLF 110). As in the "unending conversation" of which Burke
speaks, credibility in Revelation scholarship demands that the difficult progress that has been achieved be acknowledged and assimilated before proceeding. Building upon the progress of Revelation
scholars such as R. H. Charles, Elisabeth Schüssler Fiorenza, J. M.
Ford, and G. B. Caird, this is an effort to move Revelation research
beyond its present stage. The methodologies utilized until now have
brought scholars to a very close and yet still unacceptably imprecise
"knowledge" of this most difficult book. This is a further methodological step. Burkean entelechial methodology is an approach that
can provide enlightenment to the study of Revelation.

Although words are produced "cooperatively," the specific "symbol system" of a given human is unique. Burke argues that "knowing" what a given symbol/term means in a given work cannot be
accomplished by the use of a " 'symbolist dictionary' already written
in advance." Instead, "by inductive inspection of a given work," the
analyst must discover the particular contexts in which the symbol/
term occurs. "You cannot, in advance, know in what equational
structure it will have membership." Once the analyst has inspected
the work, s/he may propose his/her "description of th[e] equational structure" of the work (PLF 89). In the essay, "On Stress, Its
Seeking," Burke outlines three orders of motives—the poetic, the
psychological, and the sociological. Along with the rhetorical, this
book considers these three orders of motives as they may be detected in the Apocalypse of John.

By applying Burke's statistical method to Revelation, the "symbol
system" of John is seen to be synecdochically constructed around
the protagonist "woman" and the antagonist "dragon." The dragon
is identified by John as that archetypal serpent, the Devil, or Satan.

The agon, or contest, that is being presented in John's drama is the contest between Eve and the serpent in Eden. However, readers of Genesis would know that Eve is not called Eve until she is forced to leave Eden. Prior to that time, she is called "woman." The anecdote of woman vs. serpent informs the entire plot of Revelation. However, the woman synecdochically becomes at various points Israel, Mary, the mother of Jesus, and the Church. The serpent, meanwhile, synecdochically becomes at various points Satan, the beast (Rome), various individual Roman emperors, and possibly (through *porneia*) the "husband" of the Jewish priestly party (which is the harlot Babylon).

From a poetics perspective, John's drama may be seen as the ultimate human drama. The *telos* of this drama seems to be a new creation. Thus, thinking symmetrically and cyclically, John may be viewed as prophesying the future by looking into a mirror. If "in the beginning, God created the Heavens and the Earth," John is saying that in the end, God will create a new heavens and a new earth. He may be seen as tying his symmetric structure to a popular millennial schema of first-century Jewish thought, the *Weltwochenschema* of the school of Elias. Although this schema purports to be a seven-stage structure—the history of mankind as a week, with each day lasting 1000 years—it is, practically speaking, more on the order of a Greek trilogy-turned-tetralogy. The school of Elias taught that human history would be divided into three periods—two days with the Law, two days without the Law, and two days with the Messiah. The seventh day of this week, being Sabbath, would usher in a qualitatively different existence for mankind, the period of "rest." This structure can be compared quite easily to the Greek trilogy, and the satyr play that followed it.

Not only does John track down and perfect his plot, but he also perfects his characters. The woman who (in Eden) was torn between her two choices has, by the end of Revelation, completely split into two women—a good woman (or virgin) who yields her life in faithfulness to God, and a bad woman (or harlot) who perfects her unfaithfulness so fully that she commits *porneia* synecdochically with the serpent's representative. The dragon is progressively (entelechially) defeated. First, s/he (the dragon) is cast out of Heaven. Then, s/he is chained and confined in the abyss. Finally, s/he is cast into the lake of fire.

Since Burke equates "psychology" with his theory of "form," in addressing Revelation from the psychological perspective, the focus is on finding entelechial ways in which John "arouses" and "fulfills" expectations in the minds of his auditors. Besides the "cyclical" and "symmetrical" and "trilogy/tetralogy" expectations that John uses, an extremely entelechial form that dominates John's structuring of Revelation—the "seven" form—is analyzed. As is the case with his representative anecdote, John borrows the "expectational" strength of this form from Genesis. Since God created the world in six days and "rested" on the Sabbath, John uses the "psychology" of the number six to create in his auditors a sense of expectation—being on the brink of Sabbath. The slogan "TGIF" is no mere nicety to auditors steeped in Jewish "forms." Once the sixth day is completed, "creation" is finished, so, John pauses at the number six in two of his four septets. After the sixth seal, John pauses to seal the foreheads of the 144,000 from the tribes of Israel who will be protected. After the sixth trumpet, John pauses to eat a scroll and measure the temple. Furthermore, John places his audience (and his date of writing) in the reign of the sixth emperor. He gives the number of the beast as six six six. Psychologically, John places his audience on the brink of *telos*.

Next Leland Griffin's social movements model/adaptation from Burkean theory is applied to the authoritative texts of first-century Christianity. These texts contain nearly all of the elements that Griffin-following-Burke sees in social movements. The specific sociopolitical order in which Christianity is placed is the Jewish order. Christianity's struggle is toward the replacement of a hierarchy ruled by the high priestly party in Jerusalem. The so-called "anti-Jewish slander" of the Book of Revelation is directed not against all "Jews," but against the top echelon of the hierarchy: the high priestly party. Since the so-called "slander" is coming from the pen of a "Jew" (John, the author of Revelation), it should be considered not "anti-Semitic," but "social movement rhetoric." Placing the date of Revelation prior to A.D. 70, the struggle of Christianity to replace the "high priestly" order may be seen to be nearing an end. With the destruction of the Temple in A.D. 70, the "high priestly party" with its Temple cult ceased. Revelation seeks to replace this "social order" with a more egalitarian system, in which all Christians are "priests" and "kings" and "servants." Burke would be skeptical of any purportedly egalitarian system and John's heavenly system does present a certain hierarchal order.

The new heavenly order (of Revelation 4 and 5) does not "replace" God the Almighty (*pantokratôr*) with a new God—Jesus. Instead, it makes both God and the Lamb worthy of praise—God, because he is the Creator; the Lamb who was slain, because he is a "perfected" second Adam. With the new Eve (New Jerusalem) the Lamb may "rule" the new earth, just as the first Adam "ruled" over the first earth.

Entelechial rhetoric in RM is related to "living the dying life." This is precisely the rhetorical injunction of Revelation for John's primary audience. John encourages his primary audience to be willingly "slain" as the Lamb was "slain." In order to "persuade" his audience to become "martyrs," he appropriates the "conquest" terminology of the enemy. Whereas, prior to Revelation, a "conqueror" is one who "slays" his enemy/ies, in Revelation, a true "conqueror" is one who "is slain." John accomplishes this "transcendence" of the "conquest" dichotomy—conqueror vs. conquered—by widening the circumference from the realm of mortal humanity to the realm of the kingdom of Heaven. While Christian "martyrs" may appear to be the "conquered" from the perspective of the realm of mortal humanity, they are nothing less than "conquerors" from the perspective of the realm of the kingdom of Heaven. They are "brought back to life" and "reign" with God. John may then contrast these "conquerors" with the "cowards" (the high priestly party) who say concerning the Roman Empire, "Who can war against the Beast?" Unlike the high priestly party "cowards" who conclude, "If you can't beat them, join them," and the Zealots and Sicarii who actually thought they could "beat" the Romans in war, the Christians were encouraged to "conquer" by "being slain." They "conquer" as the Lamb has "conquered."

These various entelechial critiques of Revelation are offered for two purposes. First, the critiques may serve as a pedagogical illustration of some ways in which Burkean entelechial criticism might be conducted. Second, the critiques offer some enlightenment of what has been called "the most difficult book of the Bible." The four entelechial perspectives used—poetics, psychological, sociopolitical, and rhetorical—are basic, but are by no means exhaustive of the various disciplinary perspectives that might profit by application of an entelechial methodology.

Notes

CHAPTER 1. INTRODUCTION

1. R. H. Charles, *Lectures on the Apocalypse* (London: Oxford University Press, 1923), 1.

2. Stan A. Lindsay, *Implicit Rhetoric: Kenneth Burke's Extension of Aristotle's Concept of Entelechy* (Lanham, MD: University Press of America, 1998).

3. Borrowing one of Burke's favorite Latin expressions, Burke, as he extends entelechy to the realm of symbolic action, makes the necessary adjustments, "*mutatis mutandis.*" When Burke considers a "dramatic," "tragic," or "narrative" form, he converts *mutatis mutandis* the "chord" (instantaneous expression) of the sculpture into the "arpeggio" (expression spread out over time) of the drama. Therefore, Burkean form becomes a process as opposed to a fixed state.

4. George Kennedy, *The Art of Persuasion in Greece* (Princeton, NJ: Princeton University Press, 1963), 297.

5. Elisabeth Schüssler Fiorenza, *The Book of Revelation: Justice and Judgment* (Philadelphia: Fortress Press, 1985), 166.

6. Fiorenza, 10.

7. Ibid. (A good dramatic analysis of Revelation is found in commentary form in David L. Barr, *Tales of the End.* (Santa Rosa, CA: Polebridge Press, 1998).

8. Adela Yarbro Collins, *Cosmology and Eschatology in Jewish and Christian Apocalyptism in Supplements to the Journal for the Study of Judaism,* ed. John J. Collins (Leiden: E. J. Brill, 1996), 217.

9. Adela Yarbro Collins, *Crisis and Catharsis: The Power of the Apocalypse* (Philadelphia: Westminster, 1984), 15–16.

10. Ibid., 18–19.

11. Ibid., 84–110.

12. Ibid., 76.

13. Ibid., 77.

14. Ibid.

CHAPTER 2. REVELATION BACKGROUND

1. Paul Billerbeck, *Die Briefe des Neuen Testaments und die Offenbarung Johannis,* vol. 3 of *Kommentar zum Neuen Testament aus Talmud und Midrasch* (Munich: C. H. Beck'sche, 1961), 826–827.

2. Henry A. Fischel, *Rabbinic Literature and Greco-Roman Philosophy* (Leiden: E. J. Brill, 1973), xi.

3. Elisabeth Schüssler Fiorenza, *The Book of Revelation: Justice and Judgment* (Philadelphia: Fortress Press, 1985), 166.

4. Adela Yarbro Collins, *Crisis and Catharsis: The Power of the Apocalypse* (Philadelphia: Westminster, 1984), 55–56.

5. Ibid., 51.

6. Ibid., 57–58.

7. Ibid., 58.

8. J. Massyngberde Ford, *Revelation*, vol. 38 of *The Anchor Bible* (Garden City, NY: Doubleday & Company, Inc., 1975), 26–27.

9. Ibid., 244.

10. Ibid., 285.

11. Yarbro Collins, *Crisis*, 65.

12. Ibid.

13. Ibid., 54.

14. Ibid., 67.

15. Ibid., 76.

16. Ibid., 63.

17. R. H. Charles, *Lectures on the Apocalypse* (London: Oxford University Press, 1923), 1.

18. Fiorenza, 114.

19. R. H. Charles, *The Revelation of St. John*, vol. 1 of *The International Critical Commentary* (1920 Edinburgh: T. & T. Clark, 1975), 1:xxi.

20. Ford, 4.

21. S. G. F. Brandon, *The Fall of Jerusalem and the Christian Church* (London: S. P. C. K., 1957), 28.

22. Allen Wikgren, *Hellenistic Greek Texts* (Chicago & London: University of Chicago Press, 1947), 117, and G. B. Caird, *A Commentary on the Revelation of St. John the Divine*, a vol. of *Harper's New Testament Commentaries*, ed. Henry Chadwick (New York, Hagerstown, San Francisco, London: Harper & Row, 1966), 3.

23. Justin, "Dialogue with Trypho," dialogue 79 from *Iustinus Philosophus et Martyr*, ed. Otto, 3rd ed., vol. 1 of *Corpus Apologetarum Christianorum* (Ienae: Prostat in Libraria Hermanni Dufft., 1876).

24. F. F. Bruce, "The Revelation to John," in *A New Testament Commentary*, ed. G. C. D. Howley (Grand Rapids, MI: Zondervan Publishing House, 1975), 629.

25. Bruce, 631.

26. Ibid.

27. John A. T. Robinson, *Redating the New Testament* (Philadelphia: Westminster Press, 1976), 225.

28. Robert M. Grant, "Redating the New Testament (Book Review)," *Journal of Biblical Literature* 97 (1978): 294.

29. Robinson, 225.

30. Ford, 4.

31. Charles, *Lectures*, 1.

32. Ibid., 2.

33. Ibid., 4.

34. Ibid., 5–6.

35. Ibid., 3.

36. Ibid., 6.
37. Ibid., 6–7.
38. Ibid., 7.
39. Ibid., 8.
40. Ibid., 8.
41. Fiorenza, 161.
42. Ibid., 159.
43. Charles, *Commentary*, 1:338.
44. Ibid., 1:339.
45. Ibid.
46. Ibid., 1:345.
47. Ibid., 1:346.
48. Caird, 164.
49. Ford, 211f.
50. Fiorenza, 20.
51. Louis Finkelstein, ed. *The Jews: Their History*, 4th ed. (New York: Shocken Books, 1970), 144.
52. Ibid., 95.
53. Solomon Zeitlin, *The Rise and Fall of the Judean State*, 3 vols. (Philadelphia: Jewish Publication Society of America, 5729–1969), 2:252–53.
54. Erwin Nestle and Kurt Aland eds., *Novum Testamentum Graece* (London: United Bible Societies, 1969), 662.
55. Martin Kiddle, *The Revelation of St. John*, a vol. of *The Moffatt New Testament Commentary* (New York and London: Harper and Brothers Publishers), v.
56. Ibid., xlix.

CHAPTER 3. BURKE'S STATISTICAL METHOD

1. Stan A. Lindsay, *Implicit Rhetoric: Kenneth Burke's Extension of Aristotle's Concept of Entelechy* (Lanham, MD: University Press of America, 1998).
2. Ibid., 5.
3. Ibid., 17–18.
4. Ibid., 18–19.
5. Ibid., 10–11.
6. Kenneth Burke, "Freedom and Authority in the Realm of Poetic Imagination," in *Freedom and Authority in Our Time*, ed. Lyman Bryson, Louis Finkelstein, R. M. MacIver, and Richard McKeon (New York & London: Harper & Brothers, 1953), 374.
7. Lindsay, *Implicit*, 89.
8. R. H. Charles, *Lectures on the Apocalypse* (London: Oxford University Press, 1923), 3.
9. G. B. Caird, *A Commentary on the Revelation of St. John the Divine*, a vol. of *Harper's New Testament Commentaries*, ed. Henry Chadwick (New York, Hagerstown, San Francisco, London: Harper & Row, 1966), 13.
10. Kenneth Burke, "Poetics and Communication," in *Perspectives in Education,*

Religion, and the Arts, ed. Howard E. Kiefer and Milton K. Munitz (Albany: State University of New York Press, 1970), 415.

11.   Ruth Anne Clarke and Jesse G. Delia, "Topoi and Rhetorical Competence," *Quarterly Journal of Speech* 65 (1979): 195.

12.   *Rhetorica ad Herennium* (by Cicero?), trans. Harry Caplan in *Loeb Classical Library* (London: Heinemann, 1954), 3:10.

13.   Charles, *Lectures,* 5–6.

CHAPTER 4. SYNECDOCHE AND JOHN'S REPRESENTATIVE ANECDOTE

1.   G. B. Caird, *A Commentary on the Revelation of St. John the Divine, a vol. of Harper's New Testament Commentaries,* ed. Henry Chadwick (New York, Hagerstown, San Francisco, London: Harper & Row Publishers, 1966), 13.

2.   Ibid., 196–197.

3.   Ibid., 243.

4.   Ibid., 48.

5.   George Kennedy, *The Art of Persuasion in Greece* (Princeton: Princeton University Press, 1963), 297. Kennedy continues: "A trope is a single word used in a novel way either because the idea to be expressed has no idea of its own (no 'proper' word) or for the sake of embellishment. The difference between a trope and a figure is parallel to the difference between barbarism and solecism: a figure, like a solecism, involves at least two words; a trope, like a barbarism, consists of only a single word: a metaphor is a trope, a simile is a figure. . . . Grammatical treatises display a basic set of eight tropes: onomatapoiia, katachresis, metaphora, metalepsis, synekdoche, metonymia, autonomasia, and antiphrasis."

6.   Hayden White observes that "any history which endows the last event in the series (e), whether real or only speculatively projected, with the force of full explanatory power (E) is of the type of all eschatological or apocalyptical histories." Cf. Hayden White, "The Historical Text as Literary Artifact," chap. 2 in *Tropics of Discourse: Essays in Cultural Criticism* (Baltimore, MD: Johns Hopkins University Press, 1978), 93. Cf. also Hayden White, *The Content of the Form: Narrative Discourse and Historical Representation* (Baltimore & London: John Hopkins University Press, 1987). Thus, in a single sentence, White has both accepted apocalyptic as a type of text appropriate for applying historiographical methodologies and provided an indication of the plot structure that one might expect to find when considering an apocalyptical history.

Revelation scholars have agreed that the Apocalypse itself is a historically based text. R. H. Charles notes the close affinity of Revelation to Jewish apocalypses, indicating that, like them, it should "be taken as referring first and chiefly to the times in which it was originally written." Cf. R. H. Charles, *Lectures on the Apocalypse* (London: Oxford University Press, 1923), 1. Jewish apocalypses characteristically describe events contemporaneous with their times of writing.

White cites a private conversation with Geoffrey Hartman in which Hartman remarked, along a similar vein, that "to write a history meant to place an event with a context, by relating it as a part to some conceivable whole." He goes on to suggest that, as far as he knows, there are only two ways of relating parts to wholes, by metonymy and by synecdoche. Cf. White, *Tropics*, 94. This comment prompts White to further consider the thought of Giambattista Vico on the importance of the "four principal modes of figurative represention." Cf. White, *Tropics*, 95. Vico's "four modes" are what Kenneth Burke calls the four master tropes.

7.   Kennedy, in explaining the classical use of the terms, does not make the same distinction between synecdoche and metonymy that Burke does. Writes Kennedy: "*synekdochê* is use of the whole for a part or a part for the whole . . . ; *metonymia* is a wider term where a word associated with an object in almost any way is used for the object" (298). Even if I follow Kennedy's classical distinction, the arguments that I make remain valid. I simply combine the tropes synecdoche and metonymy and follow Burke in claiming that a distinction remains to be made between those uses of synecdoche and metonymy that are representative and those that are reductionist.

8.   Cf. Kenneth Burke, "Poetics and Communication" in *Perspectives in Education, Religion, and the Arts*, ed.

Howard E. Kiefer and Milton K. Munitz (Albany: State University of New York Press, 1970), 402.

9.   G. F. Moore, *Judaism in the First Centuries of the Christian Era*, 2 vols. (Cambridge: Harvard University Press, 1927–30), 1:414.

10.   Louis Ginzberg, *The Legends of the Jews*, 7 vols. (Philadelphia: Jewish Publication Society of America, 5728–1968), 5:21.

11.   Ibid., 5:37.

12.   Ibid., 5:125.

13.   Cf., for example, Stephen D. O'Leary, "A Dramatistic Theory of Apocalyptic Rhetoric," *The Quarterly Journal of Speech* 79 no. 4 (November 1993): 387. O'Leary claims: "The ultimate struggle is, of course, between God and 'that serpent of old that led the whole world astray, whose name is Satan, or the Devil'." Persian dualism taught that the cosmic conflict was between a good divinity and an evil divinity. The projected outcome of this conflict was always somewhat in doubt.

14.   Martin Hengel, *Judentum und Hellenismus* (Tubingen: J. C. B. Mohr, 1969), 347–48.

15.   For a discussion of the new directions in the fallen angel story taken by Jewish midrashists in the period of the Roman Empire, cf. Stan Lindsay, "Anamartetous Fallen Angels" (Masters thesis, Indiana University 1977).

16.   J. Massyngberde Ford, *Revelation*, vol. 38 of *The Anchor Bible* (Garden City, NY: Doubleday & Company, Inc., 1975), 191.

17.   F. F. Bruce, "The Revelation to John," in *A New Testament Commentary*, ed. G. C. D. Howley (Grand Rapids, MI: Zondervan Publishing House, 1975), 651.

18.   Foerster, "ophis," *Theological Dictionary of the New Testament*, 9 vols., ed. Gerhard Kittel, trans. G. W. Bromiley (Grand Rapids, Michigan: Wm. B. Eerdmans Publishing Company, 1967), 5:581.

19.   Bruce, 650.

20.   John's final use of the word "twelve" is found in 21:14. John speaks of the twelve foundations of the wall of the New Jerusalem, stating that "in them" are "the names of the twelve apostles of the Lamb." While this is not an explicit ref-

erence to Israel, it may be evidence of a terministic bridge whereby the old Israel has become a new (Christian) Israel.

21. Bruce, 650–651.

22. I am indebted to Neil Anderson for this insight. The Symbol, Exodus, "appeals [here] as the interpretation of a situation." Cf. CS 154. There are multiple allusions to the Exodus, throughout Revelation, functioning as an interpretation of the flight of the Church from Jerusalem. In 18:4, John says, "Come out of her, my people, that you do not receive her plagues." In 11:8, the "great city" is "spiritually called . . . Egypt, where their lord was crucified."

23. R. H. Charles, *The Revelation of St. John*, vol. 1 of *The International Critical Commentary* (1926 Edinburgh: T. & T. Clark, 1975), 299.

24. Caird, 149.

25. Bruce, 652, comments on the language in 12:15–16, which discussed the serpent casting water "out of his mouth like a river" that the earth "swallowed": "This may refer to some incident of the war of A.D. 66–73 no longer identifiable which threatened to cut off the church's escape." Here, again, there may be Exodus allusions. Crossing the Jordan to escape from Israel may be tied in by John, symbolically, to the parting of the Jordan on entering the promised land, or the parting of the Red Sea upon leaving Egypt. The latter event is infused with "dragon-Leviathan" imagery and implications in the Old Testament.

26. John may have finally arrived at an identification that his audience in Asia Minor might appreciate. After the (Palestinian?) church is protected from the Gentile domination (of Jerusalem for three and a half years?), the reference may now be to the church in dispersion of which those in Asia Minor are a part.

27. The *marturia* reference in 12:17 also links them to (i.e., indicates that they represent) the conquerors, the heroes of the letters to the seven churches, in the first chapters of Revelation.

28. Martin Kiddle, *The Revelation of St. John*, a vol. of *The Moffat New Testament Commentary* ed. James Moffat (New York & London: Harper and Brothers Publishers), 216.

29. Caird, 147.

30. Ibid., 149.

31. Bernard J. Bamberger, *Fallen Angels* (Philadelphia: Jewish Publication Society of America, 5712-1952), 90.

32. For a discussion of this rivalry between "angels" and "humans," see Peter Schafer, *Rivalität zwischen Engeln und Menschen*, vol. 8 of *Studia Judaica*, ed. E. L. Ehrlich (Berlin and New York: Walter De Gruyter, 1975).

33. But note that, while the dragon has seven diadems on his heads, the beast has ten diadems on his horns, and names of blasphemy on its heads. John does not say that either the dragon or the ten horns of the beast are blasphemous, and the diadems would suggest that the dragon and the ten horns had been given some sort of authority. The only other character in Revelation who has diadems is the rider of the white horse, who is called "Faithful and True" (19:11–12), and "the Word of God" (19:13), and "King of Kings and Lord of Lords" (19:16), who will "shepherd" the "nations with an iron rod" (19:15)—thus identifying him completely with the son of the woman in chapter 12. This rider has "many diadems" on his head (19:12).

34. Caird, 164.

35. Bruce, 652.

36. Ford, 211.

37. An abbreviated version of Domitian's title would in Greek letters equal 666. There is strong external evidence that Domitian's reign was the referent for the symbols of Revelation, but there is no strong evidence of a Christian persecution under Domitian. The worship of the beast and his image has been tied to emperor worship, which Caird (166) says "was never, before Domitian, forced by an arrogant imperialism on a reluctant populace."

38. Caird, 164. Suetonius, writing on Vespasian in his *Lives of the Caesars*, speaks of Vespasian as a miracle-working divine man because he is the first of a new line of emperors. This might relate him to the signs of 13:13–15. If the Jewish war of 66–73 A.D. is considered to be the historical referent for the destruction of Babylon (Ford suggests that Babylon is Jerusalem), then Vespasian would appear to be a leading candidate for a revived Nero, since Nero had instigated the war, and his commanding officer for executing the war was Vespasian. Rumors of Vespasian ascending to emperor would have the effect (for Jews all over the world) of bringing Nero back to life.

39. Charles, *Commentary*, 1:338. There is a textual variant of the number of the beast that would total 616. Gaius Caesar (Caligula's official title and name) spelled in Greek would equal this total but this is not the preferred textual reading.

40. Kiddle, 216.

41. John may be justified in painting his composite villain as the epitome of syncretism, but John cannot allow his own ideology to be tainted with the evil which he so forcefully opposes. Thus, although he borrows a syncretistic theological motif such as the fallen angel story, he may have reworked it to purge the syncretistic elements from it.

John's syncretistic description of the dragon from many cultures is filtered through the interpretive screen of the biblical dragon/serpent in order to identify this Jewish archetypal villain as an international enemy. There are the Jews and there are the Gentiles/heathen/*goiim*. Any nationality and all nationalities (other than Jewish) are heathen, for the Jew.

42. Belteshazzar is a name that philologists cite as evidence for a later date for the book because the "t" should not be in the spelling. However, if the Jewish scribes who resisted syncretism added the "t" to the name Belshazzar in order to avoid the association of the hero Daniel with the Babylonian god, Bel, in the same way that the scribes added an extra "y" to Jerusalem, making it Yerushalayim, thus avoiding a pagan deity association, then the misspelling of Belshazzar is further evidence of an antisyncretistic sentiment related to the Book of Daniel.

43. Apparently, John saw the possibility of salvation for some of the kings of the earth, but generally these nations/heathen/Gentiles/*goiim* were the evil ones with whom the conquerors should not commit *porneia*/syncretism.

That John viewed some heathen as candidates for salvation is seen in 5:9: "You were slain and purchased us to God by your blood out of every tribe and tongue and people and nation." A formula similar to this is used in 7:9, referring to an innumerable crowd of (saved) Lamb worshippers. This group (including kings, in this instance only) is the proper audience for John's prophecy in 10:11. And, in

14:6, the group is the proper audience for the everlasting gospel. Some out of this group will rejoice at the death of the two witnesses in 11:9. (Does this mean that not all of the group feel that way?) In 13:7, authority over this group is given to the beast, but that does not necessarily mean that the group was comprised of all beast worshippers. Indeed, there was always another option for the group, as seen a few verses later in 13:15—they could refuse to worship and be killed. In 17:15, this group (minus tribes) is the "waters" on which the harlot sits.

The heathen may be considered somewhat innocent dupes, in that they were "misled" by Babylon in 18:23, and by the Devil/Satan in 20:3, 8. They are to be "healed" by the "leaves" of the tree of life in 22:2. And in 15:4, all the "nations" shall worship before the Lord God *pantokratôr*.

The issue as to whether the term "earth" is to be taken as generally referring to the entire world or specifically as referring to Palestine is unresolved. The only specific "kings of the earth" that are identified in the Acts 4 passage were Herod and Pilate, both of whom ruled over the "land" of Israel, although they received their authority from Rome. If Babylon is Jerusalem, the location of the *porneia* would appear to be in the "land" of Israel. Since the "inhabitants of the earth/land" are connected to the "kings of the earth/land" in 17:2, perhaps the earth/land of the kings and the earth/land of the inhabitants are one and the same. Certainly, if the kings are to be connected to the inhabitants, either interpretation—Palestine or earth—is possible, as Charles acknowledges (*Commentary*, 1:289).

The fact that not enough evidence has been considered yet to resolve this issue in no way diminishes its importance. The earth/land is to be the focus of the seven last plagues in 16:1. Hence, this is a very important interpretive issue. If John is speaking of a destruction that comes upon the land of Israel, rather than the entire earth, it is possible to find historical referents in the Jewish war of 66–73 A.D.

44. Ford, 218–19.

45. Kiddle, 253. It was taken by Caird (171) to be "the commune Asiae, a provincial council consisting of representatives from the major towns, . . . at least as old as Mark Antony, who found it already in existence." This commune included Asiarchs and, Caird surmises, "probably local priests of the imperial cult as well." Charles reports, "This Beast, according to Wellhausen and Mommsen, represents the imperial power exercised in the provinces by the state officials" (*Commentary*, 1:339).

46. Charles, *Commentary*, 1:342–43. Here, Charles is agreeing to an extent with J. Weiss who, according to Charles, saw this beast as referring originally to "a Jewish Antichrist or False Prophet, but the final author . . . transformed him into . . . the priesthood of the imperial cult" (Charles, *Commentary*, 1:340). Charles likewise concludes that the identity was reworked into the heathen imperial priesthood.

47. Ibid., 1:339.

48. Ford, 219.

49. Kiddle, 174–175.

50. In line with Ford, and the original sense understood by Weiss and Charles, the second beast should be understood as a Jewish entity. Since it, in 11:13, "causes fire to come down out of heaven" (a sacrificial function), it is possibly the high priest, or the priestly family. In its role as the ruler of the temple economic system (compare Jesus' cleansing the temple), it controls "buying and selling" (13:17).

The mark that it causes the "inhabitants of the earth/land" to have on their right hand and forehead (13:16) would be the phylacteries, which Jews wore on their left hand and forehead. Along with Charles, interpreters might understand the "mark on their right hand and brow—an antichristian travesty of the practice of orthodox Judaism, which required the faithful to wear it on the left hand and forehead" (Charles, *Commentary*, 1:342–43).

51. Ginzberg, 5:85.

52. Louis Finkelstein, ed., *The Jews: Their History*, 4th ed. (New York: Shocken Books, 1970), 95.

53. Ibid., 126.

54. Solomon Zeitlin, *The Rise and Fall of the Judaean State*, 3 vols. (Philadelphia: Jewish Publication Society of America, 5729-1969), 2:7.

55. Ibid., 2:91.

56. Ibid., 2:252–53.

57. Charles, *Commentary*, 1:lxvi.

58. Zeitlin, 2:252–53.

59. Josephus, *Wars of the Jews*, book 1, chapter 20.3–4, in *Josephus Complete Works*, trans. William Whiston (Grand Rapids, MI: Kregel Publications, 1974), 497.

60. Ibid., 1:20. 3–4.

61. Zeitlin, 2:253.

CHAPTER 5. THE POETICS OF REVELATION

1. Harold Bloom, *The Western Canon: The Books and School of the Ages* (New York: Harcourt Brace, 1994), 249.

2. Kenneth Burke, "On Stress, Its Seeking," in *Why Man Takes Chances (Studies in Stress-Seeking)*, ed. Samuel Z. Klausner (Garden City, NY: Anchor Books, 1968), 76.

3. Burke, "On Stress, Its Seeking," 77.

4. Kenneth Burke, "Poetics and Communication," in *Perspectives in Education, Religion, and the Arts*, eds. Howard E. Kiefer and Milton K. Munitz (Albany: State University of New York Press, 1970), 408. In a footnote on page 26 of PLF, Burke appears to equate "culminating" with "representative," and by extension "synecdoche," in the sense that the top of a political hierarchy, such as monarch or tribal chief, not only "perfects" the hierarchy, but also "represents" the entire hierarchy.

5. Burke, "Poetics and Communication," 401.

6. Aristotle, Poetics, trans. T. S. Dorsch, *Classical Literary Criticism* (London: Penguin Books, 1965), 50.

7. I am indebted to John T. Kirby for this insight.

8. George A. Kennedy, *New Testament Interpretation through Rhetorical Criticism* (Chapel Hill and London: University of North Carolina Press, 1984), 12.

9. Ibid., 28.

10. Ibid., 28

11. Ibid., 28–29.

12. John T. Kirby, "The 'Great Triangle' in Early Greek Rhetoric and Poetics,"

Rhetorica 8 (1990): 216–17. This essay also appears in *Landmark Essays on Classical Greek Rhetoric*, ed., Edward Schiappa, (Davis, CA: Hermagoras Press, 1994).

13.   Elisabeth Schüssler Fiorenza, "Composition and Structure of the Revelation of John," *The Catholic Biblical Quarterly* 39 (1977): 358–66. This essay (revised) also appears as chapter 6 of Elizabeth Schüssler Fiorenza's *The Book of Revelation Justice and Judgment* (Philadelphia: Fortress Press, 1985).

14.   Kirby, "The 'Great Triangle,' " 217.

15.   J. Massyngberde Ford, *Revelation*, a vol. of *The Anchor Bible* (Garden City, NY: Doubleday & Company, Inc., 1975), 51, 93, 165.

16.   Fiorenza, 365.

17.   Ibid., 364–65.

18.   Paul Billerbeck, *Die Briefe des Neuen Testaments und die Offenbarung Johannis*, vol. 3 of *Kommentar zum Neuen Testament aus Talmud und Midrasch* (Munich: C. H. Beck'sche, 1961), 826. Sanhedrin 97a is quoted by Billerbeck, stating that in the school of Elias, it is taught that the world will stand for six thousand years: two thousand years without the Law, two thousand years with the Law, and two thousand years with the Messiah. The final thousand years of this "Weltwochenschema" is the "Weltensabbat," as Billerbeck interprets.

19.   Fiorenza, 353.

20.   Billerbeck, 826.

21.   Henry A. Fischel, *Rabbinic Literature and Greco-Roman Philosophy* (Leiden: E. J. Brill, 1973), xi.

22.   Burke, "On Stress, Its Seeking," 85.

23.   Stan A. Lindsay, *Implicit Rhetoric: Kenneth Burke's Extension of Aristotle's Concept of Entelechy* (Lanham, MD: University Press of America, 1998), 47–48.

24.   N. P. Bratsiotis, "ish," *Theological Dictionary of the Old Testament*, ed. G. J. Botterweck and H. Ringgren, trans. John T. Willis (Grand Rapids, MI: William B. Eerdmans Publishing Company, 1974), I:230.

25.   J. Massyngberde Ford, *Revelation*, vol. 38 of *The Anchor Bible* (Garden City, NY: Doubleday & Company, Inc., 1975), 173, et passim.

26.   Burke, "On Stress, Its Seeking," 88.

27.   G. B. Caird, *A Commentary on the Revelation of St. John the Divine*, a vol. of *Harper's New Testament Commentaries*, ed. Henry Chadwick (New York, Hagerstown, San Francisco, London: Harper & Row, 1966), 32–33.

CHAPTER 6. THE PSYCHOLOGY OF REVELATION

1.   G. B. Caird, *A Commentary on the Revelation of St. John the Divine*, a vol. of *Harper's New Testament Commentaries*, ed. Henry Chadwick (New York, Hagerstown, San Francisco, London: Harper & Row Publishers, 1966), 235–236.

2.   J. Massyngberde Ford, *Revelation*, vol. 38 of *The Anchor Bible* (Garden City, NY: Doubleday & Company, Inc., 1975), 92–94.

3.   Elizabeth Schüssler Fiorenza, "Composition and Structure of the Book of Revelation," *The Catholic Biblical Quarterly* 39 (1977): 354. This essay (revised) also appears as chapter 6 of Elizabeth Schüssler Fiorenza's *The Book of Revelation: Justice and Judgment* (Philadelphia: Fortress Press, 1985).

4. Fiorenza, CBQ, 39:365.

5. Caird, 236.

6. R. H. Charles, *The Revelation of St. John*, 2 vols. of *The International Critical Commentary* (1920 Edinburgh: T. & T. Clark, 1975), 1:287ff.

7. Ford, 146.

8. F. F. Bruce, "The Revelation to John," in *A New Testament Commentary*, ed. G. C. D. Howley (Grand Rapids, MI: Zondervan Publishing House, 1975), 652. Cf. also Ford, 146; Caird, 122–23; and Bruce, "Revelation," 648.

9. Caird, 122–23.

10. Paul Billerbeck, *Die Briefe des Neuen Testaments und die Offenbarung Johannis*, vol. 3 of *Kommentar zum Neuen Testament aus Talmud und Midrasch* (Munich: C. H. Beck'sche, 1961), 826.

11. Ibid., 826–827.

12. Barry Brummett, Review of *Arguing the Apocalypse: A Theory of Millennial Rhetoric*, by Stephen D. O'Leary, *Rhetoric Society Quarterly* 24 (1994): 132.

CHAPTER 7. THE SOCIOPOLITICS OF REVELATION

1. Elisabeth Schüssler Fiorenza, *The Book of Revelation: Justice and Judgment* (Philadelphia: Fortress Press, 1985), 114.

2. Ibid., 20–21.

3. Luke Johnson, "The New Testament's Anti-Jewish Slander and the Conventions of Ancient Polemic," *The Journal of Biblical Literature* 108 (1989): 419.

4. Ibib 429.

5. Ibid., 422.

6. Ibid., 427.

7. R. H. Charles, *Lectures on the Apocalypse* (London: Oxford University Press, 1923), 9ff.

8. Johnson, 424.

9. Charles J. Stewart, Craig Allen Smith, and Robert E. Denton, Jr., *Persuasion and Social Movements*, Third Ed. (Prepublication form, 1994), 5.

10. Elizabeth Schüssler Fiorenza, "Composition and Structure of the Book of Revelation," *The Catholic Biblical Quarterly* 39 (1977): 344. This essay, (revised also appears as chapter 6 of Elizabeth Schüssler Fiorenza's *The Book of Revelation Justice and Judgment* (Philadelphia: Fortress Press, 1985).

11. J. Massyngberde Ford, *Revelation*, vol. 38 of *The Anchor Bible* (Garden City, NY: Doubleday & Company, Inc., 1975), 3–4.

12. Leland M. Griffin, "A Dramatistic Theory of the Rhetoric of Movements," in *Critical Responses to Kenneth Burke*, ed. William Rueckert (Minneapolis: University of Minnesota Press, 1969), 456–78.

13. Ibid., 457.

14. Ibid., 458

15. Ibid.

16. Ibid., 463.

17. Ibid.

18. Ibid.

19. Ibid.
20. Ibid., 464
21. Ibid.
22. Ibid.
23. Ibid.
24. Ibid.
25. R. H. Charles, *A Critical and Exegetical Commentary on the Revelation of St. John*, 2 vols. (1920 Edinburgh: T. & T. Clark, 1975), 1:54 makes the identification and Caird, Kiddle, Fiorenza, and Ford concur for the most part.
26. Griffin, 465.
27. Ibid., 466.
28. Solomon Zeitlin, *The Rise and Fall of the Judaean State*, 3 vols. (Philadelpia: Jewish Publication Society of America, 5729-1969), 2:252–53.
29. Stewart, Smith, and Denton, 79.
30. Griffin, 457.
31. William Rueckert, ed., *Critical Responses to Kenneth Burke* (Minneapolis: University of Minnesota Press, 1969), 478.

CHAPTER 8. THE RHETORIC OF REVELATION

1. Charles J. Stewart, Craig Allen Smith, and Robert E. Denton, Jr., *Persuasion and Social Movements*, 3rd ed. (Prepublication form, 1994), 263–282.
2. Stewart, Smith, and Denton, 264.
3. Ibid.
4. Gerhard Kittel, ed. *Theological Dictionary of the New Testament*. Translated and edited by Geoffrey W. Bromiley (Grands Rapids, MI: Wm. B. Eerdmans Publishing Company, 1967), s.v. *"nikaô, nikê, nikos, hupernikaô,"* by O. Bauernfeind, 4:942.
5. Bauernfeind, 942.
6. G. B. Caird, *A Commentary on the Revelation of St. John the Divine*, a vol. of *Harper's New Testament Commentaries*, ed. Henry Chadwick (New York, Hagerstown, San Francisco, London: Harper & Row, 1966), 32–33.
7. R. H. Charles, *A Critical and Exegetical Commentary on The Revelation of St. John*, 2 vols. (Edinburgh: T. & T. Clark, 1920), 1:54.
8. Martin Kiddle, *The Revelation of St. John* (New York and London: Harper and Brothers Publishers, 1940), 28.
9. Elisabeth Schüssler Fiorenza, *The Book of Revelation Justice and Judgment* (Philadelphia: Fortress Press, 1985), 198.
10. Fiorenza, *Justice*, 125.
11. J. Massyngberde Ford, *Revelation*, vol. 38 of *The Anchor Bible* (Garden City, NY: Doubleday & Company, Inc., 1975), 279.
12. Ibid., 90.
13. Ibid., 100.
14. Marcus Jastrow, *A Dictionary of the Targumim, the Talmud Babli and Yerushalmi, and the Midrashic Literature*, 2 vols. (Brooklyn, N.Y.: P. Shalom Pub. Inc., 1967), 1:125.
15. Charles, *Commentary*, 1:289.

16. Kiddle, 153.
17. Caird, 87.
18. Fiorenza, *Justice*, 115–116.
19. Caird, 38–39.
20. Ibid., 39.
21. Ford, 390.
22. Kiddle, 33.
23. Ibid., 38.
24. Charles, *Commentary*, 1:52–53, 64, 70.
25. Ford, 391.
26. Caird, 31.
27. Kiddle, 34.
28. Charles, *Commentary*, 1:52–53.
29. Ford, 173, passim.
30. Fiorenza, *Justice*, 118.
31. Ibid.
32. Kiddle, 26–27, 48.
33. Caird, 35.
34. Charles, *Commentary*, 1:57.
35. Fiorenza, *Justice*, 115–116.
36. Caird, 38–39.

Bibliography

WORKS BY KENNETH BURKE

Burke, Kenneth. *Attitudes toward History*. 3rd ed. Berkeley, Los Angeles, London: University of California Press, 1984. (Abbreviated: **ATH**)

———. *Attitudes toward History*. 2 vols. New York: New Republic, 1937.

———. *The Complete White Oxen*. Berkeley, Los Angeles, London: University of California Press, 1968. (Abbreviated: **CWO**)

———. *Counter-Statement*. Berkeley, Los Angeles, London: University of California Press, 1968. (Abbreviated: **CS**)

———. "Dramatism." In *Communication: Concepts and Perspectives*, edited by Lee Thayer, 327–360. Washington, D.C.: Spartan Books, 1967.

———. *Dramatism and Development*. Barre, MA: Clark University Press with Barre Publishers 1972. (Abbreviated: **DD**)

———. "The Five Master Terms: Their Place in a 'Dramatistic' Grammar of Motives." *View* 3, no. 2 (1943): 50–52.

———. "Freedom and Authority in the Realm of the Poetic Imagination." In *Freedom and Authority in Our Time*, edited by Lyman Bryson, Louis Finkelstein, R. M. MacIver, and Richard McKeon, 365–375. New York and London: Harper & Brothers, 1953.

———. *A Grammar of Motives*. Berkeley, Los Angeles, London: University of California Press, 1969. (Abbreviated: **GM**)

———. *Language as Symbolic Action: Essays on Life, Literature, and Method*. Berkeley, Los Angeles, London: University of California Press, 1966. (Abbreviated: **LSA**)

———. "On Catharsis or Resolution, with a Postscript," *Kenyon Review* 21 (1959): 337–75.

———. "On Human Behavior Considered 'Dramatistically.'" In *Permanence and Change: An Anatomy of Purpose*. 2nd ed., 274–294. Indianapolis: Bobbs-Merrill Company, Inc., 1975.

———. "On Stress, Its Seeking." In *Why Man Takes Chances: Studies in Stress-Seeking*, edited by Samuel Z. Klausner, 75–103. Garden City, NY: Doubleday, 1968.

———. *On Symbols and Society*. Edited by Joseph R. Gusfield. Chicago and London: University of Chicago Press, 1989.

———. "Othello—An Essay to Illustrate a Method." In *Perspecives by Incongruity*, edited by Stanley Edgar Hyman, 152–195. Bloomington: Indiana University Press, 1964.

————. *Permanence and Change: An Anatomy of Purpose.* 2nd ed. Indianapolis: Bobbs-Merrill Company, Inc., 1975. (Abbreviated: **PC**)

————. *The Philosophy of Literary Form: Studies in Symbolic Action.* 3rd ed. Berkeley, Los Angeles, London: University of California Press, 1973. (Abbreviated: **PLF**)

————. "Poetics and Communication." In *Perspectives in Education, Religion, and the Arts,* edited by Howard E. Kiefer and Milton K. Munitz, 401–418. Albany: State University of New York Press, 1970.

————. "Questions and Answers about the Pentad." *College Composition and Communication* 29 (1978): 330–335.

————. *A Rhetoric of Motives.* Berkeley, Los Angeles, London: University of California Press, 1969. (Abbreviated: **RM**)

————. *The Rhetoric of Religion.* Boston: Beacon Press, 1961. (Abbreviated: **RR**)

————. "Rhetoric—Old and New." In *New Rhetorics,* edited by Martin Steinmann, Jr., 59–76. New York: Scribner's Sons, 1967.

————. "Rhetoric, Poetics, and Philosophy." In *Rhetoric, Philosophy, and Literature,* edited by Don M. Burks, 15–33. West Lafayette, IN: Purdue University Press, 1978.

————. "The Rhetorical Situation." In *Communication: Ethical and Moral Issues,* edited by Lee Thayer, 263–275. London, New York, Paris: Gordon and Breach Science Publishers, 1973.

————. *The Selected Correspondence of Kenneth Burke and Malcolm Cowley, 1915–1981.* Edited by Paul Jay. Berkeley and Los Angeles: University of California Press, 1990.

————. "Theology and Logology (Abstract)." *Journal of the American Academy of Religion* 47 (1979): 298.

————. *Towards a Better Life.* Berkeley, Los Angeles, London: University of California Press, 1982. (Abbreviated: **TBL**)

WORKS ABOUT KENNETH BURKE

Burks, Don M. "Dramatic Irony, Collaboration, and Kenneth Burke's Theory of Form." *Pre/Text* 6 (1985): 255–273.

————. *Rhetoric, Philosophy, and Literature: An Exploration.* West Lafayette, IN: Purdue University Press, 1978.

Cowley, Malcolm. "Prolegomena to Kenneth Burke." In *Critical Responses to Kenneth Burke,* edited by William R. Rueckert, 247–251. Minneapolis: University of Minnesota Press, 1969.

Donoghue, Denis. "American Sage." *The New York Review* 26 (September, 1985): 39–42.

Foss, Sonja K., Karen A. Foss, and Robert Trapp. *Contemporary Perspectives on Rhetoric*. 2nd ed. Prospect Heights, IL: Waveland Press, 1991.

Griffin, Leland M. "A Dramatistic Theory of the Rhetoric of Movements." In *Critical Responses to Kenneth Burke*, edited by William R. Rueckert, 456–478. Minneapolis: University of Minnesota Press, 1969.

Hart, Roderick P. *Modern Rhetorical Criticism*. Glenview, IL and London: Scott, Foresman/Little, Brown, 1990.

Howell, Wilbur Samuel. *Poetics, Rhetoric, and Logic*. Ithaca and London: Cornell University Press, 1975.

Jennerman, Donald L. "Kenneth Burke's Poetics of Catharsis." In *Representing Kenneth Burke*, edited by Hayden White and Margaret Brose, 31–51. Baltimore and London: Johns Hopkins University Press, 1982.

———. "The Literary Criticism and Theory of Kenneth Burke in Light of Aristotle, Freud, and Marx." Ph.D. diss., Indiana University, 1974.

Lindsay, Stan A. "The Burkean Entelechy and the Apocalypse of John." Ph.D. diss., Purdue University, 1995.

———. *Implicit Rhetoric: Kenneth Burke's Extension of Aristotle's Concept of Entelechy*. Lanham, NJ: University Press of America, 1998.

———. *The Twenty-One Sales in a Sale*. Grants Pass, OR: Oasis Press/PSI Research, 1998.

Nichols, Marie Hochmuth. "Burkeian Criticism." In *Essays on Rhetorical Criticism*, edited by Thomas R. Nilsen. New York: Random House, 1968.

———. "Kenneth Burke and the 'New Rhetoric.' " In *Contemporary Theories of Rhetoric: Selected Readings*, edited by Richard L. Johannesen. New York, Evanston, San Francisco, London: Harper and Row, 1971.

Rueckert, William H. *Critical Responses to Kenneth Burke*. Minneapolis: University of Minnesota Press, 1969.

———. *Encounters with Kenneth Burke*. Urbana and Chicago: University of Illinois Press, 1994.

———. *Kenneth Burke and the Drama of Human Relations*. 2nd ed. Berkeley: University of California Press, 1963.

———. "The Rhetoric of Rebirth: A Study of the Literary Theory and Critical Practice of Kenneth Burke." Ph.D. diss., University of Michigan, 1956.

Schiappa, Edward. "Burkean Tropes and Kuhnian Science: A Social Constructionist Perspective on Language and Reality." *Journal of Advanced Communication* 13 (1993): 401–422.

White, Hayden, and Margaret Brose, eds. *Representing Kenneth Burke*. Baltimore and London: John Hopkins University Press, 1982.

Winterowd, W. Ross. "Kenneth Burke: An Annotated Glossary of His Terministic Screen and a 'Statistical' Survey of His Major Concepts." *Rhetoric Society Quarterly* 15 (1985): 145–77.

WORKS BY AND ABOUT ARISTOTLE

Aristotle. *De Anima*. Translated by J. A. Smith. Oxford: At the Clarendon Press, 1931. Reprinted in *The Works of Aristotle Translated into English*. Edited by W. D. Ross. Oxford: At the Clarendon Press, 1968.

———. *On Sophistical Refutations, On Coming-to-Be and Passing away*. Translated by E. S. Forster. Cambridge: Harvard University Press, 1955.

———. *Physica*. Translated by R. P. Hardie and R. K. Gaye. In *The Basic Works of Aristotle*, edited by Richard McKeon. New York: Random House, 1941.

———. *Poetics*. Translated by T. S. Dorsch. In *Classical Literary Criticism*. London: Penguin Books, 1965.

———. *The Rhetoric and the Poetics of Aristotle*. Edited by Friedrich Solmsen. New York: Random House, 1954.

Kennedy, George A. *Aristotle on Rhetoric*. New York and Oxford: Oxford University Press, 1991.

McKeon, Richard. *The Basic Works of Aristotle*. New York: Random House, 1941.

———. *Introduction to Aristotle*. 2nd ed. Chicago and London: University of Chicago Press, 1973.

Randall, John Herman, Jr. *Aristotle*. New York: Columbia University Press, 1960.

Ross, W. D. *Aristotle (A Complete Exposition of His Works and Thought)*. New York: Meridian Books, 1960.

———. *Aristotle De Anima*. Oxford: At the Clarendon Press, 1961.

———. *Aristotle's Metaphysics*. 2 vols. Oxford: At the Clarendon Press, 1966.

———. *Aristotle's Physics*. Oxford: At the Clarendon Press, 1966.

———. *Metaphysica*. Vol. 8 of *The Works of Aristotle Translated into English*. Oxford: At the Clarendon Press, 1966.

Williams, C. J. F. *Aristotle's De Generatione et Corruptione*. Oxford: At the Clarendon Press, 1982.

VARIOUS WORKS

Allen, James. *The First Year of Greek*. Rev. ed. Toronto: MacMillan, 1931.

Berko, Roy M., Lawrence B. Rosenfeld, and Larry A. Samovar. *Connecting: A Culture-Sensitive Approach to Interpersonal Communication Competency*. 2nd ed. Fort Worth, TX: Harcourt Brace College Publishers, 1997.

Best, Stephen, and Douglas Kellner. *Postmodern Theory: Critical Interrogations*. New York: Guilford Press.

"Bible Scholar Claims Branch Davidian Disaster Could Have Been Avoided." *Religious Studies News* 10, no. 3 (1995): 3.

Bloom, Harold. *The Western Canon: The Books and School of the Ages*. New York: Harcourt Brace, 1994.

Cassirer, Ernst. *Language and Myth.* Translated by Susanne K. Langer. New York: Dover Publications, Inc., 1946.

Clarke, Ruth Anne, and Jesse G. Delia. "Topoi and Rhetorical Competence," *Quarterly Journal of Speech* 65 (1979): 195.

Di Sante, Carmine. *Jewish Prayer: The Origins of the Christian Liturgy.* Translated by Matthew J. O'Connell. New York and Mahwah, NJ: Paulist Press, 1991.

Fischel, Henry A. *Rabbinic Literature and Greco-Roman Philosophy.* Leiden: E. J. Brill, 1973.

Fisher, Walter R. "Narration as a Human Communication Paradigm: The Case of Public Moral Argument." *Communication Monographs* 51 (1984).

Fishman, Isidore. *Gateway to the Mishnah.* Hartmore, CT: Prayer Book Press, Inc., 1970.

Frisk, Hjalmar. *Griechisches Etymologisches Woerterbuch.* 2 vols. Heidelberg: Carl Winter Universitatsverlag, 1960.

Higgins, Alexander G. "48 in Swiss Religious Sect Die." *Journal and Courier,* 6 October 1994, sec. A.

Homer. *The Iliad of Homer.* Translated by Richmond Lattimore. Chicago and London: University of Chicago Press, 1961.

Junior Classic Latin Dictionary. Chicago: Follett Publishing Co., 1960.

Kirby, John T. "Classics 593R: Classical Concepts of Rhetoric and Poetics," lecture delivered in graduate seminar at Purdue University, West Lafayette, IN, 3 February 1994.

———. "The 'Great Triangle' in Early Greek Rhetoric and Poetics." *Rhetorica* 8 (1990): 213–28.

———. "Rhetorical Theory in Bronze-Age Greece?" lecture delivered at the Purdue University Colloquium for Center for Humanistic Studies, West Lafayette, IN, 18 April 1994.

Kittel, Gerhard, ed. *Theological Dictionary of the New Testament.* 9 vols. Geoffrey W. Bromiley, trans. Grand Rapids, MI: Wm B. Eerdmans Publishing Company, 1964. s.v. "*euchomai, euchê, proseuchomai, proseuchen* by Heinrich Greeven.

———. *Theological Dictionary of the New Testament.* 9 vols. Geoffrey W. Bromiley, trans. Grand Rapids, MI: Wm B. Eerdmans Publishing Company, 1964. s.v. "*zôopoieô,*" by Rudolph Bultmann.

Koresh, David. "Letter from David Koresh to Richard DeGuerin [14 April 1993]." *Religious Studies News* 10, no. 3 (1995): 3.

Lardner, George, Jr. "U.S. Argues Idaho Can't Prosecute FBI Sniper: Case Stems From 1992 Ruby Ridge Siege." *Washington Post,* 14 March 1998, sec. A.

Liddell, Henry George, and Robert Scott, comps. *A Greek-English Lexicon.* Revised by Henry Stuart Jones. Oxford: At the Clarendon Press, 1968.

———. *A Lexicon Abridged from Liddell and Scott's Greek-English Lexicon.* Oxford: At the Clarendon Press, 1966.

Lightfoot, J. B. *The Apostolic Fathers.* Edited by J. R. Harmer. Grand Rapids, MI: Baker Book House, 1956.

Miller, Mark. "Secrets of the Cult." *Newsweek,* 14 April 1997, 28–37.

Ogden, C. K., and I. A. Richards, *The Meaning of Meaning: A Study of the Influence of Language upon Thought and of the Science of Symbolism.* New York: Harcourt Brace Jovanich, 1923.

Plato. *Plato: Phaedrus and The Seventh and Eighth Letters.* Translated by Walter Hamilton. New York: Penguin Books, 1973.

Poulakos, John. "Interpreting Sophistical Rhetoric: A Response to Schiappa." *Philosophy and Rhetoric* 23 (1990): 160–71.

———. "Rhetoric, the Sophists, and the Possible." *Communication Monographs* 51 (1984): 215–25.

———. "Toward a Sophistic Definition of Rhetoric." *Philosophy and Rhetoric* 16 (1983): 35–38.

Schiappa, Edward. "History and Neo-Sophistic Criticism: A Reply to Poulakos." *Philosophy and Rhetoric* 23 (1990): 307–15.

———. "Neo-Sophistic Rhetorical Criticism or the Historical Reconstruction of Sophistic Doctrines?" *Philosophy and Rhetoric* 23 (1990): 192–217.

———. "*Rhetorikê*: What's in a Name? Toward a Revised History of Early Greek Rhetorical Theory." *Quarterly Journal of Speech* 78 (1992): 1–15.

———, ed. *Landmark Essays on Classical Greek Rhetoric.* Davis, CA: Hermagoras Press, 1994.

Sheler, Jeffery L. "The Theology of Abortion." *U. S. News and World Report,* 9 March 1992, 54.

Swanson, David L., and Jesse G. Delia. "The Nature of Human Communication." In *Modcom/Modules in Speech Communication.* Chicago: Science Research Associates, Inc., 1976.

Tabor, James D. "Introductory Remarks." *Religious Studies News* 10, no. 3 (1995): 3.

Tabor, James D., and Eugene V. Gallagher. *Why Waco?: Cults and the Battle for Religious Freedom in America.* Berkeley: University of California Press, 1995.

Revelation and Apocalyptic Studies

Astour, Michael C. "Ezekiel's Prophecy of Gog and the Cuthean Legend of Naram-Sin." *Journal of Biblical Literature* 95 (1976): 567–79.

Aune, David E. *Revelation 1–5.* Vol. 52 of *Word Biblical Commentary.* Edited by Bruce M. Metzger. Dallas: Word Books, 1997.

———. *Revelation 17-22.* Vol. 52C of *Word Biblical Commentary.* Edited by Bruce M. Metzger. Nashville: Thomas Nelson Publishers, 1998.

———. *Revelation 6–16.* Vol. 52B of *Word Biblical Commentary.* Edited by Bruce M. Metzger. Nashville: Thomas Nelson Publishers, 1998.

Barr, David. *Tales of the End: A Narrative Commentary on the Book of Revelation.* Santa Rosa, CA: Polebridge Press, 1998.

Beale, G. K. *The Book of Revelation: A Commentary on the Greek Text.* Vol. of *The New International Greek New Testament Commentary.* Edited by I. Howard Marshall and

Donald A. Hagner. Grand Rapids, MI:Wm. B. Eeidmans, Publishing Company, 1999.

———. *John's Use of the Old Testament in Revelation.* Sheffield: Sheffield Academic Press, 1998.

Billerbeck, Paul. *Die Briefe des neuen Testaments und die Öffenbarung Johannis.* Vol. 3 of *Kommentar zum neuen Testament aus Talmud und Midrasch.* Edited by Hermann Strack and Paul Billerbeck eds. Munich: C. H. Beck'sche Verlagsbuchhandlung, 1961.

Boring, M. Eugene. "Narrative Christology in the Apocalypse." *Catholic Biblical Quarterly* 54 (1992): 702–23.

———. *Revelation.* Vol. of *Interpretation: A Bible Commentary for Teaching and Preaching.* Edited by James Luther Mays. Louisville: John Knox Press, 1989.

Bousset, Wilhelm. *The Antichrist Legend.* A chapter in *Christian and Jewish Folklore.* Translated by A. H. Keane. London: Hutchinson and Co., 1896.

Bruce, F. F. "The Revelation to John." In *A New Testament Commentary.* Edited by G. C. D. Howley. Grand Rapids, MI: Zondervan Publishing House, 1975.

Brummett, Barry. Review of *Arguing the Apocalypse: A Theory of Millennial Rhetoric,* by Stephen D. O'Leary [Book Review]. *Rhetoric Society Quarterly* 24 (1994): 132–34.

Caird, G. B. *A Commentary on the Revelation of St. John the Divine.* A vol. of *Harper's New Testament Commentaries.* Edited by Henry Chadwick. New York: Harper & Row, 1966.

Charles, R. H. *The British Academy Lectures on the Apocalypse.* London: Oxford University Press, 1923.

———. *The Revelation of St. John.* 2 vols. of *The International Critical Commentary.* 1920 Edinburgh: T. & T. Clark, 1975.

Collins, Adela Yarbro. *Cosmology and Eschatology in Jewish and Christian Apocalypticism.* Leiden: E. J. Brill, 1996.

———. *Crisis and Catharsis: The Power of the Apocalypse.* Philadelphia: Westminster Press, 1984.

———. "The History-of-Religions Approach to Apocalypticism and the 'Angel of the Waters' (Rev. 16:4–7)." *The Catholic Biblical Quarterly* 39 (1977): 367–81.

———. "The Political Perspective of the Revelation to John." *Journal of Biblical Literature* 96 (1977): 241–56.

Collins, John J. "Pseudonymity, Historical Reviews and the Genre of the Revelation of John." *The Catholic Biblical Quarterly* 39 (1977): 329–43.

Crawford, Barry S. "Near Expectation in the Sayings of Jesus." *Journal of Biblical Literature* 101 (1982): 225–44.

Fekkes, Jan III. " 'The Bride Has Prepared Herself:' Revelation 12–21 and Isaian Nuptial Imagery." *Journal of Biblical Literature* 109 (1990): 269–87.

Fiorenza, Elisabeth Schüssler. "Apocalyptic and Gnosis in the Book of Revelation." *Journal of Biblical Literature* 92 (1973): 565–81.

———. *The Book of Revelation Justice and Judgment.* Philadelphia: Fortress Press, 1985.

————. "Composition and Structure of the Revelation of John." *The Catholic Biblical Quarterly* 39 (1977): 344–66.

Ford, J. Massyngberde. *Revelation.* Vol. 38 of *The Anchor Bible.* Garden City, NY: Doubleday, 1975.

Gammie, John G. "Spatial and Ethical Dualism in Jewish Wisdom and Apocalyptic Literature." *Journal of Biblical Literature* 93 (1974): 365–85.

Grant, Robert M. Review of *Redating the New Testament,* by John A. T. Robinson. *Journal of Biblical Literature* 97 (1978): 294–96.

Hanson, Paul D. "Rebellion in Heaven, Azazel, and Euhemeristic Heroes in I Enoch 6–11." *Journal of Biblical Literature* 96 (1977): 195–33.

Jervis, L. Ann. " 'But I Want You to Know . . .': Paul's Midrashic Intertextual Response to the Corinthian Worshipers (1 Cor 11:2–16)." *Journal of Biblical Literature* 112 (1993): 231–46.

Johnson, Luke T. "The New Testament's Anti-Jewish Slander and the Conventions of Ancient Polemic." *Journal of Biblical Literature* 108 (1989): 395–18.

Kerkeslager, Allen. "Apollo, Greco-Roman Prophecy, and the Rider on the White Horse in Rev. 6:2." *Journal of Biblical Literature* 112 (1993): 116–21.

Kiddle, Martin. *The Revelation of St. John.* A vol of *The Moffat New Testament Commentary.* New York: Harper and Brothers.

Kurz, William. "Acts 3:19–26 as a Test of the Role of Eschatology in Lukan Christology." Society of Biblical Literature Seminar Paper, 1977.

Lim, Timothy H. "The Wicked Priests of the Groningen Hypothesis." *Journal of Biblical Literature* 112 (1993): 415–25.

Marcus, Joel. "The Jewish War and the Sitz im Leben of Mark." *Journal of Biblical Literature* 111 (1992): 441–62.

Nickelsburg, George W. E. "The Apocalyptic Message of I Enoch 92–105." *The Catholic Biblical Quarterly* 39 (1977): 309–28.

O'Leary, Stephen D. "A Dramatistic Theory of Apocalyptic Rhetoric." *Quarterly Journal of Speech* 79 (1993): 385–26.

Perkins, Pheme. "The Genre and Function of the Apocalypse of Adam." *The Catholic Biblical Quarterly* 39 (1977): 382–95.

Perrin, Norman. "Eschatology and Hermeneutics: Reflections on Method in the Interpretation of the New Testament." *Journal of Biblical Literature* 93 (1974): 3–14.

Reader, William W. "The Twelve Jewels of Revelation 21:19–20: Tradition History and Modern Interpretations." *Journal of Biblical Literature* 100 (1981): 395–18.

Robinson, John A. T. *Redating the New Testament.* Philadelphia: Westminster Press, 1976.

Russell, D. S. *Divine Disclosure: An Introduction to Jewish Apocalyptic.* Minneapolis: Fortress Press, 1992.

Saldarini, Anthony J. "The Uses of Apocalyptic in the Mishna and Tosepta." *The Catholic Biblical Quarterly* 39 (1977): 396–09.

Scherrer, Steven J. "Signs and Wonders in the Imperial Cult." *Journal of Biblical Literature* 103 (1984): 599–10.

Snyder, Graydon F. "Sayings on the Delay of the End." *Journal of the Chicago Society of Biblical Research* 20 (1975): 19–31.

Talbert, Charles H. *The Apocalypse: A Reading of the Revelation of John.* Louisville: Westminster John Knox Press, 1994.

Tenney, Merrill C. *New Testament Survey.* Grand Rapids, MI: Eerdmans, 1961.

Thiering, B. E. "Once More the Wicked Priest." *Journal of Biblical Literature* 97 (1978): 191–05.

Wilkinson, Richard H. "The STYLOS of Revelation 3:12 and Ancient Coronation Rites." *Journal of Biblical Literature* 107 (1988): 498–01.

Wittstruck, Thorne. "The Influence of Treaty Curse Imagery on the Beast Imagery of Daniel 7." *Journal of Biblical Literature* 97 (1978): 100–02.

TEXTS AND TRANSLATIONS

New Testament

Aland, Kurt, Matthew Black, Bruce M. Metzger, and Allen Wickgren, eds. *The Greek New Testament.* London: United Bible Societies, 1966.

Nestle, Erwin and Kurt Aland, eds. *Novum Testamentum Graece.* London: United Bible Societies, 1969.

Greek Old Testament

Rahlfs, Alfred, ed. *Septuaginta (Id est Vetus Testamentum graece iuxta LXX interpretes).* 8 ed. 2 vols. Stuttgart: Wurttembergische Bibelanstalt, 1935.

Hebrew Bible

Kittel, Rud., ed. *Biblia Hebraica 3.* Stuttgart, Germany: Wurttembergische Bibelanstalt Stuttgart, 1966.

Intertestamental and Sectarian

Black, M., ed. *Apocalypsis Henochi Graece.* Vol 3 of *Pseudepigrapha Veteris Testamenti Graece.* Edited by A. M. Denis and M. de Jonge. Leiden: E. J. Brill, 1970.

Bonner, Campbell, ed. *The Last Chapters of Enoch in Greek.* London: Christophers, 1937.

Bonwetsch, Gottlieb Nathanael, ed. *Die Apokalypse Abrahams (Das Testament der Vierzig Märtyrer).* Leipzig: Scientia Verlag Aalen, 1897.

Charles, R. H., ed. and trans. *The Apocalypse of Baruch.* London: Society for Promoting Christian Knowledge, 1917.

———, ed. *The Apocrypha and Pseudepigrapha of the Old Testament.* 2 vols. Oxford: Clarendon Press, 1913.

———, ed. *The Ascension of Isaiah.* London: Adam and Charles Black, 1900.

————, ed. *The Assumption of Moses*. London: Adam and Charles Black, 1897.

————, trans. *The Book of Jubilees*. New York: MacMillan & London: Society for Promoting Christian Knowledge, 1917.

————, ed. *The Greek Versions of the Testaments of the Twelve Patriarchs*. Hildesheim: Georg Olms Verlagsbuchhandlung and Oxford University Press, 1960.

Davenport, Gene L. *The Eschatology of the Book of Jubilees*. Leiden: E. J. Brill, 1971.

Fitzmyer, Joseph A., ed. *The Genesis Apocryphon of Qumran Cave I*. 2nd ed. Rome: Biblical Institute Press, 1971.

Kahana, Avraham, ed. *Sefarim ha-Hizonim*. 2 vols. Tel Aviv, 1959.

Kautzsch, E., ed. *Die Apocryphen und Pseudepigraphen des Alten Testaments*. 2 vols. Tubingen: Verlag von J. C. B. Mohr (Paul Siebeck), 1900.

Schechter, S., ed. *Fragments of a Zadokite Work*. Vol. 1 of *Documents of the Jewish Sectaries*. New York: KTAV Publishing House, Inc., 1970.

Von Tischendorf, Konstantin, ed. *Apocalypses Apocraphae (Mosis, Esdrae, Pauli, Ioannis, item Mariae dormitio, additis Evangeliorum et Apocryphorum supplementis)*. Hildesheim: Georg Olms Verlagsbuchhandlung, 1966.

Christian and Hellenistic

Caplan, H., trans. *Rhetorica ad Herennium*. Cambridge: Harvard University Press and London: William Heinemann Ltd., 1989.

Hennecke, Edgar. *New Testament Apocrypha*. Edited by Wilhelm Schneemelcher. Trans. R. McL. Wilson. Philadelphia: Westminster Press, 1963.

Josephus. *The Works of Flavius Josephus*. Whiston's translation, rev. by A. R. Shilleto. London: George Bell & Sons, 1890.

Lightfoot, J. B. *The Apostolic Fathers*. Edited by J. R. Harmer. 1891. Reprint, Grand Rapids, MI: Baker Book House, 1976.

McCown, Chester Charlton, ed. *The Testament of Solomon*. Leipzig: J. C. Hinrichs, 1922.

Oates, Whitney J., ed. *The Stoic and Epicurean Philosophers*. New York: Modern Library (Random House, Inc.), 1940.

Otto, ed. *Iustinus Philosophus et Martyr*. 3rd ed. Vol. 1 of *Corpus Apologetarum Christianorum*. Ienae: Prostat in Libraria Hermanni Dufft., 1876.

Philo Judaeus. *The Works of Philo Judaeus*. Trans. C. D. Yonge. London: Georg Bell & Sons, 1890.

Philonis Judaei. *Opera Omnia*. Pars II of *Patrum Ecclesiae Graecorum*. Lipsiae: Sumtibus E. B. Schwickerti, 1828.

Roberts, Alexander, and James Donaldson, eds. *The Ante-Nicene Fathers*. American reprint of the Edinburgh edition., rev. by A. Cleveland Coxe. Vols. 1–3. Grand Rapids, MI: Wm. B. Eerdmans Publishing Co.

Whiston, William, trans. *Josephus Complete Works*. Grand Rapids, MI: Kregel Publications, 1974.

Wikgren, Allen. *Hellenistic Greek Texts*. Chicago and London: University of Chicago Press, 1947.

Rabbinic

Akiba. *Sefer Otiot* de Rabbi Akiba. ВАРЖАВА, 1871.

Albeck, Ch., ed. *Midrash Bereshit Rabbati.* Jerusalem: Mekize Nirdamim, 1940.

Braude, William G. and Israel J. Kapstein, trans. *Pesikta de-Rab Kahana.* Philadelphia: Jewish Publication Society of America, 1975.

Buber, Salomon, ed. *Agadat Bereshit.* Reprint of Cracow edition, 1902. New York: Menorah, 1958–59.

———. *Midrash Tanhuma.* New York, 1946.

———. *Midrash Tehillim (Schocher Tob).* Vilna: Romm, 1891.

———. *Pesikta de-Rab Kahana.* Reduced photo offset of Lyck 1868 ed., 1962.

Epstein, I., ed. *The Babylonian Talmud.* London: Soncino Press, 1935–48.

Freedman, H. and Maurice Simon, eds. *Midrash Rabbah.* 10 vols. London: Soncino Press, 1939.

Friedmann, M., ed. *Pesikta Rabbati.* Wien: Josef Kaiser IX, 1880.

———. *Seder Eliahu rabba and Seder Eliahu Zuta (Tanna d'be Eliahu): Pseudo-Seder Eliahu Zuta.* Jerusalem: Bamberger & Wahrman, 1960.

Gaster, M. trans. *The Chronicles of Jerahmeel.* New York: KTAV Publishing House, Inc., 1971.

Goldschmidt, Lazarus, ed. *Der Babylonische Talmud.* Haag: Martinus Nijhoff, 1906–35.

Horovitz, H. S., ed. *Siphre ad Numeros adjecto Siphre zutta.* Fasciculus primus from *Siphre de'be Rab.* Jerusalem: Wahrmann, 1966.

Jellinek, Ad., ed. *Bet ha-Midrasch: Sammlung kleiner Midraschim und vermischter Abhandlungen aus der ältern jüdischen Literatur.* Reprint, Jerusalem: Wahrmann, 1967.

Lieberman, S., ed. *Midrash Devarim Rabbah.* 2nd ed. Jerusalem: Wahrmann, 1964–95.

Luria, David, ed. *Sefer Pirke Rabbi Eli'ezer.* Reprint, Jerusalem, 1963.

Malter, Henry, ed. *The Treatise Ta'anit of the Babylonian Talmud.* Philadelphia: The Jewish Publication Society of America, 1967.

Margulyot [Margulies], Mordecai, ed. *Midrash Ha-Gadol 'al Hamishah Humshe Torah: Sefer Bereshit.* Jerusalem: Rabbi Kook Foundation, 1946–47.

———. *Midrash Wayyikra Rabbah.* 3–5 vols. Jerusalem: Wahrmann, 1972.

Mekilta de-Rabbi Ishmael. 3 vols. Philadelphia: Jewish Publication Society of America, 1933–35.

Midrash Tanchuma. (Mantua Edition, 1563). Reprint, Jerusalem: Makor Publishing Ltd.

Noah, Mordecai Manuel, trans. *The Book of Yashar.* New York: Hermon Press, 1972.

Odeberg, Hugo, ed. *3 Enoch or The Hebrew Book of Enoch.* Vol. of *The Library of Biblical Studies.* Edited by Harry M. Orlinsky. New York: KTAV Publishing House, Inc., 1973.

Schechter, Solomon, ed. *Aboth de Rabbi Nathan.* New York: Philipp Feldheim, 1945.

———. *Midrash Hag-Gadol: Genesis.* Cambridge: At the University. Press, 1902.

Sefer Zohar Hadash. Leghorn, 1866.

Sperber, A., ed. *The Pentateuch According to Targum Onkelos.* Vol. 1 of *The Bible in Aramaic.* Leiden: Brill, 1959.

Talmud Babli. Vilna: Romm, 1886.

Theodor, J. and Ch. Albeck, eds. *Bereschit Rabba.* 3 vols. Reprint, Jerusalem: Wahrmann, 1965.

Wünsche, Aug., ed. *Midrasch Tehillim.* Trier: Sigmund Mayer, 1892.

Yadler, I. Z., ed. *Sefer Midrash Rabbah.* Tel Aviv: Lipa Fridman, 1958–63.

Yalkut Shimoni al Ha-Torah. Jerusalem.

Zuckermandel, M. S., ed. *Tosefta.* Jerusalem: Bamberger and Wahrmann, 1937.

Moslem

Ali, Abdullah Yusuf. *The Holy Qur-an, Text, Translation and Commentary.* 3 vols. Lahore: Shaikh Muhammad Ashraf.

WORKS ON ANGELS AND/OR SATAN

Bamberger, Bernard J. *Fallen Angels.* Philadelphia: Jewish Publication Society of America, 5712–1952.

Bietenhard, Hans. *Die himmlische Welt im Urchristentum und Spätjudentum.* Vol 2 of *Wissenschaftliche Untersuchungen zum Neuen Testament.* Edited by J. Jeremias and O. Michel. Tubingen: J. C. B. Mohr, 1951.

Botterweck, Johannes, and Helmer Ringgren, Eds. *Theological Dictionary of the Old Testament.* Grand Rapids, MI: Wm. B. Eerdmans Publishing Company, 1975. s.v. "bên," by H. Haag.

Brandon, S. G. F. *Religion in Ancient History.* London: George Allen & Unwin Ltd., 1973.

Davidson, Gustav. *A Dictionary of Angels (Including the Fallen Angels).* New York: Free Press, 1967.

Encyclopedia Judaica. Jerusalem: MacMillan Company, 1971. s.v. "Angels and Angelology."

Fox, Samuel J. *Hell in Jewish Literature.* Merimack College Press, Northbrook, IL: Whitehall Co., 1972.

Ginzberg, Louis. *The Legends of the Jews.* Translated by Henrietta Szold. 7 vols. Reprint, Philadelphia: Jewish Publication Society of America, 5728–1968.

Haag, H. *"bên."* *Theological Dictionary of the Old Testament.* Edited by Johannes Botterweck and Helmer Ringgren. Vol. 2. Grand Rapids, MI: Wm. B. Eerdmans Publishing Company, 1975.

Hengel, Martin. *Judentum und Hellenismus.* Vol. 10 of *Wissenschaftliche Untersuchungen zum Neuen Testament.* Edited by J. Jeremias and O. Michel. Tubingen: J. C. B. Mohr, 1969.

Jung, Leo. *Fallen Angels in Jewish, Christian and Mohammedan Literature.* New York: KTAV Publishing House, Inc., 1974.

Kittel, Gerhard, ed. *Theological Dictionary of the New Testament.* 9 vols. Edited and translated by Geoffrey W. Bromiley. Grand Rapids, MI: Wm B. Eerdmans Publishing Company, 1964. s.v. *"aggelos,"* by Grundmann

————. *Theological Dictionary of the New Testament.* 9 vols. Edited and translated by Geoffrey W. Bromiley. Grand Rapids, MI: Wm B. Eerdmans Publishing Company, 1964. s.v. *"daimôn,"* by Foerster.

————. *Theological Dictionary of the New Testament.* 9 vols. Edited and translated by Geoffrey W. Bromiley. Grand Rapids, MI: Wm B. Eerdmans Publishing Company, 1964. s.v. *"diabolos,"* by Foerster.

Theodor Klauser, ed. *Reallexikon für Antike und Christentum.* Vol. 5. Stuttgart: Anton Hiersemann, 1962. s.v. *"engel,"* by J. Michl.

Lindsay, Stan A. *"Anamartêtous* Fallen Angels." Masters thesis, Indiana University, 1977.

Michl, J. *"Engel." Reallexikon für Antike und Christentum.* Edited by Theodor Klauser. Vol. 5. Stuttgart: Anton Hiersemann, 1962.

Moore, G. F. *Judaism in the First Centuries of the Christian Era.* 2 vols. Cambridge: Harvard University Press, 1927–30.

Schäfer, Peter. *Revalität zwischen Engeln und Menschen.* Vol 8 of *Studia Judaica.* Edited by E. L. Ehrlich, Basel. Berlin and New York: Walter De Gruyter, 1975.

Urbach, E. E. *The Sages: Their Concepts and Beliefs.* 2 vols. Translated by Israel Abrahams. Jerusalem: Magnes Press (Hebrew University), 1975.

Volz, Paul. *Die Eschatologie der Jüdischen Gemeinde im neutestamentlichen Zeitalter.* Hildesheim: Georg Olms, 1966.

Wickham, L. R. "The Sons of God and the Daughters of Men: Genesis VI.2 in Early Christian Exegesis." In *Language and Meaning,* edited by J. Barr, et al. Vol. 19 of *Oudtestamentische Studien,* 135–147. Leiden: E. J. Brill, 1974.

HISTORIES

Baron, Salo Wittmayer. *Christian Era: The First Five Centuries.* Vol. 2 of *A Social and Religious History of the Jews.* 2nd ed. Philadelphia: Jewish Publication Society of America, 1952.

Brandon, S. G. F. *The Fall of Jerusalem and the Christian Church.* London: S P C R, 1957.

Finkelstein, Louis, ed. *The Jews: Their History.* 4th ed. New York: Shocken Books, 1970.

Johnson, Luke. "The New Testament's Anti-Jewish Slander and the Conventions of Ancient Polemic." *Journal of Biblical Literature* 108 (1989): 419–41.

Katz, Steven T. "Issues in the Separation of Judaism and Christianity after 70 C.E.: A Reconsideration." *Journal of Biblical Literature* 103 (1984): 43–76.

Goldenberg, Robert. "The Broken Axis: Rabbinic Judaism and the Fall of Jerusalem (Abstract)." *Journal of the American Academy of Religion* 45 (1977): 353.

Levine, Lee I. *Caesarea under Roman Rule.* Vol 7 of *Studies in Judaism in Late Antiquity.* Edited by Jacob Neusner. Leiden: E. J. Brill, 1975.

Schürer, Emil. *The History of the Jewish People in the Age of Jesus Christ.* Revised and edited by Gesa Vermes and Fergus Millar. Edinburgh: T. & T. Clark Ltd., 1973.

Zeitlin, Solomon. *The Rise and Fall of the Judean State.* 3 vols. Philadelphia: Jewish Publication Society of America, 5728–1969.

QUMRAN

Black, Matthew. *The Scrolls and Christian Origins.* New York: Charles Scribner's Sons, 1961.

Braun, Herbert. *Qumran und das Neue Testament.* 2 vols. Tubingen: J. C. B. Mohr, 1966.

———. *Spätjüdisch-haretischer und Frühchristlicher Radikalismus.* 2 vols. Tubingen: J. C. B. Mohr, 1957.

Bruce, F. F. *Second Thoughts on the Dead Sea Scrolls.* Grand Rapids, MI: Wm. B. Eerdmans Publishing Co., 1961.

Burgmann, H. "The Wicked Woman: Der Makkabaer Simon?" *Revue de Qumran* 31 (1974): 323–59.

Burrows, Millar. *The Dead Sea Scrolls.* New York: Viking Press, 1955.

———. *More Light on the Dead Sea Scrolls.* New York: Viking Press, 1969.

Cross, Frank Moore Jr. *Ancient Library of Qumran.* Garden City, NY: Anchor Books, 1961.

Danielou, Jean. *The Dead Sea Scrolls and Primitive Christianity.* Translated by Salvatore Attanasio. Baltimore: Helicon Press, Inc., 1958.

Dead Sea Scrolls Research. *A Symposium.* Jerusalem, 21 April 1965.

Driver, G. B. *The Judean Scrolls.* Oxford: Basil Blackwell, 1965.

Dupont-Sommer, A. *The Essene Writings from Qumran.* Translated by G. Vermes. Oxford: Basil Blackwell, 1961.

———. *The Jewish Sect of Qumran and the Essenes.* Translated by R. D. Barnett. New York: MacMillan Company, 1956.

Eisenman, Robert H., and Michael Wise. *The Dead Sea Scrolls Uncovered.* New York: Barnes & Noble Books, 1994.

Fitzmyer, Joseph A. *The Genesis Apocryphon of Qumran Cave Y.* 2nd ed. Rome: Biblical Institute Press, 1971.

Lohse, Eduard, ed. *Die Texte aus Qumran.* Munchen: Kosel-Verlag, 1964.

Mowry, Lucetta. *The Dead Sea Scrolls and the Early Church.* Notre Dame and London: University of Notre Dame Press, 1966.

Thiering, B. E. "Once More the Wicked Priest." *Journal of Biblical Literature* 97 (1978): 191–05.

Yadin, Yigael. *The Scroll of the War of the Sons of Light against the Sons of Darkness.* Oxford: Oxford University Press, 1962.

GNOSTICISM

Fiorenza, Elizabeth Schüssler. "Apocalyptic and Gnosis in the Book of Revelation." *Journal of Biblical Literature* 92 (1973): 565–81.

Yamauchi, Edwin. *Pre-Christian Gnosticism.* Grand Rapids, MI: Wm B. Eerdmans Publishing Co., 1973.

JUDAISM

Fischel, Henry A. *Rabbinic Literature and Greco-Roman Philosophy.* Vol. 21 of *Studia Post-Biblica.* Edited by J. C. H. Lebram. Leiden: E. J. Brill, 1973.

Gesenius, Wilhelm. *Hebräisches und Aramäisches Handwörterbuch über das Alte Testament.* 15th ed. Leipzig: F. C. W. Vogel, 1910.

Grünbaum, Max. *Gesammelte Aufsatze zur Sprach-und Sagenkunde.* Edited by Felix Perles. Berlin: S. Calvary & Co., 1901.

Jastrow, Marcus. *A Dictionary of the Targumim, the Talmud Babli and Yerushalmi, and the Midrashic Literature.* 2 vols. Brooklyn: P. Shalom Publishing, 1967.

Levy, Jacob. *Neuhebräisches und Chaldäisches Wörterbuch (über die Talmudim und Midraschim).* 4 vols. Leipzig: F. A. Brockhaus, 1867–89.

Strack, Hermann L. *Introduction to the Talmud and Midrash.* Atheneum, NY: A Temple Book, 1969.

GREEK

Allen, James Turney. *The First Year of Greek.* Rev. ed. New York: MacMillan, 1931.

Arndt, William F., and F. Wilbur Gingrich, trans. *A Greek-English Lexicon of the New Testament and Other Early Christian Literature.* Edited by Walter Bauer. Chicago: University of Chicago Press, 1957.

Moulton, W. F., and A. S. Geden, eds. *A Concordance to the Greek Testament (According to the Texts of Wescott and Hort, Tischendorf and the English Revisers).* 4th ed. Edinburgh: T. & T. Clark, 1967.

RHETORICAL CRITICISM AND THE BIBLE

Fiorenza, Elisabeth Schüssler. "The Ethics of Interpretation: De-Centering Biblical Scholarship." *Journal of Biblical Literature* 107 (1988): 3–17.

Kennedy, George A. *New Testament Interpretation through Rhetorical Criticism.* Chapel Hill: University of North Carolina Press, 1984.

Ong, Walter J. *The Presence of the Word.* New Haven and London: Yale University Press, 1967.

Perelman, Chaim. *The New Rhetoric and the Humanities.* Translated by William Kluback. Dordrecht, Holland: D. Reidel Publishing Co., 1979.

Robbins, Vernon K., and John H. Patton. *"Rhetoric and Biblical Criticism."* *Quarterly Journal of Speech* 66 (1980): 327–37.

Robbins, Vernon K. "Structuralism in Biblical Interpretation and Theology." *The Thomist* 42 (1978): 349–71.

Tannehill, Robert C. *The Sword of His Mouth.* Philadelphia: Fortress Press, and Missoula, MT: Scholars Press, 1975.

Wilder, Amos N. *Early Christian Rhetoric: The Language of the Gospel.* London: SCM, 1964; Cambridge: Harvard University Press, 1971.

———. *Theopoetic.* Philadelphia: Fortress Press, 1976.

Wuellner, Wilhelm. "Where is Rhetorical Criticism Taking Us?" *The Catholic Biblical Quarterly* 49 (1987): 448–63.

MISCELLANEOUS METHODOLOGICAL WORKS

Beardslee, William A. *Literary Criticism of the New Testament.* Philadelphia: Fortress Press, 1970.

Bloom, Harold. *The Western Canon: The Books and School of the Ages.* New York: Harcourt Brace, 1994.

Dana, H. E., and Julius R. Mantey. *A Manual Grammar of the Greek New Testament.* Toronto: MacMillan Company, 1957.

Kennedy, George. *The Art of Persuasion in Greece.* Princeton: Princeton University Press, 1963.

Krentz, Edgar. *The Historical-Critical Method.* Philadelphia: Fortress Press, 1975.

Noll, Mark A. *Between Faith and Criticism: Evangelicals, Scholarship, and the Bible in America.* San Francisco: Harper & Row, 1986.

Perrin, Norman. *What is Redaction Criticism?* Philadelphia: Fortress Press, 1969.

Stewart, Charles J., Craig Allen Smith, and Robert E. Denton Jr. *Persuasion and Social Movements.* 3rd ed. (prepublication form, 1994).

White, Hayden. *The Content of the Form: Narrative Discourse and Historical Representation.* Baltimore and London: Johns Hopkins University Press, 1987.

———. "The Historical Text as Literary Artifact.: In *Tropics of Discourse: Essays in Cultural Criticism.* Edited by Hayden White Baltimore: John Hopkins University Press, 1978.

MISCELLANEOUS WORD STUDIES

Kittel, Gerhard, ed. *Theological Dictionary of the New Testament.* 9 vols. Edited and translated by Geoffrey W. Bromiley. Grand Rapids, MI: Wm B. Eerdmans Publishing Company, 1964. s.v. *"agnos, agnizô, agneia, agnotês, agnismos,"* by Hauck.

———. *Theological Dictionary of the New Testament.* 9 vols. Edited and translated by Geoffrey W. Bromiley. Grand Rapids, MI: Wm B. Eerdmans Publishing Company, 1964. s.v. *"molunô, molusmos,"* by Hauck.

———. *Theological Dictionary of the New Testament.* 9 vols. Edited and translated by Geoffrey W. Bromiley. Grand Rapids, MI: Wm B. Eerdmans Publishing Company, 1964. s.v. *"nikaô, nikê, nikos, hupernikaô,"* by O. Bauernfeind.

———. *Theological Dictionary of the New Testament.* 9 vols. Edited and translated by Geoffrey W. Bromiley. Grand Rapids, MI: Wm B. Eerdmans Publishing Company, 1964. s.v. *"ophis,"* by Foerster.

Botterweck, Johannes, and Helmer Ringgren, Eds. *Theological Dictionary of the Old Testament.* Grand Rapids, MI: Wm. B. Eerdmans Publishing Company, 1975. s.v. *"ish,"* by N. P. Bratsiotis.

Subject and Author Index

Note: Some entries that appear throughout the book, such as Burke, Church, Drama, Entelechy, Jesus Christ, Jew, John (the Author of Revelation), Rome, Roman, and Seven are not listed in the index.

Scriptural Index